THE PRICE OF PITY

By the same author:

British Warship Designs since 1906
Sea Battles in Close Up
Poems of the First World War
The Fighting Admirals
English Literature
Studying Shakespeare
Best of Saki

THE PRICE
OF PITY

Poetry, History and Myth in the Great War

by

Martin Stephen

LEO COOPER
LONDON

First published in Great Britain in 1996 by
- LEO COOPER
190 Shaftesbury Avenue, London WC2H 8JL
an imprint of
Pen & Sword Books Ltd,
47 Church Street,
Barnsley, South Yorkshire S70 2AS

A CIP record for this book is available from the British Library

ISBN 0 85052 450 4

Typeset by Phoenix Typesetting, Ilkley, West Yorkshire.

Printed in Great Britain by Redwood Books, Trowbridge, Wilts

This book is dedicated to the memory of
Charles Hamilton Sorley
(1895–1915)
and to
Mary Macpherson

Contents

Acknowledgements

This book would not have appeared without Leo and Jilly Cooper, Beryl Hill, Tom Hartman and Georgina Harris. Cherry Ekins has gone through the book with a painstaking attention to detail, and if there are good things in it then many of them have been rendered visible through her perception and editing of the text: thank you. Equally to blame for it are Toby Buchan and Dominique Enright, whose willingness to publish the anthology *Never Such Innocence* gave direct impetus to this new book. Timothy Webb, Alastair Stead, Geoffrey Hill, Jon Stallworthy, Dennis Welland and Philip Grover are not responsible in any way for the final product, but are responsible for ensuring my interest in the period and giving me examples of scholarship to follow. Mary Macpherson has been a constant source of encouragement and practical help, and has worked through my typescripts with marvellous rigour. So have Philip Franks and A.S. McK. Robinson, who put me right on many points I would otherwise have got wrong. Lawrence James has often put me right on certain historical aspects of the war. I am indebted to Ian Walker and Edward Towne of the King's School, Rochester, for the invaluable help they gave to research into the history of public schools. My thanks also to Ian Wood for encouragement he probably does not realize he has given. I am deeply indebted to Jenny, Neill, Simon and Henry for giving me the time and space to write.

I am also deeply indebted to the Librarian and Trustees of the Cambridge University Library and the Bodleian Library, Oxford, and Master and Fellows of Gonville & Caius College and the staff of the Churchill Archives, University of Cambridge, and the British Library.

I am grateful for permission to reprint work from the following:

Introduction

There is no more concise statement of the central myth of the Great War than that coined by Samuel Hynes:

> a generation of innocent young men, their heads full of high abstractions like Honour, Glory, and England, went off to war to make the world safe for democracy. They were slaughtered in stupid battles planned by stupid generals. Those who survived were shocked, disillusioned and embittered by their war experiences, and saw that their real enemies were not the Germans, but the old men at home who had lied to them. They rejected the values of the society that had sent them to war, and in so doing separated their own generation from the past and from their cultural inheritance.[1]

The same author describes the Myth of the War as,

> not a falsification of reality, but an imaginative version of it, the story of the war that has evolved, and has come to be accepted as true.[2]

The Myth of the Great War is essentially a literary myth, but a series of additional historical and sociological myths have attached themselves to it, symbols of a society that some believe was brought screaming into the real world between 1914 and 1918.

The origins of the myth go back beyond 1914, to Imperialist poets such as Sir Henry Newbolt and Rudyard Kipling, and books such as Hughes's *Tom Brown's Schooldays*. Kipling and Newbolt were the public manifestations of a vision of Empire that was never matched by reality, and Hughes presented an equally unreal vision of what Britain's public schools should have been like. They succeeded because in part they made a convincing pretence of imitating reality. Kipling managed to make the blood, sweat and tears of army life into a sweet cake that the middle classes could eat without guilt. Hughes somehow managed to make roasting a child before a fire, depriving him of intellectual stimulus and leaving him to be brought up in the company of his essentially uncivilized peers, a matter for sentimental affection and approval, whereas many years later William Golding in *Lord of the Flies* would make of it something rather different.

These earlier men did not know they were laying the foundations for a literary vision of the First World War, but that vision would have been far harder to create were it not for their efforts. When the war came Rupert Brooke created the first myth, that of the Young Apollo sacrificed for King and Country. Shortly afterwards Owen, Sassoon and Rosenberg created the myth of the Great War as Waste and Pity, though the Brooke myth and its many variants never succumbed totally to rival visions. After a faltering start, trench poets were discovered with increasing regularity from the 1930s onwards, their poetry summing up what society thought it had to feel about the Great War.

As with satellites round the main planet, a whole host of other literary productions revolved round the vision of the war created by Owen, Sassoon and Rosenberg. Books such as *All Quiet on the Western Front*, plays such as *Journey's End* and *Oh What A Lovely War!* pretended modernity, but in practice reinforced the vision of the war purveyed by its great poets. Rearguard actions made the battle all the more exciting, from those who thought that Rupert Brooke and not Wilfred Owen was right, to those as famous as W.B.Yeats, who insisted that passive suffering was not a proper subject for poetry and that the trench poets were 'all dirt and sucked sugar stick'. Society's vision of this historical event, the First World War, was ironically determined by a literary response to it, and it is the vision of some of the war's poets that has dominated the popular image of what that war was to those who fought in it and lived through it.

This book seeks to take the literary and historical images of the First World War and place them beside what, for want of a better word, we might call the reality of the war and the society which produced it. Reality is a commodity one presumes has been around for all of human history, but which has yet to be defined. Each generation sees it in the light of its own concerns, which helps to explain why perfectly good productions of *Hamlet* can show him as a rebellious student in the 1960s, a prematurely aged student in the 1970s, and a woman in the 1980s. Reality, for all that historians might wish it otherwise, is a variable and changing feast. Of course this book cannot change the reality of the Great War; I hope it might shift some of our perceptions of that reality.

A notable feature of writing on the First World War is the divide that exists between its historical and literary manifestations. In poetry in particular no school of verse has ever been linked more clearly to a historical event, yet very few works look at the war in both a literary and a historical context. There is a very tight-knit group of scholars and others who write about the poets of the war, and they have tended to concentrate on establishing an orthodoxy of merit among First World War poets. Only very rarely have they challenged the accepted view of the poetry of the Great War, a view that has held sway more or less intact since the late 1960s, so much so that one leading critic has worried that criticism of Great War verse faces 'death by orthodoxy'[3], the stagnation that comes about when no one can find anything new to say about a group of writers. Purely historical research has fallen into two categories, with many books taking advantage of it being such a literary war and providing immensely detailed and compelling accounts culled from contemporary writing. Others have centred on the leadership exercised in the war, consulting all the original papers of the various generals – some of whom were as generous in their production of memoirs as they were wasteful with the lives of those they commanded.

The present work has several aims. It also requires a disclaimer. In questioning some orthodox views of the war and its literature I am not attempting to set up an alternative orthodoxy, something for which I do not have the knowledge. I hope I am doing more than tilting at windmills. What I seek to do is to examine the myths concerning the generals, officers and men who fought the Great War, the poets who wrote about it, and the tactics used in the conflict. My aim is to look anew at the greatest poets and authors of the war, with a view to establishing whether or not the present orthodox view of their merit is justified, and seeing if anything new can be added to our understanding of them. It examines several well-known authors who have not usually been associated with the war, and several who have clearly been misrepresented. Truly popular poetry, such as that by John Oxenham, 'Woodbine Willie' and those who wrote for *The Wipers Times*, is also examined, as is the largely neglected poetry by women, and poetry about the war in the air. I have with much sadness, for reasons of space, had to leave out any examination of the considerable body of poetry written about campaigns outside Europe, and the war at sea. The myths of pre-war England, and in particular those relating to the public schools, pre-war poetry and the so-called Edwardian Summer, are scrutinized.

On the military aspects of this book I have consulted mainly published material. The literary conclusions are based on research undertaken for my doctoral thesis, and twenty-one years of reading both obscure and well-known authors of the war, talking to survivors and burying my head in the mass of slim volumes that gather dust in most libraries and second-hand bookshops. I am grateful to all those people who sent me unpublished material after the publication of my anthology *Never Such Innocence*, now the Everyman *Poems of the First World War*. In many respects this book is a companion volume to that anthology, the selection of poetry in which illustrates many of the points I am trying to make here. The First World War has attracted the cream of British historians and some of its sanest literary critics; I am indebted to them all.

It is a matter of some concern to me that two people who have read the text thought that Chapter 2 (an examination of the career and personality of General Haig) and Chapter 7 (an examination of the major trench poets) should be omitted. The reason in both cases is the same. The chapters are too specialized; military history and literary criticism do not sit easily side by side; they imbalance the book.

I have decided to retain these two chapters because their polarity goes more distance than anything else in explaining why this book was written in the first place. In them I pretend to be a military historian and pretend to be a literary critic. In terms of recent work, and even the best to have come from the American Universities, these are two alien cultures, as sympathetic to each other as matter and anti-matter. My curse has been to take a first degree in both English and History. Why was it that when I read about General Haig as a historian the conclusions seemed to clash with what I would have felt were I reading about him as a student of English Literature? Why was it that when I read about Owen and Sassoon as poets no one seemed to see them as heroic and decorated soldiers? The start of my interest in the poetry of the First World War came when in the course of a week or so I interviewed two men who had known Siegfried Sassoon. One was a soldier. One was a 'literary man'. Both sang his praises. Both spoke as if talking about people from different galaxies. At the heart of this dichotomy there are two stark facts. Wilfred Owen went back to the front to lead his men and to kill Germans as a soldier, despite knowing within himself that he was the poet who could lead society out from carnage into sanity. Siegfried Sassoon was the most committed pacifist of any published author in the Great War, and at

the same time the most committed and the bravest of fighting soldiers. The post-war tendency to categorize people and issues, and
place each in a lead-lined box, has not helped us to reconcile the
glaring differences that existed among those who fought and who
wrote about the Great War. There is a central dichotomy in the
Great War, the dichotomy that saw poets finding out to their great
surprise that they were good soldiers, and the dichotomy that saw
soldiers finding out to their great surprise that they were good
poets. The fear for any author is that he will be panned as an
'amateur' military historian by those who specialize in that field,
and as an 'amateur' literary critic by the respective specialist in that
area. As my own career does not depend particularly on appro-
bation from either camp, I am lucky enough to be able to write a
book that suggests poets and soldiers had a lot in common. I apolo-
gize therefore for a cocaine-like snort of military history in Chapter
2, and the equivalent dose of literary criticism in Chapter 7. Wise
readers, like those who consulted medieval maps, should avoid
these areas, on the basis that they contain the warning 'Here Be
Dragons'. For those who care to pause and gather flowers by the
wayside, the dragons can be heard to play an interesting tune. The
theme of that tune is that the First World War did not recognize
distinctions between literary critics or academic historians. The
experience that was the First World War was universal. If at times
in this book I take a stance as a military historian or as a literary
critic it is in the hope that in general my stance is simply that of
the informed observer, and that the time has come to amalgamate
with honour both visions of the Great War.

No one will have the last word on the First World War, least of
all this book. Itself a tragedy played out on the greatest possible
canvas, the meaning of the First World War to us shifts and
changes as does the message of a great play or a great painting. If
this book has one overriding aim it is to present a picture of various aspects of the First World War that reflects the variety of
viewpoint found among those who fought in it. It would be a proud
and probably a mistaken man who felt that any one book could
achieve that aim, but I hope what follows may at least postpone
death by orthodoxy for a few years more.

Notes
1 Hynes, *A war Imagined*, p. x
2 *ibid.*, p. ix
3 Parfitt, *English Poetry of the First World War*, p. ix

CHAPTER ONE

Before the War

The Edwardian Summer

> Viewed across half a century of war and economic crisis the England of Edward VII stands out in the mind of a later generation as an era of peace and prosperity – a brief Indian summer at the close of a century of British political and economic pre-eminence.[1]

Such is the myth, and myths are resilient creatures, more than proof against most of the weapons that accurate and informed opinion can hurl against them. They ignore time and, because they present us with stories that we either need or feel we ought to believe, they can scorn academic criticism and an earnest command of the facts.

The myth of the Edwardian Summer, 'the dear dead days beyond recall',[2] is a relative latecomer on the scene, but it is both potent and apparently destined to be very long-lasting. One can judge this by virtue of the fact that it has been dismissed by almost every historian who has written on the period 1900–1914 to no noticeable effect, Asa Briggs commented that,

> during certain years of the Edwardian period . . . there was violent and open conflict . . . the happiness of the few was tempered by the misery of the many.[3]

Many other similar comments have not destroyed the myth. In the words of the Curator of Art at the Barbican Gallery, trying to launch another demolition of it:

It is a period which has . . . attracted an increasingly glamorous array of misconceptions. In the latter half of the century the world of film and television has cast a romantic haze over its first decade. From such a distance, sentimental hindsight has given the period a stability to which, in these seemingly more turbulent times, it has been reassuring to look back.[4]

The key to this comment is the phrase 'the world of film and television'. Academic historians have railed against the vision of pre-war England as an idyll of peace, but the popular media have long been used to ignoring academic history. The picture of an ordered world, where country houses were venues for startling and comforting displays of wealth and civilization and poor folk lived close to nature and knew their place, is beguiling. Academic historians have not dented its shine. The academic literary establishment has actively helped it to glow.

It is all very well for those who know about such things to hail as the greatest poet of the twentieth century a man who writes of 'smell of steaks in passageways', 'patient etherised upon a table' and talks of lives measured out with coffee spoons (T.S. Eliot, 'Preludes' and Prufrock). But when you add the accolade of most significant novelist going to someone whose central female character talks at length about whether or not men wash their penises after intercourse (James Joyce, Ulysses), and the accolade of most influential dramatist to a playwright who bases his most significant play on two tramps with bladder problems waiting for someone who never turns up (Samuel Beckett, Waiting for Godot), then it is hardly surprising that the man (and woman) on the Clapham omnibus looks for a little more romance and sentimentality.

Eliot, Joyce and Beckett spoke with immense strength and skill for the age of irony, but irony is a strong and bitter sauce and a mass of people still looked for some sugar in what they read as well as what they ate. Earnest reformers in the 1930s, when the Depression was at its height, could never understand why so many working-class families blew their money on jam, instead of using it to buy sensible (and boring) foodstuffs. The answer is that Man Shall Not Live By Logic Alone, any more than by boiled nettles. A film such as The Railway Children, in effect creating a world of magical simplicity where miracles can still happen, is a potent vision of what the Edwardian era can be made to represent, and a reminder that, however hard historians try, we will continue to see in that period what we need to see, and not what was there. Even films that seek directly to give a tragic flavour to the period, such as Greystoke (Tarzan) and The Shooting Party, still leave the audience with a rose-tinted vision of the certainty and order of the Edwardian era, often filmed in soft focus. Films and books seek to glorify the period. An influential but by no means exceptional example was Siegfried Sassoon's *The Old Century*,

> *The Old Century* revived purely happy memories of the late Victorian and early Edwardian 'golden afternoon', of the peaceful, slow years before the bursting of the dykes on August 4th, 1914. For younger readers, perhaps, the tranquil world it portrayed symbolised their birthright, which had been cast away by the folly of the Great War and utterly submerged beneath the social upheaval and widespread disillusion that followed it.[5]

The need to believe in the Edwardian summer survives the rigours of academic history just as a patch of oil on water survives a child's attempts to sink it by hurling stones. Each new academic work creates a great splash, but when the ripples die down the stone has sunk and the oil is still there.

There were, of course, major advances in the Edwardian era. Golden the age may not have been, but there was a lot of polished brass around. Provincial universities were founded (Birmingham in 1900, Liverpool 1903, Leeds 1904, Sheffield 1905 and Bristol 1909). Haldane's army reforms and Fisher's revolution for the Royal Navy did as much as anything else to ensure a country that could emerge from the first modern war as victor. Surprisingly, these reforms were supported by the corpulent figure of King Edward VII,[6] who, whilst he may never (in the Irish joke of the time) 'be half the man his mother was' still had much to offer Europe, not least of all his command of French and German. There were major advances in education for the masses and in the provision of pensions for the elderly, and the first National Insurance Act was established. It was the age that saw the emergence of the quantum and relativity theories, the first stirrings of interest in nuclear energy, and the invention of aspirin, teddy bears and vacuum cleaners, as well the development of effective aircraft, telephones and motor cars.

Successes these may have been, but for even the casual observer the signs of 'a deeply felt unrest of heart and mind'[7] were clear. Between 1911 and 1913 a staggering 464,000 people emigrated from Britain, the clearest possible illustration of the hardship faced by many of those living in the country. The combination of this emigration and a declining birth rate due to greater use of birth control produced an ageing population, itself a cause of great concern in both Britain and France. In 1841 a little under half the population of England and Wales were aged under twenty; by 1911 those under twenty numbered less than a third of the total.

A declining population was one problem; an increasingly troubled economy was another. There was marvellous innovation. Hardly ten years separated the first appearance of Parsons' steam turbine in the diminutive *Turbinia* from the same invention's use in a huge ocean liner, the *Mauretania*. But it was clear that the economies of the United States and Germany were catching up on Britain. Between 1900 and 1910 Germany's steel output doubled and that of the USA rose by 150 per cent; Britain's increased by one-fifth. An upper and upper-middle class, educated predominantly in the classical tradition, needed no reminding that all empires were subject to decay. Already Britain was paying the price for being the first country in the world to undergo an industrial revolution. There was no real infrastructure of scientific or technical education to underpin British industry, which relied on inspired amateurism and was still bedevilled by class division and unwillingness to change old practices.

A significant part of the economy was heavily dependent on the Empire, both for markets and for raw materials, yet in economic terms the Empire was starting to be hoist by its own petard. Its avowed aim (or at least one of the morally acceptable aims) had been to civilize primitive countries, but what to do when one had clearly been at least partially successful was a problem when one's economy depended to a large extent on subservience and not equality. The word 'Commonwealth' was starting to enter common usage in the Edwardian era, though with no clear notion of what it might imply for Britain's economic future. Those who were ignorant of the economic imperatives increasingly being asserted by the Empire could not remain ignorant of the threat to the myth of the Empire's invulnerability. The Boer War (1899–1902) had shattered complacency and that myth. The almost savage rejoicing at the relief of the siege of Mafeking showed just how close a nation's heart and mind had been brought to the unthinkable, a British defeat by one of its colonies.

Industrial unrest peaked in the Edwardian period. The Industrial Revolution had produced great wealth based on a mass of working-class labour, only one in four of whom lived in the country in 1911. It has been argued that the average industrial worker was considerably better off than his rural counterpart, but comparisons based on income can be misleading. The farm worker could live off the land in a way denied his urban equivalent. Despite this, it is clear that the average purchasing power of the working class rose by forty per cent between 1875 and 1895, and

4

remained more or less constant thereafter, partly as a result of cheap food imports. The average member of the working class may have been better off and better fed, but he was also more militant. The number of days lost through strike action between 1901 and 1907 varied from one-and-a-half to four million. In 1912 the figure, aided by the coal strike, was forty-one million, and figures of ten to eleven million were not uncommon after 1907. In 1911 alone there was a major strike by the seamen and dockers, a two-day national rail strike which shut the network down and a ten-month strike by South Wales miners.

Underpinning the industrial action was the awareness that up to thirty per cent of the Edwardian population lived in or near a state of extreme poverty. The word 'poverty' has a meaning in the Edwardian period which can be difficult to convey. It was not the poverty we associate with those sleeping rough in London or the thousands of homeless in the UK at the present time; it was closer to the poverty we see on television in third world countries, where the stark choice is between the aid agencies or death. Of course the modern age has not banished poverty, suffering or deprivation. But institutions such as the National Health Service and the welfare state have created a belief that there should be a safety net and a system whereby it is morally, socially and politically wrong for anyone to die of starvation or a curable illness. Nowadays we rightly view it as a national scandal if, after a visit to a hospital, an elderly patient dies because treatment is not forthcoming in time, whereas then there was likely to be no hospital to visit in the first place, and no money to pay for the visit even if it had been possible. The Jarrow marchers were complaining about starvation, not unemployment.

The militancy of the working class in the Edwardian period was a forerunner of the comradeship seen in the First World War. Both soldiers and working class were often united by their suffering, and could rely only on each other, a state which made collective action inevitable. The clearest sign of all that the Establishment was seriously worried by the growth of industrial unrest was the fact that in 1910 the King started to make frequent tours of industrial districts to combat fierce industrial unrest and 'working class bitterness'.[8]

The bitterness was understandable. The 1911 edition of the *Encyclopaedia Britannica* described 'unemployment' as 'a modern term', and the Edwardian period has the dubious distinction of introducing British society to the concept. In 1908 a higher number of the wage-earning population were unemployed than had been the case since 1886, the year of Bloody Sunday in

Trafalgar Square. To make matters worse, the cost of living rose by nearly nine per cent between 1909 and 1913.

Fear of war dominated much public thinking in the period 1901–14. Modern commentators have a tendency to point to the outbreak of war in 1914 as a surprise, or put it down simply to the assassination of an unpopular Archduke in Sarajevo. The truth is that no war had been more often predicted that the First World War, and its outbreak was no more due to the assassination of Archduke Ferdinand than catching the plague is due to meeting one rat: if the illness is current one will meet it at the next street corner if one does not meet it at the present one. The fear of war was present in high and low society alike. In 1909 King Edward VII asked Asquith if his Cabinet, in considering the budget proposals, had taken into account the possibility of financing a European war.[9] Some historians have seen this impending sense of doom as a prime feature of the Edwardian period,

> Indeed, their sense of what was coming, their feeling of apprehension, gives the Edwardians their particular fascination.[10]

In the mad and largely uncontrolled rush to industrialization much had been achieved and fortunes made. The Edwardians started to pick up the bill. Major items were gross inequalities in the distribution of wealth (half Britain's total national income went to one-ninth of the population, one-third to one-thirtieth), amateur management and feudal relationships between management and workforce. Old machinery and old practices dominated too much of British industry, not a new theme now but certainly a new one then, and one which trips to the USA by industrialists did little to dispel. Additional problems were too great a dependence on a secure and economically unsophisticated market, and the presence of a vast housing stock erected without planning and often to the lowest of standards.

The health and living conditions of many of the working class were appalling. In 1900 half those who applied were found unfit for military service on grounds of ill health or bad physical condition – and this after the undemanding standards had been reduced in 1883 and 1900. The Edwardian working-class schoolboy was five inches shorter than his public schoolboy counterpart and at the age of thirteen was eleven pounds lighter. Edwardian England was a divided society. One of the lesser ironies of the First World War was the extent to which it served to bring the extremes together.

Two final issues made Edwardian England a turbulent and

violent time. The Irish problem threatened to split governments and society, and bring civil war to Britain. The suffragette movement challenged a concept of male superiority that was as old as the species itself, and it was clear to any thinking person in the period 1901–14 that, for very different reasons, neither the Irish problem nor the issue of women's rights were going to go away.

When another great English Queen, Elizabeth I, died, the age which followed her was typified by massive contrasts, or what Paul Fussell in *The Great War and Modern Memory* would call antithesis. A long and essentially prosperous reign by a great queen was followed by a great revolution, the English Civil War in the case of Queen Elizabeth I and the First World War in the case of Queen Victoria. There never was an Edwardian Summer, but it took only thirteen years from the death of Queen Victoria for a horrific, four-year winter to be inflicted on British Society.

The Public Schools

The myth of the Edwardian Summer contains a sub-section, the myth of the English public school. The phrase itself is a notorious misnomer, as by 1901 any school that called itself public did so because it made strenuous efforts to exclude the general public. Most of the 'public' schools were old grammar school foundations, enlarged at the start of the nineteenth century to meet the increasing demand for education in a country which had no state education worth speaking of, and dependent for their survival on charging fees for the education they offered to the majority of their pupils. Certain of the newer schools managed by dint of much hard work and some luck to put themselves in the front rank, such as Wellington, Haileybury, Lancing and Marlborough.

A class-ridden society ranked its schools as rigidly as its people. In the top league were Eton, Harrow, Westminster, Winchester and St Paul's, though many other schools would claim to be up there with the best. Rugby was thrust to prominence firstly by having a very famous headmaster, Thomas Arnold, and secondly by having an old boy write a very famous book about him and the school, *Tom Brown's Schooldays*. Manchester Grammar School was, as it still is, a law unto itself, because, despite constant pressure from some of its High Masters, it never agreed to accept boarding pupils and therefore confused horribly all those who sought to rank the great schools of England. There were, as there still are, idiocies in the ranking of schools. Uppingham gained a fame rather in excess of the known facts through its great headmaster, Edward Thring. One of the great schools of the twentieth century, Oundle, was out of the reckoning until it acquired Sanderson, its charismatic headmaster. Sedbergh, in the top thirty in the 1970s for schools gaining scholarships and exhibitions to Oxford or Cambridge, was described as a mere encumbrance on the ground on which it stood by the Clarendon Commission in the 1860s. From all this confusion, and the avid public interest that the English give to any socially elitist institution, certain truths emerge. What has also emerged is the Myth of the Public School in England prior to the First World War.

The myth holds most dear the idea that the public schools prepared, in readiness for 1914, an unthinking group of right-wing automatons, ready to go 'over the top' for King, Country, the Established Church and, probably, the MCC.

> The class of 1914 had been prepared both implicitly, by the codes to which the schools subscribed, and explicitly, by the junior branch of the Officers' Training Corps, for the eventuality of war. What they had not been prepared for was this particular war, which brutally exposed the inadequacy both of an outmoded set of ideals and an archaic and optimistic concept of warfare.[11]

No myth is born without some truth, and there is an extent to which the English failings of

> emotional inadequacy and rootlessness unless defined by institutions (usually single-sex).[12]

were created by the public school system. But to see this as the only truth does not give an accurate picture of public schools in the period 1901–14, nor of how they prepared their pupils.

From 1845 onwards vast changes occurred in the public school system, changes which have come to be associated with great Victorian headmasters such as Thomas Arnold and Edward Thring. In part these changes were in response to two different but linked national scandals: the widespread embezzlement of the charitable funds owned by many of the schools (the universities of Oxford and Cambridge were particularly culpable), and the wholly licentious and riotous behaviour of public schoolboys. Early public schools were far from being havens of Arnoldian perfection, but were instead,

> tribes of self-governing boys that waged irregular warfare, generation after generation, against titular adult overlords endeavouring to trench upon their independence.[13]

Pupils at Marlborough were branded on the arm with an anchor mark by their fellows. Deaths at school were so common as hardly to merit a mention. In 1818 rebellions broke out in nearly every public school, and troops were not infrequently called in to suppress such events. Nor were riots restricted to the bad old days; Uppingham held one when the headmaster refused to give a half-holiday on the news that Mafeking had been relieved. Drunkenness, bullying and every variant of sexual abuse were rife. Arnold, and many headmasters in his mould, sought to change this anarchic regime beyond recognition. Staff were paid decent salaries to be present in the school, individual boarding houses built, and a heavy emphasis placed on religion and sport – both methods of taming the wildness of pupils.

From these reformed schools came the myth of the public schools, and inevitably some parts of it are accurate. Though it was not Arnold's idea (he was largely oblivious to games, unlike Edward Thring, who started his reign at Uppingham by hitting a six off a boy bowler, flung down the bat and announced, 'Now I am Headmaster!'), sport began to exert an almost overpowering influence on schools and school life. The hero of Alec Waugh's *The Loom of Youth* spots this after only a few days as a new boy at Fernhurst (a thinly-disguised Sherborne).

> The only thing he realised was that for those who wore a blue and gold ribbon ('colours' for rugby) laws ceased to exist. It was apparently rather advantageous to get into the Fifteen. He had not looked on athletics in that light before. Obviously his preparatory school had failed singularly to keep level with the times. He had always been told by the masters there that games were only important for training the body. But at Fernhurst they seemed the one thing that mattered. To the athlete all things are forgiven. There was clearly a lot to learn.[14]

Arnold unashamedly put character development before intellectual achievement, something easy enough in the days when a public schoolboy of even moderate intellect could expect to walk into the universities of Oxford or Cambridge. His emphasis on religion gave rise to the image of 'muscular Christianity', and so to the image of thousands of unthinking good chaps going over the top because it was the right thing to do and they had been told to do it. The arrival in schools of the OTC (Officers' Training Corps) was a godsend to historians who wished to present the public schools as factories for later cannon fodder. Pictures of row upon row of Edwardian schoolboys in uniform have a tragic poignancy when we know what was to happen to so many of them between 1914 and 1918. The OTC, the emphasis on games and being part of a team (something heavily emphasized by the house system), an essentially anti-intellectual approach and a distrust of individuality, were all present in the Edwardian public schools, and can make them seem as if they were little more than Sandhurst without the official military link, and a perfect training ground for the military.

The truth is very different and pointers to it lie very close to the surface of history, so much so that it is difficult to understand why the myth has grown as it has. Perhaps it is because the public schools as presented in a book such as *The Old Lie* by Peter Parker are like ghosts, something we need to believe in regardless of facts. Yet a cursory glance at some of the greatest poets of the First World War shows that whatever else they may have done the public schools turned out men of fierce independence and originality.

Siegfried Sassoon went to Marlborough and appears to have thoroughly enjoyed himself. As well as winning the MC and being a superbly aggressive officer, he risked being shot for a public condemnation of the war and went on to work as a journalist for a left-wing newspaper. Rupert Brooke was public school twice over. He attended Rugby, where again he was extremely happy. His father, a Haileyburian, was a Rugby housemaster. Brooke was also a Fabian, a trenchant critic of the middle classes and very much an individual. Edmund Blunden, arguably the most under-rated of all poets writing in the war, was entirely his own man and as far from the standard public school image of heartiness as man can be; he went to Christ's Hospital. Charles Sorley left Marlborough two terms early because he distrusted the tin-god effect of the final months as a sixth former at a great boarding school. He planned to become an elementary teacher, and was sufficiently individual to comment in the torrent of jingoistic verse at the outbreak of war that Germany was just like Britain.

Of all the war poets Robert Graves has most often been cited as the one at odds with the public school system. It is not surprising, it is argued, that such a fine artist should be embittered and misunderstood by so inflexible and philistine an institution as the Victorian public school. Graves himself fostered this image in his so-called autobiography, *Goodbye To All That*, and it has been picked up by modern writers:

Graves's devotion to Dick and his friendship with one of the masters, the mountaineer George Mallory, were about all he enjoyed at Charterhouse.[15]

The truth is different. Graves wrote to Edward Marsh, the founder of the *Georgian Poetry* anthologies, of 'three years misery at Charterhouse', and to Siegfried Sassoon he described his fellow officers as,

> everyone's as damnably cold-shouldered as the lower forms of a public school.[16]

The key is the phrase 'three years'. Graves was at Charterhouse for six years, 1908–14. He made a dreadful start at the school, his angularity and bloody-mindedness making him very unpopular, as they were later to do in the army. But after that three-year period the picture changes dramatically. In later years, when Graves achieved seniority at Charterhouse, he came to love it. The same was true of a great many who found in their last years at public school a peace and a happiness they would never be able to repeat in later life. Graves wrote to Edward Marsh about a projected new book that it,

> has nothing highfalutin' about it which would make it ridiculous in the eyes of the regiment and of Ch'house, which is most important.[17]

Charterhouse mattered to Graves, and he desperately needed to retain its approval. He was a frequent visitor after he had left, and was welcomed back: 'I had two wonderful days down at Charterhouse'[18] he wrote in 1916, and whilst his perhaps latent homosexuality was part of the attraction (the next sentence reads, 'Peter was exquisite as usual'), Graves appears to have a genuine love for the school which had put him through such hell when he was a young boy. Someone who asks one of his schoolteachers to be his best man cannot be wholly embittered by his schooldays. Graves simply left that love out of *Goodbye To All That*, just as Sassoon omitted his poetry from *Memoirs of a Fox-Hunting Man* and *Memoirs of an Infantry Officer*. One presumes both had the same reason: the books sold better and were more convincing without, despite the fact that Charterhouse to Graves and poetry to Sassoon were central parts of their being. Perhaps as two very private men they both felt a need to leave out what privately mattered most to them.

A very different picture of public school life is given by Charles Hamilton Sorley. One of the lesser tragedies of the First World War is that later generations have tended to see Rupert Brooke as the symbol of his generation. Brooke was a rather fine poet and a very interesting man, but typical of nothing. He was a public schoolboy who adopted left-wing politics, a homosexual who conducted passionate, loving and destructive relationships with women, a self-doubter who spoke in poetry with cutting certainty, a caring and sensitive man who embraced life as a soldier. If Brooke was typical of his generation, the mental hospitals prior to 1914 would have been England's largest growth industry. Far more typical was Charles Hamilton Sorley.

Sorley was the son of a Scottish academic who settled in Cambridge, and whose family tree includes various bishops and Rab Butler. Sorley was sent to Marlborough. He was in Germany when war was declared in 1914, filling in a year before going up to Oxford as a scholar of University College. He joined up and was killed by a machine-gun bullet through the head at the battle of Loos in 1915. He produced one very slim volume of poems, *Marlborough and Other Poems*. His father allowed what was almost a private collection of his *Letters* to be published after his death, and both this and the poems ran to several editions at a time when bookstalls were full of slim volumes and letters from dead officers. Sorley loved Marlborough, as Sassoon had loved it and as Graves loved Charterhouse at the end and Brooke loved Rugby. At the same time, he was more than capable of seeing through its pretensions,

> When one reaches the top of a public school, one has such unbounded opportunities of getting unbearably conceited that I don't see how anyone survives the change that must come when the tin god is swept off his little kingdom and becomes an unimportant mortal again. And besides I am sure it is far too enjoyable, and one is awfully tempted to pose all the time and be theatrical.[19]

Dr Wynne Wilson, headmaster of Marlborough in Sorley's last two years, used Sorley as a symbol of his generation when he wrote,

> With all his keen radical theories and sympathies, which he held in common with most clever boys, he was – a frequently occurring paradox – doggedly conservative in all that affected his own environment. He had a passionate love for Marlborough as he found it, a love which was not inconsistent with a mordant power of criticism. This love and this criticism alike are displayed in his poems and letters. . . . He was a rebel against mere convention,[20]

In that respect Sorley was typical. The Edwardian public schools have rarely been given credit for their capacity to command the love of such individuals as Sorley without constraining their power to criticize, their rebelliousness or their independence. Alec Waugh was in exactly the same mould.

Sorley shows us schools that probably depended too much on athleticism and a simplistic Christianity. Yet he also shows us schools that allowed inspired leadership from young teachers to young men, and schools which were bonded by an underlying and sometimes very obvious homosexuality. Sorley's school bred a tremendous love in him, but a love which never obscured his intelligence or his capacity to perceive its weaknesses. It made him value scholarship and learning, individuality and caring, as well as athletic success, and see no contradiction in the combination. It provoked a healthy awareness of some of the grosser idiocies of military life, rather than any unthinking devotion to militarism:

> The examination is divided into three parts – Company Drill, Tactical and Musketry. . . . I entered with fear and trembling. Twenty questions I was asked, and I looked sheepish and said 'Don't know' to each one. Then he said, 'Is there anything you do know?' and I gave him the two pieces of knowledge I had come armed with – the weight of a rifle and episodes in the life of a bullet from the time it leaves the breech till it hits its man. Then I saluted really smartly, and the gentleman gave me 60 out of a hundred.[21]

It produced a liberal awareness that did not reject privilege, but which took on board an obligation to relieve suffering. Sorley wrote to his mother in 1913:

> This is no new idea of mine – to become an instructor in a Working Man's College or something of that sort. Why I didn't tell you before I don't know. But until today it was only a hazy dream – I had no idea of how or when to do it. But now that Dyson [on the Marlborough teaching staff] has given me facts, it seems much nearer than before.[22]

The family idea had been for him to join the Indian Civil Service. Undoubtedly Sorley's school also produced a large number of dunderheads, idiots and jail-bait. That it and schools like it helped to produce Sorley, Sassoon, Graves, Blunden and Brooke has never been properly acknowledged. However, it is not only the great poets of the war who suggest that the public schools were a richer and more varied breeding ground for individuality and talent than has often been supposed.

Christianity was a central pillar of Arnold's reforms. The great Victorian headmasters almost to a man built large chapels at the first opportunity, some of them (Lancing and Cheltenham are two examples) giving expression in brick and stone to the spiritual splendour they expressed so often in words. *Tom Brown's Schooldays* gives especial prominence to this aspect of life at Rugby, the memory of 'The Doctor's' sermon at evensong being one of Tom's most lasting. Undoubtedly some public school pupils were deeply affected by the religious diet they were offered. It is, after all, easy to be a Christian when one comes from a family wealthy enough to afford school fees, and lives intensively for several years with other equally privileged young men. My experience, and that of the many others whose letters and memoirs I have read, suggests that once again Alec Waugh hits the nail on the head in *The Loom of Youth*.

> As is the case with most boys, Confirmation had little effect on Gordon. He was not an atheist; he accepted Christianity in much the same way that he accepted the Conservative party. All the best people believed in it, so it was bound to be all right; but at the same time it had not the slightest influence over his actions. If he had any religion at the time it was House football.[23]

With extracts such as this, one begins to question the assertion by the historian Correlli Barnett that public schoolboys cast in the Arnoldian mould lost Britain the Empire. Barnett's argument can be summarized as a belief that one could be moral, and one could hold on to an Empire, but one could not do both. Britain's public schoolboys were 'enfeebled by decency'. If they were, it was not through any widespread conversion to evangelical Christianity, though their teachers might have wished posterity to take a different view.

It is true that the arguments for a real Christian influence in Britain's public schools are outwardly overwhelming. They are first and foremost very visible, in occasionally beautiful and more often horrific monuments in brick and stone. Either way, the chapels of the English public school cannot be ignored. Nor can the writings and the sermons of the Establishment. Thring believed that hitting a six at cricket made him a headmaster; most of his contemporaries (and almost all his successors) seemed to believe they had not proved themselves until they had preached a sermon that had the Shell rocking in the aisles. Public school head-masters preached from morn till night, and left manifold evidence of their work behind them. The impression they tried to give was that Jones Mi. in Shell A had been altered for life by his head-master's sermons. Jones Mi., when he came to write his version of his schooldays, usually did so because they had been the happiest days of his life, after which he had obtained nothing but studied mediocrity. The evidence for which a historian thirsts – the written evidence stored in the libraries of venerable institutions – thus points to an unthinking Christianity on the part of public schoolboys.

The seeds of doubt in at least one writer were sown by the fact that his belief in Christianity came about despite, rather than as a result of, the sermons he heard at public school. When we have a memorial of public-school life it has tended to come to us either through a teacher, or through an adult who passed through those schools as a child. Alec Waugh's *The Loom of Youth* is an excep-tion, written as it is by a youth who was still a youth at the time of writing. As a youth Waugh can comment,

> 'I don't think it matters very much,' said Hunter, 'what masters think; most of them here have got into a groove. They believe the things they ought to believe; they are all copies of the same type. They've clean forgotten what it was like at school. Hardly any of them really know boys. They go on happily believing them "perhaps a little excitable, but on the whole, perfectly straight and honest." Then a row comes. They are horrified. They don't realize all of us are the same. They've made them-selves believe what they want to believe.'[24]

'They' were vocal and powerful, and historians have tended to take their view. This is unfortunate. Certainly neither Waugh nor Sorley accepted without question the *Boy's Own* Christianity they were offered at public school. There is good reason to believe that for most public schoolboys Christianity was simply a part of the Establishment, to be accepted like cold showers, school food and beating. Those whose commitment to Christianity was formed at school tended to write about it. The mass of boys who were left null and void about the whole business did not choose to write novels, but simply got on with life. Alec Waugh was rather differ-ent; in order to get on with life he had to write a novel. His novel is one of a number which make it clear that there was throughout the Edwardian period a massively powerful boy sub-culture, operating largely independently of the staff and of which the staff were largely ignorant.

Homosexuality was a large part of that sub-culture. One of the few great truths of life seems to be that the male sexual urge is proof against anything that can be put in tea. Soldiers and sailors have been told for years that the authorities doctor the tea to reduce the sex drive, and I was told exactly the same thing (and almost believed it) in the early 1960s when I was at public school. In both cases whatever substance was added failed miserably. Put a group of males into a residential or communal setting, and deprive them of female companionship or female role models, and the inevitable result, be it in prison or in public school, seems to be an obsessional homosexuality.

This homosexuality differs in important respects from the feelings of the true homosexual, who cannot bond sexually with a female. Institutional homosexuality, particularly in a school setting, does not place males as equal sexual partners, but creates 'little boys' as substitutes for women. The younger boy does not exist solely as a physical substitute, though he most certainly is that, but also as an emotional substitute: beauty, delicacy, sensitivity, all the 'softer' or more 'female' virtues that are denied in the daily currency of *macho*, all-male communities are admitted in the relationship between older and younger boys in a public school.

One comparison is with the courtly love genre of stories in the early Middle Ages. In that society the male exercised a brutal domination over women, the man in effect owning the woman completely in marriage, body, wealth and soul. This was the Establishment view. The literary world came up with the courtly love form, where the women exercised total domination over the man, who was reduced to pleading for 'mercy', and where the formal beauty of extra-marital love affairs held the fragile beauty of the finest tracery in a medieval stained-glass window. The beauty and fragility thus created offset and compensated for what was true in reality, and so the harsher and more brutal aspects of an Edwardian public school were offset by idolization of the beautiful younger boy, who whilst an object of sexual desire was also a thing of beauty and unspoilt innocence.

So many years on it is difficult to know where refined and idealized love affairs left off and sweaty tangling between the sheets took over. Certainly biographers of Robert Graves have sought to persuade us, as he did himself, that his love of other boys at Charterhouse was a devine, tender and idealized affair, and that Graves was actually horribly revolted by any grossness or physical excess. The following is typical, both of Graves and of those who have written about him,

> Johnstone was the first scholar of his year . . . it was not long before Robert fell idealistically and romantically in love with this 'exceptionally intelligent and fine-spirited' fellow. Their relationship, which Robert later called 'pseudo-homosexual', was also described by him as 'chaste and sentimental'.[25]

Who knows and, one might add, who cares? An open admission that one was a sodomite was no guarantee of immediate social or economic success in the post-war period. Graves's love affairs with boys may have been as chaste and spiritual as he would have us believe, or they may have sometimes descended into what his Charterhouse contemporaries would have called 'fast' behaviour, or even 'beastliness'. He would have been very unwise to admit to the latter: the trial of Oscar Wilde was comparatively recent history, and an author such as Hector Hugh Monro ('Saki') lived in permanent fear that his homosexuality would be exposed.

Either way, Graves's experience points us to a world where very strong bonding took place between boys, and women were largely excluded. At almost the same time as Graves was falling in love with Johnstone, a very pretty and spirited Irish girl fell in love with him. Graves's panic-stricken response to her attentions was to state, 'I was so frightened I could have killed her.'[26] Rather a lot of his generation seemed to share that fear.

Alec Waugh paints a possibly more honest picture of public school homosexuality. Very early on in *The Loom of Youth* there is a long and compelling complaint from a boy who has been expelled for homosexuality that his school has a double standard, and throughout the novel boys are being asked to leave their studies so that their study-mate can use the room to meet a junior pupil. Rupert Brooke's letters to his friend Geoffrey Keynes show a thoroughly playful, salacious and gossipy attitude to homosexual 'scandals' within the small world of the school:

> This term, as you may have heard, has been enlivened by a scandal. The unsuspected [. . .] has been discovered (a) showing up proses done for him by a wee and terrified Sixth (b) writing love letters to a small child in another house. For these offences his XV [first rugby fifteen colours] has been taken away, and he has been requested [asked to leave the school]: reason (b), however, has not been published.[27]

A short while later Brooke is giggling in a letter to his friend that a boy in another house has requested a photograph of him. The boy turns out to be,

> one with the form of a Greek God, the face of Hyacinthus, the mouth of Antinous, eyes like a sunset, a smile like dawn.[28]

It was impossible to attend an Edwardian public school without at the least a heightened awareness of homosexual behaviour. The smoke-screen put up by Graves and Establishment figures from public schools at the time that these relationships were pure, chaste and holy is not in keeping with what we now know and face up to about male sexuality, which is that it is far from chaste, pure and holy, and is often bestial, wholly physical and overwhelmingly demanding.

However, it would be a serious mistake to assume that public schools held a monopoly of homosexual feeling. Sassoon, Graves, Brooke and possibly Sorley all went through what would now be unequivocally seen as a phase of homosexuality; it seems likely that Sassoon never came out of it. At the same time the greatest of the war poets, Wilfred Owen, was spotted immediately as a homosexual by Robert Graves and described in the first American edition of *Goodbye to All That* as 'an idealistic homosexual with a religious background'.[29] Owen never went near a public school.

Another great Edwardian figure, the short-story writer and journalist 'Saki' was homosexual long before he spent two scant years at Bedford School. The Edwardian period was one in which men were encouraged by circumstances, social conditions and an overriding ethos to bond closely with fellow men. The public schools merely put some icing on that cake, and a greater opportunity to eat it. It was also an age of great naivety, and this combination of strong male bonding and an essential innocence is one of the things that Paul Fussell has got right in *The Great War and Modern Memory*.

Perhaps more surprisingly the public schools bred a healthy scepticism about themselves. This can be seen in Sorley's letters, where affection does not hide an awareness of the fallible nature of the institution. It can be seen in Alec Waugh, who in writing honestly about life at Sherborne ensured that his brother, Evelyn, would have to go to Lancing instead. Waugh's preface in the 1984 edition of *The Loom of Youth*, first published in 1917, could speak for Sorley, Graves and most of their generation.

Intensely though I had enjoyed my four years at Sherborne, I had been in constant conflict with authority. That conflict, so it seemed to me, had been in the main caused and determined by authority's inability or refusal to recognise the true nature of school life. The Public School system was venerated as a pillar of the British Empire and out of that veneration had grown a myth of the ideal Public School boy – Kipling's Brushwood boy. In no sense had I incarnated such a myth and it had been responsible, I felt, for half my troubles. Those moods of nostalgia and rebellion fused finally in an imperious need to relive my school days on paper.[30]

Alec Waugh wrote to destroy a myth. For all the fuss that was made over *The Loom of Youth* at the time, and for all that it is rather a good book and infinitely better than the execrable *Tom Brown's Schooldays*, the myth has lived on, possibly because a flood of memoirs in the post-war period gave in retrospect a picture of school life that was often not apparent at the time.

A wave of anger and bitterness broke [against public schools] in 1926 with a spate of novels and memoirs in which the author's days as schoolboys and subalterns were recalled in a jaundiced frame of mind.[31]

Yet Waugh's ability to love his school and simultaneously cock a snook at it is not unusual. Arnold Lunn's *The Harrovians* (1913) is in much the same mould as *The Loom of Youth*. Public schoolboys were well able to laugh at themselves, as a reminiscence by Professor R. H. Tawney shows,

The general was talking loudly about Winchester.
'Were you there?' I whispered to my neighbour.
'No, thank God,' he muttered.
'Same here. We're not of the elect. It may comfort you to reflect that the most important Wykehamist of the last two hundred years was an eighteenth century bishop. They don't do things. They are.'[32]

Geoffrey Fisher, headmaster at Repton, supported *The Pubber* magazine from June, 1917, to 1918, despite its frequent expressions of anti-war sentiment. The magazine was finally banned after intense pressure from the War Office, but the mere fact of its existence is remarkable. In 1915 the Eton Debating Society argued that in a democracy the lower classes must be led to join the army, not driven. In 1911 Shrewsbury boys passed a motion justifying war by only two votes. Lyttelton, headmaster of Eton, appears to have been in effect fired after preaching a school sermon in 1915 arguing for a negotiated peace. The public schools knew their boys and worshipped their successes. The suffering inflicted on those schools by the loss of their brightest and best cannot be underestimated, and the schools responded much as did society, with intense sadness and weary resignation, and occasional outflowings of bitter rebellion.

Very many of those who attended public schools remembered dreary lessons by uninspired teachers. Very many also remembered inspirational teaching, and teachers who hated anything that had not been thought through. Harold Nicolson wrote of Dr Pollock, Headmaster of Wellington in the 1890s,

> He knew that the system of the school had scored upon our brains deep grooves of habit which were in danger of becoming rigid: he set himself to render those grooves more flexible, to create new channels and associations in our minds.[33]

Of a Headmaster of Eton in the 1860s it was said,

> He taught contempt for cant and despised the commonplace.[34]

There was cant and humbug in public schools; there was also much else. In particular there was a tendency to produce individuals capable of going against the conventional political *mores* of upper class society, and capable of the most intensely radical thought. Clement Attlee, Labour Prime Minister from 1945–1951, went to Haileybury. The Marxist physicist J.D. Bernal was educated at Stonyhurst and Bedford, the Fabian and academic G.D.H. Cole educated at St Paul's. Hugh Dalton was an Etonian. Others include Lord De La Warr, Labour Minister in the 1930s and thereafter, the biochemist and Communist J.B.S. Haldane, the 6th Earl of Lucan, a Labour Junior Minister in 1945 and John Strachey, also a Labour Minister in 1945. Harrow produced Lord Gardiner, Labour Lord Chancellor from 1964. C.E.M. Joad, the Fabian and broadcaster, went to Blundell's School. The left-wing academic and well-known Labour supporter Harold Laski went to the Manchester Grammar School. This is not an exhaustive list, but it shows how dangerous it is to categorize the product of the public schools under too easy a list of headings.

The supposed military link between public schools and adult life is also a false myth. Sorley sums up the attitude of most public schoolboys to the OTC in the extract quoted earlier. It was often a rival to games, and in the spirit of the day there was far more glory in games than in being in the OTC. In 1900 only sixteen per cent of a sample of army officers had attended public school. Most boys who wanted to join the army or go to Dartmouth were sent to special military crammers designed solely for that purpose. Those that were left on the 'army side' at school were often the dregs, the army side a dumping ground for the least intelligent pupils. In *The Loom of Youth* Alec Waugh wrote,

> As a whole everything connected with the corps was 'a hell upon earth'. . . . No one knew what was happening; no one cared. It was a sheer waste of time.[35]

Sassoon's experience at Marlborough was hardly more inspiring,

> Only about a third of the School belonged to the Rifle Corps, and I sometimes wondered why I had joined it myself, since it was obvious that I had no prospect of getting into the Shooting Eight and going to Bisley.[36]

Despite this lack of respect for the armed forces, a large number of public schoolboys were tremendous officers. R.C. Sherriff could hardly be expected to be a fan of the public schools. He served in the army on leaving grammar school in 1914, and went on to a distinguished career as an author, producing, among other works, the play *Journey's End*, which has become one of the classics of the Great War. Sherriff was humiliated when he first tried to join up, being rejected because he had not been educated at one of the 'recognized' public schools. Initially he resented this bitterly, before coming to see why the edict had gone out in 1914 that only those from recognized public schools could be considered for officer training.

> But the need was pressing. Officers had to be made quickly, with the least possible trouble. The Army command had to find some sort of yardstick, and naturally they turned to the public schools. Most of the generals had been public school boys before they went to military academies. They knew from first-hand experience that a public school gave something to its boys that had the ingredients of leadership. They had a good background. They came from good homes. At school they gained self-confidence, the beginnings of responsibility through being prefects over younger boys. Pride in their schools would easily

translate into pride for a regiment. Above all, without conceit or snobbery, they were conscious of a personal superiority that placed on their shoulders an obligation towards those less privileged than themselves. All this, together with the ability to speak good English, carried the public school boy a considerable way towards the ideals that the generals aimed at for good officers. And so the edict went out that all young men selected for training as officers in the New Army must come from public schools.

But these young men never turned into officers of the old traditional type. By hard experience they became leaders in a totally different way and, through their patience and courage and endurance, carried the Army to victory after the generals had brought it within a hairsbreadth of defeat.[37]

Without raising the public schoolboy officers onto a pedestal it can be said with certainty that it was they who played the vital part in keeping the men good-humoured and obedient in the face of their interminable ill-treatment and well-nigh insufferable ordeals.[38]

It had nothing to do with wealth or privilege. Very few of the public school boys came from the landed gentry or distinguished families. For the most part they came from modest homes, the sons of local lawyers, doctors or schoolmasters – hardworking professional men. Some were the sons of country clergymen who lived on the verge of poverty and sold their precious family heirlooms for the money to send their boy to public school.[39]

These comments are not unusual. Indeed, in over twenty years of reading contemporary journals and letters the number of comments praising the product of the public school far, far outweigh any criticism. One typical example is,

At intervals the gun fired, time of flight, twenty-seven seconds. I gave the Captain roughly where the shell burst and damage, if any. My word, he didn't bat an eyelid, another of these Public School boys![40]

Another reads,

He was one of those trained in the big public schools and the Royal Military College at Camberley in those far-off days before the war, men who thought they were indestructible, untouchable – and, by God, the way some of them acted, we sometimes

22

thought so too. Marvellous men they were, men one could follow. Sometimes one thought they did not possess a scrap of human kindness, but when it came to the pinch, especially if the honour of the regiment was at stake, they would go through hell and high water to help their own men.[41]

An almost-final word might go to another relatively neglected public school classic, Kipling's *Stalky and Co.* It is a flawed book, because Kipling had to leave the United Services College fairly early on in his career and he is unconvincing in his portrayal of the sixth form public school life he never experienced. Despite that, *Stalky & Co.* is fascinating, partly because it too destroys the stereotype image of the team-member public schoolboy.

> Unlike the boys in . . . most school stories, Stalky, Beetle and McTurk are heroes because they do not conform or rally round the flag with fabricated emotionalism. Above all they are heroes because of their individuality and their ingenuity.[42]

Individuality, ingenuity and an ability to conform: there is an abundance of evidence from the writers of the First World War and from contemporary material that these were features produced by the public schools in equal measure to team spirit and mindless adherence to tradition and conformity. Even those hostile to public schoolboys had to find a grudging admiration in the less-than-inspiring products of the system, as in Richard Aldington's frequently hilarious description of one such in *Death of a Hero*:

> Evans was the usual English public-school boy, amazingly ignorant, amazingly inhibited, and yet 'decent' and good-humoured. . . . Evans was an 'educated' pre-War public-school boy, which means that he remembered half a dozen Latin tags, could mumble a few ungrammatical phrases in French, knew a little of the history of England, and had a 'correct' accent. He had been taught to respect all women as if they were his mother; would therefore have fallen easy prey to the first tart who came along, and probably have married her. He was a good runner, had played at stand-off half for his school and won his colours at cricket. He could play fives, squash, rackets, golf, tennis, water-polo, bridge and vingt-et-un, which he called 'pontoon'. . . . Evans possessed that British rhinoceros equipment of mingled ignorance, self-confidence, and complacency which is triple-armed against all the shafts of the mind. And yet

Winterbourne could not help liking the man. He was exasperatingly stupid, but he was honest, he was kindly, he was conscientious, he could obey orders and command obedience in others, he took pains to look after his men. He could be implicitly relied upon to lead a hopeless attack and to maintain a desperate defence to the very end. There were thousands and tens of thousands like him.[43]

As with so much in that war, the truth had been overlaid by the wash of cynicism and bitterness that swept over the country in the 1920s, and which was not a feature either of the Edwardian period or the war itself. The public schoolboy was a far more complicated animal than has often been supposed, and that complexity is reflected in the character and writing of the poets that the public schools produced in abundance. Even more significant is the fact that Britain's largely volunteer army was staffed at the outset by officers drawn from the public schools. They were largely untrained, and in many instances had only the most passing knowledge of anyone living outside their own class. But they bonded the British soldier to his officer more effectively than in any other European army, kept that army together and brought simple qualities of comradeship, loyalty and duty to what many now see, in Sassoon's words, as a 'dirty job'. And, as Sassoon himself comments, they 'did it fine'. Indeed, Sassoon's poem 'To Any Dead Officer', one of the most moving written of any war, is also one of the most moving and accurate pictures of the public schoolboy officer:

> You were all out to try and save your skin,
>   Well knowing how much the world had got to give.
> You joked at shells and talked the usual 'shop',
>   Stuck to your dirty job and did it fine:
> With 'Jesus Christ! When will it stop?
>   Three years . . . it's hell unless we break their line.'
>
>   . . . I'm blind with tears,
>   Staring into the dark. Cheero!
> I wish they'd killed you in a decent show.

Post-war society allowed the public schoolboys who gave their lives in vast numbers between 1914 and 1918 the sobriquets of bravery and patriotism. It did not allow them the fact that they believed they were fighting for liberty, were in many cases hugely independent and, as will be seen later, for the most part did not lose their faith in what they were fighting for. The tendency to laugh, to scorn the concept of the English amateur, has obscured the fact that an army composed of amateur officers won a war against the most professional army in Europe, and did so in a straight fight.

Georgian Poetry

Georgian poetry is the third leg in the triangle of pre-war myths. Many who believe they know all about public schools and the Edwardian Summer might confess themselves ignorant of the Georgian poetry movement. More than any other feature of Edwardian England it has suffered from the 1920s backlash, the purge of the politically incorrect that came when irony, cynicism and complexity became the only intellectually acceptable expressions of poetry.

Georgian poetry acquired its name through the titles of five *Georgian Poetry* anthologies, the first published in 1912 and the last, when the movement was a spent force, in 1922. At its centre was the dapper figure of Edward Marsh. Marsh was a descendant of the only British Prime Minister to have been assassinated, and as a recipient of money awarded to the descendants had considerable private means. A civil servant, he was for many years private secretary to Winston Churchill. A childhood illness had left Marsh impotent, and throughout his adult life he showed a need to develop strong relationships with younger men. He used his wealth to act as a patron of the arts, specializing in painting and poetry.

Marsh adopted Rupert Brooke from an early age, and it was from a late-night conversation between the two men that the idea for the *Georgian Poetry* anthologies emerged. Both felt that a great deal of exciting new poetry was being produced by young authors, and that it should receive a wider audience. Harold Monro, himself a poet and founder of the Poetry Bookshop in London, was soon brought in and the first anthology, *Georgian Poetry 1911–1912*, published by the Poetry Bookshop. It was an immediate success, and sold well over 20,000 copies in hardback.

Marsh prefaced the first anthology with the comment,

> This volume is issued in the belief that English poetry is now once again putting on a new strength and beauty . . . This collection, drawn entirely from the publications of the past two years, may if it is fortunate help the lovers of poetry to realise that we are now at the beginning of a new 'Georgian' period which may take rank in due time with the several great poetic ages of the past.[44]

Much modern criticism has queued up to dismiss Georgian poetry. Indeed, I started a doctoral thesis on the school in the firm belief that I would find a decayed and decadent romantic backwater, a voice of poetry that had actively interfered with and held back the great poets of the First World War. My mistake was actually to read the five *Georgian Poetry* anthologies (rather difficult to avoid if one is writing a 120,000 word thesis on them), which seemed to reveal just how many of those who felt able to comment on the anthologies had not done that small thing. Typical of comments which damned the Georgians was that found in the hugely influential John H. Johnston's *English Poetry of the First World War*. Johnston, who in fairness clearly had read the anthologies, gave both barrels to the movement, one from himself and one from another leading figure in critical circles:

> The *Georgian Poetry* series . . . represented not a renaissance but what David Daiches has aptly called a 'retrenchment' . . . But if they achieved 'a certain tremulous stability' in their meditative response to 'the slow-beating rustic heart of England', this stability was attained by a sacrifice which is in the long run always fatal to poetry: the loss of contact with contemporary reality.[45]

The Georgian poets would have laughed out loud at this dismissal, believing themselves to be the pioneers of contemporary reality in poetry. The 1980 edition of Bernard Bergonzi's *Heroes' Twilight* delivers an even more damning blow to Georgian poetry: it does not even mention it. The most influential book so far published on the Great War, Paul Fussell's *The Great War and Modern Memory*, condemns Georgian poetry as being concerned only with 'sunrises and sunsets'[46], a sublimely fatuous statement in the light of what the Georgians actually wrote. Fussell is one of those who feels able to comment on the Georgians without apparently having read their work. Among other commentators there has been a remarkable tendency to say that a certain poet was not a Georgian because the poet in question was good and the Georgians clearly were not.

> Robert Graves, we are assured, was not a Georgian, nor were D.H. Lawrence, Edward Thomas, Siegfried Sassoon, Wilfred Owen, Isaac Rosenberg and Edmund Blunden. Whether or not they appeared in *Georgian Poetry* is, according to such critics, totally irrelevant. What matters is the quality of their work: if it is good it cannot be Georgian; if it is Georgian it must, *ipso facto*, be feeble.[47]

26

Of the seven poets mentioned above, five appeared in the Georgian anthologies, one (Edward Thomas) lived his literary life with Georgians and was only excluded because the anthologies did not print work by dead authors and the last, Owen, marked his acceptance as a poet by crying out that he was held peer by the Georgians. Jon Silkin argued that Isaac Rosenberg was not a Georgian,[48] and F.R. Leavis believed that Edmund Blunden could not be a Georgian 'because he has some genuine talent'.[49] A series of reviews and semi-popular comment disposed of the Georgians as soon as was convenient:

> The mistake – probably unavoidable – was to regard 'Georgian poetry' as a 'movement' when . . . it was really a kind of shelter for a few poets writing poetry in a familiar style about familiar subject matter.[50]

There is rarely smoke without fire. Each of the Georgian anthologies contained its fair share of weak or lacklustre poetry, but the last two were particularly weak, despite the presence of Edmund Blunden and Robert Graves. These last two anthologies were published without the influence of Rupert Brooke and have done the most harm to the reputation of the movement.

Brooke was a vital part of the Georgian revolution and it did not survive his death. Firstly, he was an exciting and innovative poet and a symbol of the new age in poetry. Secondly, he was a social and literary jam-pot of gargantuan proportions. Even a brief list of his friends and acquaintances reads like a *Who's Who* of the Edwardian literary world – he played as a child with Virginia Stephens (Woolf), and was close friends at school with James Strachey, Duncan Grant and Geoffrey Keynes. He met and knew Thomas Hardy, Ramsay MacDonald, Alfred Austin, Hilaire Belloc, H.G. Wells and nearly all the Bloomsbury group. Without Brooke's presence and contacts, Marsh's editorship of the anthologies relapsed into unenterprising and unexciting conservatism, something clearly reflected in the sales as well as the quality of the verse.

The weakness of the last two anthologies was an exaggeration of a strand that had been visible from the start, a strand which saw the milder parts of nature, moonlight and rural calm as being at the centre of poetry. The weakness which saw the Georgians crucified was that they harked back to Wordsworth, and it was the Wordsworthian tradition that was most alien to the new conformity established by T.S. Eliot and summed up in *Prufrock* and *The Waste Land*. The Georgians were subjective; Eliot pursued objectivity. The Georgians favoured – sometimes – rural settings; Eliot favoured 'smell of steaks in passageways'. The Georgians were sometimes sentimental; Eliot, a patient etherized upon a table, was cynical. The Georgians spent much of their time leading up to an explosion of emotion, a personal revelation on the road to Damascus; the only explosion in Eliot was akin to that of a terrorist's hand grenade, only not so exciting. The Georgians used irony as an incidental technique; Eliot used irony not so much as a technique but more as a theme. A literary establishment that hailed Eliot, quite rightly, as the major poetic talent of the twentieth century was always going to see the Georgians as a symbol of everything that Eliot and his poetry opposed.

Yet the Georgians, far from being the last spasm of a decayed Romanticism, were perceived in their time as being revolutionaries. No one individual has been more fair to the Georgians than C.K. Stead:

> Mr Daiches, like so many critics of the past twenty years, has seen the Georgians through spectacles provided for him by the later, more vigorous movement led by Pound and Eliot. The suggestion is that the Georgians set themselves against the natural development of modern poetry: in fact they were its precursors.[51]

To see the lie in much modern commentary on the Georgians one only has to look at the forty poets whose poems were published in the five anthologies. *Georgian Poetry* was the only agency outside vanity publishing to print anything of Isaac Rosenberg's. It published Rupert Brooke, Robert Graves, Siegfried Sassoon, Isaac Rosenberg and Edmund Blunden, and did not restrict its choice to the sanitized, 'safe' poems of those authors. It published brutal, 'realistic' poetry by the writer of *Autobiography of a Supertramp*, W.H. Davies, by Wilfrid Gibson, Lascelles Abercrombie and Gordon Bottomley. In the latter and in John Drinkwater it showed its willingness to accept the new vogue for poetic drama. It accepted D.H. Lawrence as a poet before anyone else had done so. It was prepared to print the new voice even if it came from old men, including poems from Masefield and G.K. Chesterton. It gave room to a poet whose reputation has lasted despite wholesale neglect by the literary establishment, Walter de la Mare.

Far from being backward-looking, Georgian poetry was in its time a revolutionary movement. The nature of that revolution is crucial to understanding why the young poets of the Great War were able to produce so much powerful poetry within a very short time of being presented with an experience that should have been so overwhelming and so new as to freeze their ability to translate it into poetry. Georgian poetry was the standard-bearer of the new, the vigorous and the bold. As such it acted as a model for many young poets, and helped shape how and what they wrote. The key to its revolution was realism. The Georgians were only prepared to write about what they knew and had experienced personally. Thus Brooke got into great trouble with his publishers for entitling a poem 'Lust', and for writing graphic descriptions of seasickness. Wilfrid Gibson and Walter de la Mare wrote poems about prostitutes and derelicts. Lascelles Abercrombie included lovingly-detailed descriptions of flies crawling over human bodies in his 'The Sale of St Thomas' (*Georgian Poetry 1911–1912*). He was also the author of the immortal lines,

> Pierre: I'm going to spew.
> Andrieu: Good lad! Why not?
> Jacques: For God's sake mind my legs!

and,

> Eutache: Look out, behind!
> 'Ware turds! the street's a patch of muck.

One forgets just how shocking these lines were before the First World War. Gordon Bottomley's play *King Lear's Wife (Georgian Poetry 1913–1915)* contains a cheery little song based on lice crawling out of a dead woman's body. True, there is a deal of rather uncritical and tedious nature poetry in the anthologies, but contemporary opinions of what Georgian poetry stood for are very different from the character imposed on it by the literary establishment of the 1930s.

> They [the Georgians] show a wholesome revolt against poetic cliches, a desire for directness and simplicity both of feeling and expression. They are not afraid of their imaginations or their minds.[52]

Georgian poetry was a reaction against the empty rhetoric and abstractions of the Imperialist poets and against poetry that was mere empty form. It owed a great debt to Thomas Hardy's poetry and an even greater one to what was perceived as the new realism of John Masefield, whose poem 'The Everlasting Mercy' was a major influence on Sassoon and many poets of his vintage, in particular Charles Sorley. It refused to accept any limits on what a poet might write about, and demanded that verse be written in language shorn of antique affectation,

> Every aspect of life shall be the subject of our art, and what we see we will describe in the language which we use every day. The result shall be the New Poetry, the vital expression of the new race.[53]

Robert Graves claimed that after an interview with Edward Marsh he never wrote 'thee' or 'thou' again in his poetry.[54]

Poetry can be divided into form and content – the manner in which the poet expresses what he or she wishes to say, and what he or she actually chooses to say. What Georgian poetry did not do was challenge accepted ideas of form – that verse should be loosely metrical and, more often than not, rhyme – in any serious way, though D.H. Lawrence and others interested in poetic drama pushed at the edges in this respect. Its greatest weakness was that as a movement of young poets, many of whom had lived more or less restricted lives, most of its authors did not have a strength of experience to match the strength of their lyric impulse. The result is that many young Georgians show in their poetry what T.S. Eliot in another context described as an emotion in excess of the known facts: their subject matter is simply not able to bear the load of emotion they place on it, and some Georgian poetry, Brooke's in particular, consists of a search for 'the immortal moment', an intense and almost messianic vision imposed on unconvincingly limited experience.

Left to its own devices Georgian poetry would have had its day and given way to a stronger and more widely-based vision of poetry. Speculation about what would have happened to English poetry if the war had not happened is entirely useless, and great fun. My own belief is that it would have followed a path set by Thomas Hardy far more than the one it did follow, that set by T.S. Eliot. Some would argue that this strand of poetry is in fact coming to pass in the works of poets such as Ted Hughes and Seamus Heaney, and that the dominance of irony in post-war poetry is untrue to the essential traditions of English poetry, a vast sidetrack imposed on literary culture by the war. As long ago as the 1970s at least one academic argued that literature devoted wholly to irony cannot generate the occasionally total commitment to its subject that is necessary for any true masterpiece.[55] Whilst *The Waste Land* seems to disprove that theory, it is true that irony shows the reader a succession of visions, layered one upon the other and none containing an ultimate truth. It is my impression that most great literature usually makes at least one statement which is capable of only one meaning.

In any event, the Georgians could not have done a better job of preparing for the First World War if they had been invented for that purpose. They took on board a group of young poets and told them that they could write with total honesty about whatever experience came to them. By a loose adherence to conventional form they gave those poets a ready vehicle with which to write about the war, but did not preclude experiment with form. They persuaded the poets that poetry was the most potent of all the literary media, and that poetry could change the world: Owen's vision of the poet as preacher ('Out of my mouth might many men . . .') owes something to Shelley and something to his own religious leanings, but also something to the importance ascribed to the poet by Georgian poetry.

To other poets Georgian poetry gave a vision of nature that allowed the poet to see the war in perspective, something perhaps best summed up in Edward Thomas's poem 'As the Team's Head Brass', where the tree may not be moved because the other ploughman has died in the war, but the young lovers are still emerging from the wood and there is no doubt that nature will outlive the war. This certainty gives strength to Thomas's work and also to much of that by Edmund Blunden. It has to be said also that an attempt to hide in nature cripples much of Robert Graves's war poetry.

The other, crucial impact on the poetry of the Great War from Georgian poetry has never been properly chronicled, its sole serious historian being Dominic Hibberd in an article printed in the mid-1970s.[56] The Georgians brought into their ranks, encouraged and nurtured many of the major voices of the war. They also had an immense practical influence on a number of poets who never published in the anthologies, but who owed much to the movement.

The first level of influence exerted by the Georgians was that formed by the war poets who were unequivocal members of the movement, as witnessed by publishing poetry in the anthologies. Of these the best known are Rupert Brooke, Siegfried Sassoon, Robert Graves and Edmund Blunden. Isaac Rosenberg had one extract published in *Georgian Poetry 1916–1917*, the anthology which marked the apogee of the movement. As well as 'They', 'In the Pink', 'Death Bed' and five other poems by Sassoon, this anthology contained eight poems by Robert Graves, including 'Goliath and David'. Other powerful war poems were included by

Robert Nichols, now neglected but at the time one of the first, with Sassoon, to write unashamedly realistic war poetry; J.C. Squire, whose 'To a Bull-Dog' is a neglected classic; several by Wilfrid Gibson, who is arguably the inventor of the short, colloquial and realistic war poem; and Herbert Asquith's 'The Volunteer'. The final anthology contained work by Frank Prewett, another poet neglected for many years but now increasingly being hailed as a significant talent. This list alone proves that the Georgians were willing to take on board and publish the 'new' war poetry, and had among them some of the strongest and best talent visible in the war.

However, the Georgians did as much for those who did not appear in the anthologies as for those whose poems were chosen for inclusion. Harold Monro was a major early influence on Wilfred Owen and may have been responsible for Owen's interest in the sonnet form. The key moment in Owen's development as a war poet came when he met Siegfried Sassoon at Craiglockhart. Sassoon was thoroughbred Georgian. His poetry was firmly in the Georgian mould of realism and truth to experience. Sassoon was very much the John the Baptist figure to Owen's Jesus: in Sassoon's case also a greater one was to come. If that analogy holds any truth, then the doctrine preached by the forerunner was in large measure the doctrine of Georgian poetry. It is not only the literary influence that matters in this link between two poets, but also the level of emotional support and straightforward morale boosting.

What is true for Owen is true for many other young poets of the time. The Georgians were famous, seen as being at the heart of what mattered in a poetic revival, and were hero-worshipped by younger and sometimes not-so-young poets. To be admitted into the club, to be admired by a Georgian, gave the same thrill as a debutante felt when asked to dance by a prince of the blood. It also gave young poets a crucial boost at a time when often they stood in greatest need of support and encouragement from those they admired. Thus the most moving letters Owen wrote are to his friend Sassoon.

There is evidence that Owen had not heard of the Georgian anthologies prior to August, 1915, when he expresses ignorance of Walter de la Mare, something no reader of the Georgian anthologies could have done.[57] He met Harold Monro in late October, 1915, (Monro featured regularly in the anthologies, as well as publishing them), and knew him well enough to use the room Monro kept for poor poets above his bookshop in February, 1916. Monro read Owen's poetry and advised him on it, though Owen appears not to have liked Monro particularly. It may simply be that Owen disliked criticism of his poetry; he responded in a similar manner to Robert Graves. Owen reveals that he knows Masefield's poetry in February, 1917,[58] and the first mentions of Sassoon's poetry and Georgian poetry come in his letters in August, 1917. From then dates one of the most dramatic and intense periods of creativity ever embarked upon by any major English poet. Owen met Robert Graves in October, 1917, and felt rather patronized.[59] The tension soon appeared to pass; there was extensive correspondence between the two men, and Owen was invited to Graves's wedding. Owen met Edward Marsh in January, 1918. His own comments tell how important his links with Georgian poets were,

> They believe in me, these Georgians, and I suffer a temptation to be satisfied that they read me; and to remain a poet's poet![60]

> I am held peer by the Georgians; I am a poet's poet![61]

> We Georgians are all so old. . . . Someday I'll lend you my *Georgian Poetry 1917.*[62]

Owen sees Georgian poetry as something to aspire to, something of an élite club, and is proud to be seen as one of its poets, as in the telling phrase, 'We Georgians'. Perhaps some of the pruning of excess from Owen's earlier style, one of the features that allowed him to write great poetry, can be attributed in part to his reading of work by Georgian poets. Whatever the literary influence exerted by Georgian poetry on Owen's development, its personal influence, in the shape of Sassoon, Graves and an entry into the London literary world, was immense.

It was equally immense in the case of Isaac Rosenberg, the son of a poor Jewish family. With help from Jewish organizations and individuals, he was educated as a painter and attended the Slade School. Edward Marsh initially supported him as a painter, but poetry became increasingly important to Rosenberg and overtook his painting as a primary interest.

> I believe in myself more as a poet than a painter. I think I get more depth into my writing.[63]

Rosenberg's image can tend to suggest that he spent most of his time either in synagogues or working men's clubs. In fact he came from a working-class background, inasmuch as any immigrant family from Europe can be placed immediately into the English class structure, but was much more what might now be called a Bohemian than a symbol of the working classes. He was undoubtedly Jewish, but his historical and intrinsic grasp of Jewish themes and history did not stretch to a contemporary worship of Judaism. Even with these caveats, he is an unlikely figure to be fêted by the Georgian poets, perceived largely as the epitome of English middle-class literary taste. He was introduced to Edward Marsh on 10 November, 1913, when he also met T.E. Hulme. When Marsh bought three paintings from Rosenberg it allowed Rosenberg to publish privately his pamphlet *Youth*. In November, 1915, the Georgian stalwart Lascelles Abercrombie was shown Rosenberg's poetry by Marsh, and wrote to him at the front; Rosenberg had enlisted in October, 1915. In June, 1915, R.C. Trevelyan and in July, 1916, Gordon Bottomley wrote to Rosenberg: both were leading Georgians.

These are the bare facts. They do not tell half the story. Marsh introduced Rosenberg to the Georgian anthologies, to which he responded with enthusiasm,

> What strikes me about these men [is] they are very much alive, and have personal vision – and what is so essential, can express themselves very simply.[64]

Marsh regularly criticized Rosenberg's poetry, arousing Rosenberg's thinly-veiled hostility but also pushing him towards greater simplicity and intelligibility, something which a reading of Rosenberg's less famous work suggests has to be a good thing.[65] Marsh's continuing financial support was invaluable.

> Thank you for the cheque. I love poetry – but just now the finest poem ever written would not move me as the writing on that cheque.[66]

Marsh sent chocolates to Rosenberg when he was taken ill, and was frequently called on by Rosenberg, who was almost wholly impractical and disorganized, to sort out problems with pay and other organizational matters. Indeed at times Marsh was treated much in the manner that a schoolboy might treat a generous uncle:

> Could you send me a pound to buy boots with and to get to London with [by] Xmas if my devil of an officer will give me leave as I must get another pair when my feet are better.[67]

Those who were loyal to Rosenberg required patience. He dropped most of his paintings overboard when returning from South Africa before the war, ruined others by placing them face to face with other work while they were still wet, and appeared frequently to smudge letters to his patrons. At one time he left a large parcel of paintings for Marsh without any address on it to say for whom it was intended.

In the meantime Rosenberg found the work of Lascelles Abercrombie through reading *Georgian Poetry*, and responded with wild enthusiasm;

> Who is your best living English poet? I've found somebody miles and miles above everybody – a young man, Lascelles Abercrombie – a mighty poet and a brother to Browning.[68]

Abercrombie gave immense encouragement to Rosenberg, writing early on,

> Some of your phrases are remarkable; no-one who tries to write poetry would help envying some of them.[69]

Rosenberg very soon came to place Gordon Bottomley equally high in his estimation. Writing in 1915 he states:

> I like Bottomley more than any other modern poet I have yet come across.[70]

Bottomley gave huge encouragement to Rosenberg, and Rosenberg makes clear the debt he owes when he writes in 1916:

> If you really mean what you say in your letter, there is no need to tell you how proud I am. I had to read your letter many times before I could convince myself that you were not 'pulling my leg'. . . . It is a great thing to me to be able to tell you now in this way what marvellous pleasure your work has given me, and what pride that my work pleases you.[71]

The situation is very similar to that between Sassoon and Owen, with a young and unknown poet receiving almost out of the blue the strongest possible support and encouragement from one of his literary heroes. The effect on Rosenberg was arguably even greater, because it was not two but four figures from the Georgian movement – Marsh, Bottomley, Abercrombie and Trevelyan – who poured praise on Rosenberg, starved of such praise for most of his life. It is also clear that the pressure from the Georgian poets was for greater simplicity in Rosenberg's work without sacrificing complexity of meaning. They provoked Rosenberg to define what might be seen as one of the strongest features in his best work:

> Simple *poetry* – that is where an interesting complexity of thought is kept in tone and right value to the dominating idea so that it is understandable and still ungraspable.[72]

Those who think 'Break of Day in the Trenches' and lines from 'Dead Man's Dump' to be among the finest products of any war would be hard put to find a better account of the strange power these poems exert, and it is difficult not to believe that some of the success is down to the incessant pounding by Georgian figures for Rosenberg to restrict his far from wilful obscurity. Rosenberg seems to acknowledge this when he ends a tetchy letter to Marsh by saying he has enclosed a copy of the newly-written 'Break of Day in the Trenches':

> I am enclosing a poem I wrote in the trenches, which is surely as simple as ordinary talk. You might object to the second line as vague, but that was the best way I could express the sense of dawn.[73]

Rosenberg was clearly impressed by the poetry of the Georgian Wilfrid Gibson:

> Gibson's 'Battle' was sent to me and delighted me. It is as good as Degas.[74]

Rosenberg also admitted himself 'delighted' with another poet featured heavily in the Georgian anthologies, T. Sturge Moore, and expressed admiration for W.J. Turner, J.C. Squire and Sassoon when Marsh sent him his complimentary copies of *Georgian Poetry 1916–1917*.[76] He was rather disparaging about the other work in the anthology: 'There is some good stuff in it but very little.'[77] This was at a time when Rosenberg appeared, less than a month before his death, to be very depressed. He wrote to Marsh that he considered the first two anthologies to be far better than the third, though he did find time to praise 'The Tower' by Robert Nichols.[78] The last letter Rosenberg wrote that has survived was to Edward Marsh.

Biographers and critics of Rosenberg have tended to disparage

Georgian poetry and its influence, saying, 'But the Georgians closed ranks against Rosenberg'[79] and,

> convention had to be avoided at all costs. In establishing this principle, Rosenberg precluded for himself any deep involvement in the emerging Georgian movement.[80]

There is truth in the disparagement, inevitably. Marsh became very annoyed with Bottomley for giving too much encouragement to Rosenberg, and thought *Moses* (a privately-printed pamphlet) was a 'farrago'. The worship of Rosenberg's greatest poetry has tended to overshadow the fact that he wrote huge tracts of very bad verse, among which much of the content of *Moses* might be included. His finest poetry is unlike anything produced by the Georgians, or for that matter by any other contemporary poet. The criticism of Rosenberg by Marsh, Marsh's own failure to see the genius in his poetry and the rampant individuality of Rosenberg's poems have distanced him from the Georgians. It is also hard to credit a serious and meaningful link between a visionary, poverty-stricken Jewish East End painter/poet and a poetic movement edited by an Establishment figure and populated to some extent from the middle ground of English gentile poetry.

Yet Georgian poetry can and should take some of the credit for Rosenberg's achievement. The only one of Rosenberg's biographers to acknowledge this is Jean Liddiard:

> 'Spring 1916', for example, contains not only the simplicity and finish of Georgian poetry, but another feature Rosenberg admired in it – 'personal vision'.[81]

The *Collected Works* prints 176 letters or fragments of letters from Rosenberg. Fifty-two of these are to Edward Marsh, eighteen more to Abercrombie, Bottomley or Trevelyan. It is of course dangerous to place too much weight on this: the figures might reveal more of those who kept letters from Rosenberg than those he most commonly wrote to. Nevertheless, the sheer weight of correspondence to Marsh and other leading Georgians suggests that Rosenberg's greatest mentors and guides, albeit ones he frequently disagreed with, were the Georgian editor and the poets of *Georgian Poetry*.

What cannot be denied is that it was Marsh and his poets who first spotted Rosenberg's exceptional talent, and who were the only figures other than Laurence Binyon both to recognize him and give him the artistic and financial support he craved. For example, apparent pleas for recognition to Israel Zangwill and Ezra Pound appear to have fallen on deaf ears. Georgians did not 'create' Rosenberg the poet any more than they created Wilfred Owen. They did provide recognition, support and guidance which were crucial to the final product of both poets. Whatever rows Marsh and Rosenberg might have had, Marsh remained loyal to Rosenberg throughout the latter's life. A final pointer to the place Rosenberg had in Marsh's heart is the fact that visitors to Marsh's house woke up in the guest room to the sight of one of Rosenberg's paintings; given that Marsh's life revolved round his visitors, it is difficult not to see something very personal in this placing of a painting.

Nor does the list of Georgian involvement stop there. The Georgians exerted a very significant influence over several poets who never appeared even briefly in the anthologies. One of the most famous is Edward Thomas. Thomas turned to writing poetry with help mainly from Robert Frost, a poet who would certainly have been included in the anthologies had he not been American. Other than that, his poetic links were almost entirely with Georgian poetry and poets. The list of those links is far too long to be dealt with adequately here: the correspondence between Edward Thomas and Gordon Bottomley occupies a full-length book, and this represented only one of Thomas's links with Georgian poets. Thomas was present at the opening of Monro's Poetry Bookshop in January, 1913, as a reviewer. Ironically Robert Frost, who had invited himself, was also there, though on this occasion the two did not meet. When they did, through the agency of the Georgian poet, Ralph Hodgson, Thomas's role as writer and reviewer meant that he was on first-name terms with a large number of the Georgian poets long before the publication of the first anthology in 1912.

The folly of excluding either Frost or Thomas from the Georgian poets, despite the fact that neither appeared in the anthologies, is shown by the fact of Frost's move to what was to become a famous gathering ground for Georgian poets, the village of Dymock in Gloucestershire. Wilfrid Gibson and Lascelles Abercrombie led the way in setting up house there, and the Frosts followed in April, 1914. Thomas was a frequent visitor to the area. Other regulars in this remarkable poetic colony were Rupert Brooke, W.H. Davies and John Drinkwater, the meetings being in effect a roll-call for the leading lights in the Georgian poetry movement.

Brooke had known Thomas for some years, and took him to one of Edward Marsh's literary breakfasts in London in February, 1913. The occasion was a disaster, and led in all probability to

Marsh excluding Thomas from *Georgian Poetry 1916–1917*. Ostensibly this was because Marsh had a principle that no poet should be represented posthumously, but the rejection was a cause of great friction among the Georgian poets. Walter de la Mare offered to stand down to make room for Thomas, and several other Georgians pleaded for Thomas's inclusion. It was a fair plea: Thomas the poet owed something to Georgian poetry and his frequent contacts with Georgian poets:

> Perhaps . . . his acquaintance with the poets of the Georgian fraternity in Gloucestershire had suggested that he need not consider himself a failure for ever. If they could write poetry, why not himself?[82]

Those who seek to distance Thomas from the Georgians have some justification: Harold Monro and Gordon Bottomley were both lukewarm when sent the first of Thomas's poems. Yet the triumph of the Georgians in recognizing Thomas's talent, came in 1915 with the idea of three Georgian poets – Bottomley, Lascelles Abercrombie and R.C. Trevelyan, the same three who recognized Isaac Rosenberg – to produce another anthology, *An Annual of New Poetry*. There is some reason for believing that the main aim of the project was to get Thomas's poems published. Certainly Edward Eastaway (Thomas's pen-name as a poet) had, with eighteen poems, by far the largest selection in the book. All the poems were previously unpublished. The Georgians John Freeman and Walter de la Mare then launched a plan for publishing a complete volume of Thomas's poems.

Thomas Hardy was probably a far greater influence on Thomas than the Georgian poets, but despite that Thomas repeats the pattern seen elsewhere, the pattern of a young movement that gathered to it all that was brightest and best in pre-war poetry, and nurtured it in practical as well as literary terms. Thomas's poetry has prospered since his death, that of the Georgian poets who took him to their hearts has often sunk without trace. Yet Thomas's love of nature and the English countryside, his deceptive simplicity, his dedication to traditional though loose form, his inability to speak from anything other than personal experience, are features central to Georgian poetry and all it stood for.

Ivor Gurney is another example of a major poetic talent who did not publish in the anthologies but who knew many of the Georgian poets and took at least some literary and practical succour from them. In 1916 he took leave from the front and chose to travel through Gloucestershire, sufficiently moved by the presence of

Wilfrid Gibson and Lascelles Abercrombie there to go to Dymock and introduce himself to Abercrombie's wife. Long after Gurney's death Edmund Blunden was a crucial figure in launching the first full collection of Gurney's poems. Gurney's fascination with the Georgian movement is revealed by the domination in his songs of Georgian authors. He set to music the poems of Edward Thomas, Wilfrid Gibson, Walter de la Mare, W.H. Davies, Edward Shanks, Hilaire Belloc, Robert Graves, Rupert Brooke, John Masefield, J. C. Squire, John Freeman, James Elroy Flecker, William Kerr, Edmund Blunden, Ralph Hodgson, John Drinkwater and Francis Lewidge, with Georgian poets far outnumbering others and the work of Thomas, Gibson and de la Mare given special priority. Marsh was involved, in an echo of his involvement with Rosenberg, in attempting to get a pension for Gurney. The true extent of Gurney's involvement with Georgian poets has never been fully revealed, though there is evidence that it was quite extensive:

> Though Ivor Gurney's movements and activities, other than the writing of music and poetry, are shadowy and uncertain, a letter to John Haines, postmarked 11 November, 1919, reveals that he had already become known to and accepted by several of the Georgian poets.
>
> I have seen Shanks in London 3 or 4 times, Monro, Turner at his house. And one evening Shanks, Munro [sic] and myself went to hear Steuart Wilson sing the 'Wenlock Edge' cycle of Vaughan Williams – a fine strong piece of work . . . On Saturday . . . we visited Masefield in his proper haunt at Boar's Hill, where are Graves, Nichols and Bridges also.[83]

All the poets mentioned, with the exception of Robert Bridges, appeared in one or more of the anthologies.

There is therefore much evidence to suggest that Georgian poetry was a midwife to much of the poetic talent that sprung up during the First World War, and that the true force of its impact has never been fully recorded. A criticism of this viewpoint is the argument that Georgian poetry was never a movement in the correct sense of the word, merely a loosely-connected group of poets drawn from the mildly innovative middle ground. To counterbalance this is the fact that no movement in British poetry has ever arisen without the almost simultaneous arrival of a critical body of opinion pointing out that it is in fact not a movement but merely a collection of loosely-connected poets. I can remember feeling an unreasoned juvenile anger at being asked as an undergraduate to explore the work of 'The Movement' only to find that most of the available critical material was concerned with pointing out that 'The Movement' was not a movement at all.

It does seem clear that the Georgian poets were united by an admiration for poetry of personal expression based on personal experience, that they scorned abstraction and any restriction on subject matter, and that they believed simplicity need not preclude poetry with a complex emotional and intellectual appeal. The inclusion of D.H. Lawrence as one of their number and their willingness to experiment with poetic verse drama suggest they may not have been as hidebound over form as posterity suggests. In any event, the publication of the anthologies gave them a very high public profile at a time when poets of their age and sales might not expect to be so favoured, and this high profile placed them in contact with all that was best in young British poetry.

The Georgians in general, and Marsh, Bottomley, Abercrombie, Trevelyan, Sassoon and Graves in particular, responded to their privileged position with a patrician dedication to unknown poets, encouraging, supporting and giving friendship with immense literary and occasional financial generosity. Georgian poets recognized Owen, Rosenberg and Sorley as major talents, and in the case of the first two exerted a significant influence on the form and content of their best work. Georgian poets also recognized and were the seed-bed for the poetry of Edward Thomas, as well as influencing a host of other poets, including Ivor Gurney. It is a proud record, as proud as that of any group of poets, and has never yet been given the credit it deserves. The Georgians were in some respects similar to the salmon that dies after it has spawned: the product of their spawning has a part in some of the most remarkable English poetry written in the twentieth century. Perhaps now we can recognize such an achievement, and consign another myth to history's rubbish bin.

Notes

1 Arthur J. Taylor quoted in Nowell-Smith, *Edwardian England*, p. 105
2 Nowell-Smith, p. 45
3 *ibid.* p. 46
4 Beckett and Cherry, *The Edwardian Era*, p. 7
5 Thorpe, preface to Sassoon, *The Old Century*, p. 12
6 Nowell-Smith, pp. 25–6
7 Marwick, *Deluge*, p. 26
8 Read, *Edwardian England*, p. 69
9 Nowell-Smith, p. 31

10 *ibid.*, p. 37
11 Parker, *Old Lie*, pp. 17–18
12 Philip Franks, private letter to author
13 Chandos, *Boys Together*, p. 12
14 Waugh, *Loom of Youth*, p. 21
15 Fussell, *Great War and Modern Memory*, p. 208
16 O'Prey, *In Broken Images*, p. 55
17 *ibid.*, p. 41
18 p. 45
19 Sorley, *Letters*, p. 42
20 *ibid.*, p. 58
21 p. 16
22 p. 42
23 Waugh, p. 88
24 *ibid.*
25 Graves, *Assault Heroic*, p. 88
26 *ibid.*, p.87
27 Brooke, *Letters*, p.39
28 *ibid.*, p. 41
29 Graves, *Goodbye to All That*, NY ed., 1957, p. 264
30 Waugh, p. 35
31 Parker, p. 281
32 Chapman, *Passionate Prodigality*, p. 155
33 Gathorne-Hardy, *Public School Phenomenon*, p. 185
34 *ibid.*, p. 186
35 Waugh, p. 35
36 Sassoon, *Old Century*, p. 226
37 Sherriff, quoted in Panichas, *Promise of Greatness*, p. 139
38 *ibid.*, p. 152
39 p. 154
40 McDonald, *Voices*, p. 292
41 Bert Chaney, quoted Moynihan, *People at War*, p. 118
42 Parker, p. 60
43 Aldington, *Death of a Hero*, pp. 285–6
44 *Georgian Poetry 1911–12*, np
45 Johnston, *English Poetry*, p. 5
46 Fussell, p. 55
47 Press, *Map of English Verse*, p. 105
48 Silkin, *Out of Battle*, p. 258
49 Leavis, quoted Rogers, *Georgian Poetry*, p. 2
50 *The Times Literary Supplement*, 21 November, 1952, pp. 753–5
51 Stead, *New Poetic*, pp. 80–1
52 J. Buchan, *Spectator*, 18 January, 1913, p. 107
53 A. Waugh, *Quarterly Review*, October, 1916, pp. 365–86

54 Graves, quoted O'Prey, p. 28
55 Thurley, *Ironic Harvest, passim*
56 Hibberd, 'Wilfred Owen and the Georgians', *Review of English Studies*, ns, xxx, no. 117, 1979, pp. 28–40
57 Owen, *Letters*, p. 355
58 *ibid.*, p. 437
59 p. 499
60 p. 520
61 p. 521
62 p. 526
63 Rosenberg, *Collected Works*, p. 223
64 *ibid.*, p. 200
65 p. 202
66 p. 210
67 p. 225
68 p. 208
69 p. 224
70 p. 209
71 p. 236
72 p. 238
73 p. 239
74 p. 250
75 p. 265
76 p. 267
77 p. 271
78 p. 271
79 Liddiard, *Rosenberg*, p. 224
80 Cohen, *Rosenberg*, p. 84
81 Liddiard, p. 161
82 Marsh, *Edward Thomas*, pp. 113–14
83 Hurd, *Ordeal of Ivor Gurney*, p. 138

CHAPTER TWO

Cheery Old Cards

Siegfried Sassoon did more than any other author to establish the reputation of First World War generals in the popular and literary imagination:

> 'He's a cheery old card,' grunted Harry to Jack
> As they slogged up to Arras with rifle and pack.
>
>   *   *   *
>
> But he did for them both by his plan of attack.

The general referred to was probably Sir John French, Commander-in-Chief of the British Expeditionary Force at the start of the war. Numerous commentators of a superstitious bent took great comfort in the fact that the last three letters of the French commander's name, Joffre, were the same as the first three of French's surname. The number three has great significance in numerology, and in times of crisis ordinary people take consolation from whoever it has on offer. This explains why so many charlatans profit at the start of major wars, and sometimes why so many great men are seen as charlatans.

If the consensus of popular opinion has been that the generals were fools, it is partly in defiance of a considerable strand of contemporary opinion which realized that the generals had their problems, just like the soldiers:

> I think there's a good deal of truth in it [condemnation of generals]; but after all, what is a brass-hat's job? He's not thinking of you or of me or of any individual man, or of any particular battalion or division. Men, to him, are only part of the material

he has to work with; and if he felt as you or I feel, he couldn't carry on with his job. It's not fair to think he's inhuman. He's got to draw up a plan, from rather scrappy information, and it is issued in the form of an order; but he knows very well something may happen at any moment to throw everything out of gear. The original plan is no more than a kind of map; you can't see the country by looking at a map, and you can't see the fighting by looking at a plan of attack. Once we go over the top it's the colonel's and the company commander's job. Once we meet a Hun it's our job.[1]

These lines are from Frederick Manning's *Her Privates We*, later published as *The Middle Parts of Fortune*, one of the most closely observed novels that emerged from the war, and a central tract for those who want to know what soldiers were thinking in the First World War.

The debate over the quality of leadership exercised by the senior generals on the British side has, if anything, increased in fervour over the years. At the heart of that debate, and in effect a symbol of British military leadership in the war, is Sir Douglas Haig, appointed leader of the British Expeditionary Force in succession to Sir John French in 1915, and held responsible for the offensives on the Somme and at Passchendaele. These offensives have become a symbol of what was perceived to be the senseless slaughter of the Great War. They are to the British what Verdun is to the French, or Stalingrad to the Germans. A schoolboy who told me that Hitler was a Bosnian leader knew that 60,000 British soldiers died on the first day of the Somme offensive. He was wrong on both counts: there were 60,000 casualties on the first day of the Somme, with perhaps a third of those actual deaths, but his knowledge of that figure says a great deal about the extent to which the Great War has entered popular myth.

That myth has no room for generals appearing in the front line, and even less room for generals showing sympathy for and interest in the common soldier. Yet contemporary accounts are full of such references. George Coppard was a gunner whose Vickers machine gun was so active on one day that it used up all available supplies of water:

It was on this occasion that we ran out of water for the Vickers. Our reserve supply had disappeared and there was very little drinking water left in our water bottles. As a temporary measure all the members of my team piddled into the water jacket of the gun through a funnel, to the accompaniment of much hilarity and vulgar remarks. As it was midsummer the natural sources of supply were very meagre, but with the help of other troops sufficient water was obtained to get the gun going again. The only drawback was the offensive odour.[2]

Immediately after this major action Coppard was returning to the front line after being treated for boils. On his way he met someone that the myth says he should not have encountered – a very senior officer:

> Suddenly I ran into a party of staff officers accompanying Sir Julian Byng, GOC the Third Army, on a tour of inspection. I wondered if I was seeing things. When about to pass by me, the general, noticing my bandaged head, stopped and said, 'Are you wounded?' I replied, 'No sir,' 'Boils?' queried the general. 'Yes sir,' I said, hoping that he, in an expansive mood, would wave a hand and say, 'Send this boy down to reserve for a couple of days' rest.' I had no such luck. 'Beastly things. I've had them myself,' he said, and with that the general and his entourage moved on.[3]

Many soldiers in the post-war period showed genuine anger at the myth of the absentee officer:

> Mind you, it's not true that the senior officers stayed out of the fighting. Brigadier Maxwell is a good example of one type of commanding officer. He arrived on the night before the Battle of the Somme to take his command and be in the battle, but he wasn't due to take over for another day by which time we would have been leaving. He simply felt he had to take part in the battle. Eventually he got shot in the bottom while walking across the top of a trench in full view of the enemy. The men adored him.[4]

Some generals at least were very much in evidence at the front:

> The problem was on both our flanks where the fighting was ferocious. That's where they got the worst of it. And all the time General Maxse – he was only 5ft 6in tall and his equerry was 6ft 3in – watched the battle through his field glasses. I remember he came to see us. 'Good morning gentlemen,' he said. 'Damned good show!'[5]

46

More junior officers were often very welcome in the trenches, depending on the reason for their visit:

> 'Hullo! There's Edmonds! How are you getting on?'
>
> 'Not so badly, sir, but I'd give my next leave for a whisky and soda.'
>
> 'Done!' says the Colonel, groping in his side pocket, and producing a Perrier bottle which he hands to me. 'Your next leave is mine, Edmonds.'
>
> He had taken the precaution to bring a pint of that mixture with him over the top. The little joke and the spirits restore my nerve and I feel ten times more confident that the Colonel should merely be in the trench with us.[6]

Carrington records at least one instance of a general at the front,[7] but what is frequently missed is the fact that the average officer and soldier had no desire whatsoever to see their commanders in the front line. At the least it meant spit and polish in advance and reprimands afterwards; at worst it was a preliminary to an attack.

For reasons of space I have concentrated in this chapter on Douglas Haig, Commander-in-Chief of British Forces for the majority of the war. However, as a curtain-raiser to some of the issues relating to Haig, and to suggest that the points I make about him are true on a wider canvas, it is interesting to look at one episode in the career of another leading general, Sir Henry Rawlinson.

Rawlinson would be a very easy candidate to fit into the popular image of the First World War general, the 'butcher and bungler' who combined a capacity to throw away lives with congenital stupidity. He had the conventional background of Eton and Sandhurst, came from one of the 'right' families and had the sporting ability which was so essential to survival at public school. He was seen as a cavalry man, the most socially-acceptable wing of the army, and had served in India.

In March, 1914, Rawlinson was responsible for the Neuve Chapelle offensive. From the outset his approach shows a man far more professional and thoughtful than the conventional image of the First World War general would allow. He showed no enthusiasm for Haig's vision of a grand advance, preferring to aim for limited objectives with limited casualties. He forced through the concept of a 'hurricane' barrage, whereby the advance would be preceded by ten minutes' bombardment of enemy barbed wire to break it up, and thirty-five minutes' bombardment of enemy trenches. Prior to the offensive experiments were conducted to see which guns were best for dispersing barbed wire. The bombardment worked magnificently. The concentration of guns Rawlinson was able to bring to bear on a small front was sufficient to break the wire and pulverize the trenches, not least because of Rawlinson's technical knowledge of the various guns he was deploying. The accuracy of the artillery bombardment was greatly assisted by the extensive use of aerial reconnaissance prior to the assault.

Realizing the importance of communications, Rawlinson also ordered not only three separate tracks of telephone wire to be laid as the troops advanced, but for these three lines to be cross-connected to each other to circumvent the inevitable breaks in the lines as a result of enemy fire. As well as triplicating wires, Rawlinson ordered that the lines should not be laid in trenches or roads where enemy artillery fire might be expected, but across open fields. The troops were well rehearsed in what they had to do, and were brought up into the front line without alerting the enemy. In addition they were trained to attack in columns and at the fastest possible pace, rather than in the slow 'waves' used later in the war. The attack was a remarkable success, achieving its primary objectives with a fraction of the casualties that have become associated with similar offensives later in the war.

The aftermath was less impressive. Rawlinson mishandled his reserve troops, and the next phase of the advance stalled. It has been suggested that if Rawlinson had acted with more panache after the initial success he could have made a major breakthrough, but this has been effectively disproved by a recent study of the battle.[8] Whatever came later, the first assault on Neuve Chapelle proved that a line of trenches could be broken with acceptable losses to the attacking force. So why was this not done later in the war? The answer reveals much about the nature of warfare on the Western Front.

Firstly, Rawlinson was able to bring a very heavy concentration of artillery to bear on a narrow front, had enough shells to achieve his purpose, and enough guns of the right type to achieve his double aim of forcing a path through barbed wire and breaking down enemy trenches. For many later offensives there were simply not enough guns or shells. Secondly, the targets for the artillery could be seen by the gunners. Thirdly, at this stage in the war Rawlinson still had enough experienced officers and men to advance in columns and at speed. Later in the war all generals operated with troops who had had neither the time nor the opportunity to be trained in offensive warfare. Fourthly, the objective was a limited one using relatively small numbers of troops, so the assembly of the men could just about be kept secret. Fifthly, the hurricane bombardment was long and heavy enough to pulverize the enemy, but not so long as to allow them to bring up reserves to counter the subsequent attack.

Rawlinson applied intelligence and professionalism to the problem of breaking through enemy trenches, and won a victory that was both effective and sparing in the lives of his men. It was also a victory that showed Rawlinson learning on his feet, adapting to conditions which no general had ever before had to face. This is not to paint Rawlinson as an angel. He made mistakes in the battle, particularly in the handling of his reserves, and did not make his opposition to the plan for a further advance clearly enough known. But I hope it makes an initial point that many of the generals in command of the British Army in 1914 were not fools, and that given a suitable opportunity and the necessary materials they were perfectly capable of doing a thoroughly professional job. Nor were they by instinct profligate with their men's lives. This does not explain the later appalling loss of life and series of stalled offensives, but does suggest that simply to blame the generals and categorize them as idiots is far too simple a response to some very complex issues.

The debate over the merit of Sir Douglas Haig has no equivalent on the literary side of the war. In that latter camp the last authority to challenge in any serious way the table of merit established by modern criticism for the war poets was W.B. Yeats. His complaint that passive suffering is not a subject for poetry is as old as war itself, and has been gleefully dashed by successive generations of critics. Not so with the military historians. In one corner stand most contemporary accounts, and most notably John Terraine among modern authors, arguing in support of Haig and believing that, despite the terrible losses his leadership incurred, he was in effect the military architect of victory in the war. In the other corner stand a number of historians, most notably Denis Winter. His account of Haig's command damns the man on every possible front, personal and professional. To an outsider it seems remarkable that two professional historians can take such diametrically opposed views of the same man, particularly as that man was one of the first to take decisions and exercise leadership in a glare of publicity that would have horrified Wellington, or indeed any other commander prior to the Crimean War.

The essential background to any judgement of Haig and the other commanders on the British side is an understanding of the changes that had come over the British Army and warfare in general prior to the First World War. The changes in warfare were almost exclusively the product of the Industrial Revolution. One of the most obvious was the arming of the ordinary infantryman with the bolt-action rifle. The musket used by Wellington's troops at Waterloo was slow to load, prone to accident in the heat of action, and inaccurate. Its smooth-bore barrel threw a less than perfectly round ball a relatively short distance, with precise aiming impossible. A residue of burning powder could explode the new powder charge as a soldier poured it into the barrel, before the bullet was loaded. Too much powder and the barrel exploded, too little and the bullet went off like a damp squib. Soldiers in action were known to fire guns with the ram-rod still in the barrel, or even fail to load a bullet in their panic. A lost or bent ram-rod made it virtually impossible to use the gun, which is why later models had the ram-rod permanently attached to the gun by a swivel hinge. Even in the calmest hands the priming charge that ignited the main charge could fail to go off in rain or if it was slightly damp.

Then a number of things changed. New technology allowed the priming charge, explosive and projectile to be combined into a single, metal-cased 'round'. Rifled barrels, a better understanding of projectile ballistics and tighter control of metallurgical manufacturing processes produced a weapon accurate to beyond half a mile. The famous Martini-Henry rifle was only single shot, meaning that each bullet had to be pushed into the rifle breech by hand, but it had an action that is still widely used today in target rifles and which was both fast and lethal in trained hands. It defeated an overwhelmingly numerically superior band of Zulus at Rorke's Drift. The Martini-Henry was prone to jamming though, particularly because the breech-block needed to drop down into the gun-casing and back up again if the action was to work. Relatively small amounts of sand or mud could block the action.

The next stage was the bolt-action rifle, and in particular the Lee-Enfield that, with various adaptations and improvements, served the British Army until well beyond the Second World War. Pulling back the bolt cocked a firing pin and brought a cartridge up from the magazine. Pushing the bolt forward placed the bullet in the barrel. Pulling the trigger fired it, and pulling back the bolt ejected the empty cartridge case and loaded a new bullet. The rifle was heavy, but its wooden casing made it more or less soldier-proof. Its action was simple to clean and oil, and virtually foolproof to use even if a cartridge jammed or was defective. It had a battle sight and a more refined sight for when there was more time to take aim.

The British Expeditionary Force expected its soldiers in 1914 to be able to loose off fifteen rounds of accurate fire a minute; the best could manage thirty rounds a minute. With a sensible under-standing of what appealed to the British soldier, the army paid more to those who could shoot well. With that single weapon the killing power of the average infantryman had increased tenfold or more – always provided that he could be kept supplied with the necessary amount of ammunition. This latter fact worried the army so much in the early days of the Lee-Enfield that the first models had a sliding metal cut-out which stopped new bullets being loaded from the magazine, forcing the soldier to hand-load each round as he had done with the Martini-Henry. The idea was that the bullets in the magazine would be there as a last-ditch reserve if the soldier was about to be overcome.

The machine gun was another development made possible by advances in metallurgy and propellants. An early form was the Gatling gun, adopted at one stage by the Royal Navy and placed high on the mast-head of warships that might still have to repel boarders or pepper the decks of native craft. By the turn of the cen-tury the machine gun had made very significant advances. As with all weapons its basic efficiency depended on the quality of the ammunition it used, but a well-placed machine gun could be handled with ease by two men and wreak havoc on any force advancing towards it in the open.

Next up the ladder of carnage was artillery, coming in all shapes and sizes but again well able to profit from advances in technology. The major development was the exploding shell. It takes a degree of knowledge to manufacture a metal casing that can be given instant and massive acceleration in a gun barrel and not itself explode the charge it carries in its nose. In fact the fusing of shells was not satisfactory by 1914, one of many reasons why there were so many 'duds' at the Battle of the Somme, some of which are still being dredged up today. The Royal Navy suffered just as badly. If its armour-piercing shells had managed to pierce German armour at the battle of Jutland, instead of exploding on impact or skidding off with detached nose cones, between three and six more German capital ships would have been lost, making Jutland the greatest British naval victory of modern times. That apart, the 1914 gen-eral could hurl shells with considerable accuracy over many miles, choosing from high explosive, armour-piercing or shrapnel. Later gas was added to the menu. The exploding artillery shell was the weapon that claimed nearly sixty per cent of all casualties in the First World War on the British side.

The general of 1914 had two other devices available to him. The first and simplest was barbed wire. Laid with sufficient thickness it was very hard to break and force a path through, and unless it was broken it would hold up even the strongest and bravest of men. The second was the railway engine. A general could bring up reserves at fifty or sixty miles an hour if a line existed, whilst his advancing enemy were restricted to the average infantryman's walking speed in full kit. This meant that what should have been many breakthroughs became merely temporary break-ins, stemmed by massive counter-attack using hastily assembled reserves. Once launched on an offensive troops could move at the best speed their feet could take them, whilst troops being rushed to plug the gap could move at the best speed of steel and steam.

Artillery occupied one of the most crucial positions in 1914, and in microcosm reflects many of the wider problems affecting warfare at the time. Artillery was marvellous at stopping an attack, particularly over open ground where the gunners had been able to range and register on the target area at their leisure. It could also be very effective at cutting wire, despite the myth to the contrary, and at caving-in trenches. But a different type of shell was needed to cut wire from that which was best at killing men advancing over open ground, and a different type altogether was needed for destroying strong-points. Just as there were specialist shells, so were there specialist guns, and the type of guns available to a general was often as vital as their number.

The final but most important problem was that no artillery is any use unless shells can be landed on target, whatever that target is. Technology had produced the capacity to hurl a shell many miles, but had not produced the technology to see where it landed once it was out of visual range. Even if forward spotters could be placed in visual range to see the fall of shells (very unlikely in many theatres of war on the Western Front), they had only the most primitive methods of signalling back their findings, and the most reliable (telephone) was all too likely to have its wire smashed by enemy artillery fire. Aircraft could spot for the guns, but without radio again it was appallingly difficult to get the information back to the gunners. A trench is a very narrow target, and to land a shell either in it or near enough to cave it in requires great accuracy. That accuracy was itself compromised by various technical factors. Where a shell landed could be influenced very significantly by different weather conditions, by minute variations in the thickness and width of the band around it that engaged with the rifling in the barrel, and by minute variations in its own weight. It could also be influenced by the age of, and wear and tear inflicted on, the gun that fired it; in general the longer a gun had been in service the more inaccurate it became.

The artillery could, of course, fire from map references. If the gunner knew exactly where his gun was positioned and exactly where his target was, he stood a reasonable chance of at least moderately effective 'blind' firing. However, accuracy depended on accurate maps, which simply did not exist for many areas on the Western Front. When the war started officers found that the last maps of the region had been surveyed in Bonaparte's time. Technology had given the generals a viciously effective weapon, but one which was only partially under their control.

Technology provided the means to increase vastly the defensive killing power of the ordinary soldier and of the new armies. It had also provided many more people available to be killed. The population of Great Britain in 1911 was 40.8 million. In Queen Elizabeth I's time it was probably less than five million, and in 1831 it had only been fourteen million.

What is sometimes overlooked in accounts of technological advance is how much had not been achieved in 1914. Technology gave the generals of 1914 the capacity to defend, albeit at appalling cost. It did not give them the capacity to attack. The accuracy of the bolt-action rifle was a boon to those in prepared positions able to take aim at an advancing enemy. To those advancing it was suicide to stop, aim and fire. Despite the film epics of various Hollywood stars, a machine gun cannot be fired to any great effect or for any period of time from the hip by one man. Firing from a prepared, defensive position it can hold up an attack by thousands of men.

Barbed wire never helped an army win an offensive; its use is to stop other armies doing so. The tanks used for the first time at the Somme in 1916 were slow, over-manned and very unreliable mechanically. Aircraft for most of the war simply could not carry enough bombs to blow out a trench line and did not have the communications to support an infantry advance effectively. But a comment by Major W.A. Bishop, VC, showed how useful aircraft could be:

Suddenly I heard that deadly rattle of a nest of machine guns under me, and saw that the line of our troops at one place was growing very thin, with many figures sprawling on the ground. For three of four minutes I could not make out the concealed position of the German gunners. . . . Then in a corner of a German trench I saw a group of about five men operating two machine-guns . . . I dived vertically at them . . . With hate in my heart I fired every bullet I could into the group. . . . A few minutes later I had the satisfaction of seeing our line again advancing . . .[9]

Bishop's attack did the trick, but it was pure chance that he was drawn to a situation where his guns could help. He had no effective means of communicating with the ground, nor was the ground able to call up an air strike. This predicament still bedevils modern armed forces, albeit in a different form. The public and politicians tend to want guns for their money, to load up the modern equivalent of Bishop's aircraft with as many visible weapons as the airframe can bear. Those at the sharp end of the fighting could manage with less guns and a decent radio to get the guns to where they can do some good. The problem is the same in the tank with a very good gun and a bad aiming system, or the warship with hundreds of missiles but no electronic systems to stop the enemy's missiles sinking it.

Once an assault was launched and troops went beyond the range of laid telephone lines (themselves vulnerable to fracture from explosions) the generals lost all contact with their men. In terms of communications the soldier of 1914 moved back to 1066 in a matter of moments. A general had no voice control over his soldiers once the offensive was launched; they communicated with their commanders either face to face, or by runner-delivered note, or not at all. Usually it was not at all. The ingredients of mobile warfare – aircraft, tanks, good communications – simply did not exist in 1914, and were hardly there in 1918. But there were ample means for extended defensive warfare.

What all this means is that no one, least of all those who have savaged the top commanders in the First World War, could have written the rule book for the 1914–18 war because so many other rules had been changed in the period between the Boer War and 1914. The situation was expressed rather plaintively by Sir John French:

> No previous experience, no conclusion I had been able to draw from campaigns in which I had taken part, or from a close study of the new conditions in which the war of today is waged, had led me to anticipate a war of positions. All my thoughts, all my prospective plans, all my possible alternatives of action, were concentrated upon a war of movement and manoeuvre.[10]

The game did not exist until 1914. By 1918 there were sufficient advances in armour, aircraft and communications to suggest that a new game was on its way, so the lessons of 1914–18 were already redundant.

There are interesting comparisons and similarities with the situation of the Royal Navy in 1914. It too had moved an immense distance from the fighting ships of Nelson's day. The army's Waterloo in the nineteenth century became the Somme in the twentieth; Trafalgar became Jutland for the Royal Navy. By 1914 wooden hulls had been replaced with armour plate. Battles fought on the vagaries of the wind at speeds that never went into double figures had been replaced by battles fought between ships totally independent of the wind and capable of speeds of well over twenty miles an hour. The steam engines that drove these ships required a totally new breed of engineer, and the supply of coal and oil to fire them a whole world in miniature of depots and supply lines. From smooth-bore cannons capable of little more than hurling solid shot inaccurately at an enemy in very close range, the navy had moved to battleships armed with eight fifteen-inch guns (fifteen inches being the diameter of the projectile) capable of hurling a shell well over ten miles.

The similarities with the army are numerous. Both had the technology to reach an enemy out of visible range, but not the technology to spot where he was and know if he had been hit. Radar was to come many years later. The capacity to communicate with one's units was very limited, radio communication being in its infancy and signalling by light and flag the order of the day. For both services one was only certainly in control of what one could see, and that included the enemy and one's own forces. The Royal Navy stuck to its belief in the battleship as the major weapon in its war. The army stuck to the cavalry and the massed attack. The effect of one such was recorded by an officer:

> The attack . . . started soon afterwards. It was a very pretty sight, and for a moment, we were thrilled by the line of galloping horses and pointed swords in perfect order, but the excitement was soon spent for we knew that there were no enemy in front. We saw one or two fellows whirl out of their saddles from long-range machine-gun fire, but then came a pitiful anticlimax, for on meeting with a few thin strands of wire, they were thrown into confusion . . . [we left] a line of dismounted troops leading their frightened horses across the entanglement.[11]

Both cavalry and the massed, frontal attack were becoming obsolete, but the weapons that would seal their death warrant – the submarine, the aircraft and the tank – were either in short supply in 1914 or non-existent, as well as being primitive in their technological development. They presented the potential for changing the rules of war, but in 1914 it would have been a foolish man who believed that they had the proven power to do so.

In fact the situation facing both naval and military commanders in 1914 was considerably more complex than many commentators have suggested. It is not an easy task to write a constitution for an emerging nation in the middle of a revolution, yet this was what the commanders of Britain's army and navy were expected to do. The tragedy of the First World War was not so much that it was fought with the first products of the Industrial Revolution, but rather that it was fought before those products had seen time enough to balance defensive and offensive capabilities. The generals and admirals of the First World War were caught in the situation of a commander forced to use troops or sailors of fourteen or fifteen years of age: very mature in some areas, very immature in others. The technology of war had advanced unevenly. It made it very hard to lose a war, but even harder to win one.

The first symbol of high command in the war was Kitchener. Asquith is reported to have said of him, 'He is not a great man. He is a great poster,'[12] and that image has persisted. Yet there is another view of Kitchener, and one which is so firm a part of history that it cannot be denied. As Charles Carrington has commented,

> Kitchener meant as much to the British in 1914 as Churchill meant in 1940. . . . In his first month of office, with no precedents, no staff, no political machine behind him, no authority over organised labour, no national registration, no tradition of compulsory service, but, on the other hand, a deep-rooted suspicion of militarism to overcome, Kitchener envisaged and planned the recruiting, officering, arming, equipping, and training, of a new army of thirty divisions. At the same time, he doubled the strength of the Regular Army in France, doubled the Territorial Army so that half of it could be released for service abroad, and mustered the armies from the Dominions. After a year of war he had forty British divisions in action, most of them new formations. The Americans, with all the British experience to improve upon, had only managed to get one Regular Army division into battle at the end of their first year of war.[13]

Britain was not a militarized nation, as was Germany, in 1914. Its ability to react with such speed to a total crisis of military manpower and *matériel* is one of the greatest triumphs of its armed services ever, and one of the most forgotten. Kitchener takes much of the credit for that achievement.

Haig has to be the second symbol of British command in the Great War. Outwardly there is a convincing case against him, which divides roughly into two camps; one seeing him as a callous butcher and the other as an incompetent promoted beyond his ability. Haig's case has not been helped by some extremely unpleasant facts about his personality. He was immensely spoilt by his mother, and brought up to have what many regarded as an inflated sense of his own importance. He only spent two years at public school, during which time he excelled at little and was disliked by most other pupils. He was ruthlessly ambitious.

Throughout his life Haig displayed . . . pragmatic detachment towards most institutions and almost all people. He was concerned mainly with his own progress, something from which he never more than slightly distracted.[14]

His ambition included criticizing his seniors behind their backs to influential figures, and at times he could appear both vicious to his rivals and a sycophantic snob. He wrote letters criticizing Kitchener when he was fighting alongside him to Sir Evelyn Wood, the Adjutant General, and on another occasion was actually reprimanded by the Prince of Wales for telling tales about his fellow officers.

Haig pursued royal connections with vigour and single-mindedness, refusing no opportunity to make sure everyone knew of those connections. It has been suggested that many of Haig's early patrons were homosexual, and a dark current of rumour concerns the use Haig made of them. What is certain is that Haig loaned £2,500 to Sir John French in 1899, when French was Commander of the Aldershot Brigade, to save French from certain bankruptcy. To place a figure on the modern value of that loan is to date both the loan and this book; suffice it to say that it was a small fortune. Haig was then appointed as Brigade Major of the First Cavalry Brigade, a much-coveted appointment and a crucial step up the army ladder. Servility to those above him, leavened by a measure of backbiting, was met at the other end of the scale by a tendency to appoint servile and obsequious staff officers, at least according to some biographers. One of Haig's greatest critics sees him succeeding to high command through intrigue and not ability,

a man whose rise had always owed more to intrigue and patronage than to any evidence of talent as a soldier.[15]

Haig did not help himself by being largely inarticulate at times, nor by appearing to treat his marriage in a most cursory manner. He proposed to his wife thirty-six hours after they first met, and had a reputation for disliking women. He was also an absentee parent. When he went to India for three years his children remained at home. On his return they did not recognize their parents, and on one occasion totally vandalized the Haigs' dining room.

Obsessive about appearance, he appears as something of a prude, aloof from those serving under him and opposed to any nudity among his troops and the singing of the usually obscene marching songs. It was the same coarseness among the infantry that so horrified Wilfred Owen, and it was typified by the marching song 'Do Your Balls Hang Low?'

The impression of a cold, wholly self-centred and ruthlessly ambitious career officer prepared to sneak on his colleagues and buy favour is not an attractive one. Haig's military competence can be damned in equal measure. Throughout his life he remained convinced of the importance of the cavalry, never really losing his faith in them as the deciding factor in a battle. The conditions on the Western Front seemed to make cavalry action rather a joke in cruel taste. Haig was present at what can be seen as the last triumph of the British cavalry, the charge at Kimberley, after which one biographer says that his mind was 'slammed shut'[16] to any new thoughts on the use of cavalry or its usefulness at all.

Throughout his period of command crucial wrong decisions were taken over major battles, decisions for which Haig has to be held responsible. He was opposed to the plan to advance over open ground at the Battle of Loos, but was overruled by Sir John French and the French commander, Joffre. Haig sought to place the blame for Loos on the fact that no reserves were readily available. Just as he had criticized Kitchener earlier to a senior officer, so now he wrote home to Kitchener implying that blame for the defeat rested on Sir John French.

The Somme offensive was planned at the point in the line where the French and British armies joined. Haig did not oppose this sufficiently strongly on the grounds that the French and British position was faced by some of the strongest German emplacements, nor did he withdraw from the assault when it became clear that French involvement would be less than had hitherto been supposed. Passchendaele was another bad mistake, launched over appalling ground and with too much reliance placed on inherently weak commanders such as Gough. Brigadier General John Charteris has suggested that Haig wished to launch the offensive early, before German reserves could be brought up, but that he was overruled by his senior commanders:

> D. H. wanted the attack to go on at once, and in the end he accepted the Army Commanders' view. He could, indeed, do nothing else, for they have to carry out the job.[17]

This defence carries little conviction. Armies do not run on consensus, nor are battles fought by democratic command structures. If Haig believed the offensive should have been launched early, then he should have ordered it to do so.

He knew the time and date of the 1918 German offensive, and had guessed at its style, yet still his army was nearly overrun. He had adopted the 'defence in depth' philosophy, which he copied from the Germans. Unfortunately there was insufficient time to train his army properly for the use of such a defensive system, actively disliked by the soldiers for the manner in which it split them up. Haig can also be criticized for throwing tanks into the Somme offensive when they were still at a fairly primitive level of development and only small numbers were available, thus losing the advantage of surprise for a later and more concentrated offensive based on the tank.

Judgement on these matters is not helped by the fact that Haig appears to have altered diary and other entries to support or prove his version of events. Given his ambition and self-centredness, it would perhaps have been surprising if this was not the case.

Those who support Haig see him as a hero and the architect of victory on the Western Front. Uniquely among First World War figures he has two myths centred on him, the first the callous and incompetent butcher, the second the maligned hero. As myths go, both are very good; and as myths go, it is time they went.

Haig is guilty as charged on several counts. He was undoubtedly ruthlessly self-centred and ambitious, and undoubtedly his rise to top commander was facilitated by his political skill and knowledge of the 'right' people. One suspects that this was a truth long before Haig, and will remain one long after he has been forgotten. In any event, raw ambition is never an attractive sight, for all that it is sometimes a very compelling and successful one. In Haig's case it is rendered even more rank by an accompanying insensitivity, and an almost total inability to believe that he could be wrong. From this it is not hard to divine a man who used patriotism and duty merely as socially and ethically acceptable covers for his own ambition: Haig versus Germany, with Haig winning with a knockout in the fifth round.

This vision of Haig asks more questions than it answers. Pleasant men rarely make good military commanders. Haig's predecessor, Sir John French, was a *bon viveur* and a delightful companion, but ineffective as commander-in-chief. A number of admirals in the Second World War were both pleasant and effective men, but were dumped by the wayside because of their inability to compete politically: one thinks of the victor of the Battle of the River Plate, Admiral Sir Henry Harwood. The charismatic and highly successful Admiral Cunningham was a martinet who knifed his friends in the back and steadfastly refused to accept technology, both characteristics which link him to Haig. Many historians have pointed out that Haig was spared for the most part the danger to his life faced by the officers and men under his orders. This is unfair: he had put his life on the line many times in offensive action prior to 1914, and no one can seriously doubt that he had courage. Courage was a virtue the army trained for, and one it perhaps had a right to expect from its officer recruits.

However, the army did not offer training in political skills, and one of the tragedies of the First World War was that its generals had to be politicians as well as commanders in the field. Popular accounts of the war have dealt insufficiently with the sudden-death nature of Haig's survival in political and hence command terms. The man in charge of the British army in the First World War, if he was to survive, had to be a politician more than he was a general. In particular the arrival of Lloyd George as Prime Minister and General Nivelle as French Commander-in-Chief meant that Haig was fighting for survival. Lloyd George wanted him dismissed, seeing him as a prime cause of the high casualty warfare being waged in France, which Lloyd George felt was politically unacceptable. Lloyd George was also naive about other possible theatres where the war might be won. Haig was not a pleasant man, and was adept at political manipulation and scheming. In that he was similar to Lloyd George, and had he not been so he would not have survived as commander. As has been said, 'Each man met his match in the other.'[18]

Haig's unpleasantness is a complete irrelevance to his standing as a commander; who asks if Wellington was kind to the servants? His political scheming, his paranoid fear of rivals and his use of private networks were as essential to his survival as the rifle was to a private. Support from government and political allies were the prime requirements of a top commander, who had a right to rely on officers beneath him to engage the support of the troops. The image of the general as politician goes against a treasured myth of command, which sees the officer leading from the front, eating the same food as his troops (an extremely unlikely event in Haig's case) and being first over the parapet. It is an attractive vision, but for a senior commander it was suicidal for him and for his troops.

In fact, and rather surprisingly, Haig does fit into certain aspects of this myth. He did on occasion don a greatcoat to obscure badges of rank and walk among troops. He was one of the first commanders to use a train as a base so he could get near to the front line. Charles Carrington recollects him making a personal reconnaissance of a piece of ground in Carrington's sector before deciding to launch an attack over it. Haig was under fire in 1914 and only narrowly escaped capture. He had a very active war in South Africa, was the prime agent in the crucial relief of Kimberley, and was clearly no coward.

He was undoubtedly wrong to insist on the importance of cavalry, which had had their day in modern warfare by 1914, and perhaps even earlier,

> In their advance the lines of horsemen passed over us rapidly. . . . It may have been a fine sight, but it was a wicked waste of men and horses, for the enemy immediately opened on them a hurricane of every kind of missile he had. If the cavalry advanced over us at the trot or canter, they came back at a gallop, including numbers of dismounted men, and riderless horses, and – most fatal mistake of all, they bunched behind Monchy in a big mass, into which the Boche continued to put high-explosive shrapnel, whizz-bangs, and a hail of bullets, until the horsemen dispersed and finally melted away back over the hillside from where they came.[19]

There is a further comparison with the Royal Navy here, in that the naval establishment committed itself to gunnery and the battleship long after it became clear that aircraft were taking over as the major naval weapon. The navy's commitment to the big gun and the army's commitment to the cavalry were the product of an inevitable and understandable conservatism that sought to pretend things had not changed quite as much as in fact was the case. In his defence there is no evidence that Haig saw cavalry as the main reason for victory in the Boer War, as has sometimes been suggested. He admitted that it was cordoning off by barbed wire and blockhouses which did it.[20] Furthermore, all Haig's comments on the cavalry fall into two categories: the proud officer who feels himself a part of a proud tradition, and the actual tactical use to which he saw the cavalry being put.

Throughout the war he and all those in command were obsessed with the need to make a breakthrough and so end the war. With hindsight we ignore the fact that the only section of the army able to go faster than walking pace in 1916 for any length of time was the mounted soldier: the cavalry. It was they who had the top prize for every general on the Western Front – the capacity to move faster than an infantryman on foot. The massively-fortified front line was clearly a target for artillery and infantry; Haig never considered sending cavalry 'over the top' against a defended trench position. His dream was for them to pour through a hole made by artillery and infantry, and cause havoc in the rear lines. In many respects it was not such a bad idea. If one substitutes 'tanks' for 'cavalry' many a post-war general said the same thing, the difference being that Haig had only horse-flesh whilst the post-war generals had fast and reliable tanks. The cavalry to Haig meant mobility and firepower. That both were contained in fragile horse-flesh instead of armour plate, and that his offensive arm was powered by hooves instead of engines, was not so much his fault as one of the crosses he had to bear. He had an aim in mind for the cavalry and the aim was right. The tragedy was that tradition blinded him into believing that cavalry could achieve what the machine gun and barbed wire made impossible.

In any event, the whole issue has been allowed to get out of perspective. The majority of top commanders in the army were products of the infantry, not the cavalry, just as in the Second World War the majority of top naval officers came from specializations other than gunnery. Cavalry represented a less than massive 6.6 per cent of the British Expeditionary Force in 1914. By 1916 the figure had gone down to 2.5 per cent. Perhaps in his heart of hearts Haig might have hoped for the cavalry to do the trick at the Somme or Passchendaele, but he was never guilty of overloading his army to make that wish come to pass.

Comments on Haig's supposed homosexuality and his marriage are largely unhelpful in forming an accurate picture of him as a commander. We judge Owen and Sassoon on what they wrote as poets, not as homosexuals. In the absence of any firm evidence that Haig's judgement was affected by his sexuality, he can be judged as a commander and nothing else. His marriage only appears odd if the patterns of the late twentieth century are applied to it. In the Victorian and Edwardian period it was not only acceptable but strongly desirable for a man to marry late. The marriage itself was an alliance between families, the only way of producing an heir and the only acceptable career for a certain class of woman. If the partners were lucky it was also a matter of love. If they were not it was surprisingly easy for both partners to undertake their duty to

62

produce children, and for the women to undertake further duties commanding the household, without the need for any greater closeness. In fact, it seems as if Haig and his wife were rather closer to each other than was the case in many comparable marriages.

If Haig was homosexual, a fact for which there is no firm evidence whatsoever, it was a not uncommon state for a man brought up in an all-male school and an all-male profession. It would matter if he could be shown to have corrupted those under his command in pursuit of his sexuality, or to have been corrupted in his turn by those in authority over him. It is also rather insulting to the large, complex and efficient sex industry of Victorian and Edwardian times to suggest that it could not offer sexual gratification to any taste. Victorian society tended to associate sexual pleasure either with affairs conducted with the highest discretion at country-house parties, or with prostitutes. The concept of a sub-Masonic homosexual ring granting promotion to those of its kind makes a good story for a novel. It is highly unlikely that a man as shrewd as Haig would want or need to combine his sexuality with his profession. It is more likely that he was a type of man the twentieth century finds it increasingly hard to believe in, namely one for whom sex was not a major issue. Such men have been known to exist.

In two areas Haig did undeniably major service before the war. He was ordered to destroy all the plans relating to the mobilization for a European war of Indian troops, but refused to do so. These plans were used in 1914. Rather more influentially, when Haig was serving at the War Office as head of the Directorate of Military Training he worked closely with and supported the great Secretary of State for War, Haldane. Haldane's army reforms have become famous, though they have been criticized with the benefit of hindsight. That debate belongs to another book, but what cannot be doubted about Haldane's reforms was that they were intended to make the army a more efficient and professional organization, and led directly to the creation of the British Expeditionary Force. Haldane was an archetypal new broom. Helping him sweep was Haig, hardly the thing to expect of a soldier who has been accused of thinking on rails, and set up as the unthinking guardian of tradition.

Haig's political skills can appear in a very bad light. They had a credit side. He allowed an extremely hostile trade unionist (Ben Tillett, a docker) free access to the troops at the front, and ordered officers to absent themselves when Tillett talked to the men. Tillett became Labour MP for Salford in 1917, and as a result of his visit and free access became a supporter of both the war and Haig. Haig trusted his men. Indeed, as the most regular of all regular army officers, he was fulsome in his praise of the new recruits, and throughout his life showed a genuine admiration for them. It is interesting to note that in his communications he never referred to 'officers and men', but simply to 'all ranks'. He had been brought up in colonial service, a hard school in which an officer frequently found himself cut off from base and dependent wholly on the goodwill of his troops. Officers of that school would rather have died than be on familiar terms with their men, but knew they would soon be dead if they did not know and understand them, and gain their respect. Haig's background was not that of an armchair general.

His willingness to send influential letters to his friends criticizing the performance of his seniors will never be attractive, yet it is surprising how often it was justified. Was Haig opposed to the plan for an advance over open ground at Loos? Did he argue for the reserves to be brought closer to the front line? Did his part of the battle suffer from the bad luck that produced the wrong weather for gas, and was a breakthrough only stopped by shortage of shells at a crucial moment? The allegations that evidence has been doctored make a truthful answer to all these questions impossible at present, but if even half are true it puts Haig clearly ahead of the other British commanders and explains why he was so quick to distance himself from the battle.

However, the two crucial battles on which Haig's reputation rests are likely to be the Somme and Passchendaele. The myth of the Somme is a powerful one, perhaps the all-powerful one of the Great War. This in itself is surprising, because quite clearly it was not the first battle of its type, though it was the largest. The British soldier and British people had had two years to become accustomed to hitherto unprecedented casualties and the slogging attrition of trench warfare. The Battle of Loos (at which the poet Charles Sorley was killed) had all the horrors of the Somme a year earlier. It has probably been elevated to its present status in the popular imagination because it was seen to mark the blooding of the new, volunteer army that Kitchener had helped to raise. It has also achieved its status because it represented perhaps the greatest anticlimax of the war.

What is very rarely pointed out in defence of Haig and his policies is that no one, least of all the ordinary soldiers, knew how to break out of the stalemate of trench warfare. The only answer that suggested itself was what took place on the Somme: the most massive possible concentration of artillery and men. The ordinary soldier saw the vast preparations being made for the Somme and by and large approved of them, as did the officers. Haig's Somme offensive was not a casual and callous slaughter of the innocent. It was the logical answer to an impasse, and one which had the support of those who fought in it. Most of all it offered the chance of the breakthrough, the smashing of the enemy line that would lead to open warfare and, of course, an end to the war.

We see the Somme now as the death of a generation and the end of innocence, all of which it was. It was also a ray of hope to many soldiers, who approved of its relatively simple philosophy (amass enough strength and you will smash the enemy), applauded the magic way in which the Commander-in-Chief was able to produce shells and men, and genuinely believed that the Somme would end the war. As Charles Carrington commented on Haig, 'He was trusted,'[21] because his plan for the Somme was one which any sensible man would have supported. It seemed at the time the only way forward. There is also considerable evidence that the Somme did not break the spirit of the British Army. Carrington is frequently politically incorrect but nevertheless a shrewd observer of the war:

> The Somme battle raised the morale of the British Army. Although we did not win a decisive victory, there was what matters most, a definite and growing sense of superiority over the enemy, man to man. The attacks in mid-July were more successful and better managed than those of July 1st. In August and September things went better still. When the tanks made their surprising appearance on September 15th rejoicing knew no bounds. . . .[22]

Haig was also hamstrung by politics at the Somme, the same political element that was indistinguishable from a general's life in 1916 but which has sometimes been ignored in the formation of the myth that surrounds the war's top commanders. He was forced into battle because of a very real fear that the French, who were having to shoot their own officers and men at the time, were facing total collapse at Verdun. Haig was rushed into the Somme. It is hard not to feel some sympathy for this soldier who was forced to think so politically, with no training except his own gut instincts and capacity for survival. It is, of course, much harder to feel that sympathy if one's father or grandfather was killed as a result of a political decision. Despite all that, it is difficult to argue with the logic of Haig's statements:

We discussed the nature of guns and ammunition most required. I said large numbers of heavy guns and howitzers because enemy's defences had become so strong. We ought to aim at having enough guns to engage enemy on a front line of 25 to 30 miles, while retaining in addition a strong central reserve. After wearing down the enemy the Reserve should be sent in to attack at whatever point the enemy appeared weakest. By this means the decisive attack would come as a surprise. This can never be the case if an attack is made on a narrow front. Owing to the present strong defences, the enemy is able to hold up any attack long enough to enable his Reserves to arrive before the line is pierced.[23]

Nor has sufficient credit been given to what professional soldiers like Haig knew all too well. The spirit of the new recruits was marvellous; their enthusiasm exemplary; and their skill at arms lamentably below the minimum a pre-war officer would have expected. To all intents and purposes the massed recruitment of 1914–16 produced raw recruits, men who had been miraculously trained for defensive warfare, but who were by the standards of any European army not soldiers, not fully trained and certainly not capable of independent action under fire. From this fact sprang many of the decisions of the Somme. It was left to the artillery to smash the enemy. The artillery would break up the wire, destroy the trench system and force what Germans were left underground, whence they would emerge bemused and battered to find the first wave of British troops already in their trenches. The effect of artillery shelling on those who survived was known to be savage:

> Official historian Bean saw the Australians, toughest of soldiers, shaking like leaves and weeping at Pozières on their introduction to west front shelling after Gallipoli.[24]

It was decided to advance the men in close formation with their officers, in the belief that without the company of their fellows and the close support of their officers these raw recruits would break up and become simple cannon fodder. Experience was to prove the generals right. As one of Haig's severest critics has noted, 'Isolated men in the battlefield always became fearful.'[25] Later experience suggested that 'crater-hopping', advancing men through shell-craters and other holes in the ground, was the best way forward. It was rejected on the Somme because of the time delay involved, which might allow the Germans to set up their machine guns. The priority was to get the men to the battered German front line at the maximum possible speed.

Later offensives showed the value of preliminary reconnaissance to pinpoint weak points in the enemy line; rejected on the Somme because the ground had been covered topographically more efficiently than in any other war, there were no conventional weak spots in the German line facing the British, and it was considered a waste of time and lives which would do no more than alert and inform the Germans of Allied plans. Gas was used only sparingly, because it had proved to be unreliable, far too dependent on the vagaries of climate and a threat still to troops taking the objective. All these were sensible decisions, taken by professional soldiers who knew what their men could and could not be expected to do. So what went wrong?

Firstly, British shells failed to explode, just as they failed to explode correctly at the Battle of Jutland. The reason was partly the failure of technology, partly the result of setting up a mass armaments industry when the average worker in 1916 knew as much about making shells as the average soldier did of the military arts. Secondly, artillery fire failed to break up the barbed wire nearly as effectively as had been hoped. Thirdly, the bemused and battered German soldiers won the race to man the firing step by only a few minutes, but those minutes were enough to cut down the advancing troops with machine-gun fire. Fifty or so armour-piercing shells that exploded on impact instead of penetrating enemy armour deprived the Royal Navy of the greatest victory in its history. Dud shells and a few minutes were all that separated the British Army from true victory at the Somme, that and the bravery of the German soldiers.

The extent of the victory achieved at the Somme is also called into question by the generally greater credibility given to it by German sources. A member of the German general staff commented,

> The Somme was the muddy grave of the German field army and of its faith in the ability of the German leaders.[26]

The German *Official History* wrote,

> The heavy loss of life affected Germany much more than the Allies.[27]

Tanks have become a major issue in the debate over the Somme, with hindsight arguing that Haig should have waited to release his new weapon until it was more technically advanced and available in larger numbers. It is to be doubted that such a policy would have made any difference. As late as 1918 in the Battle of Amiens 534 tanks started the battle; a mere thirty-eight were left at the end. The primitive tanks made it easier to break into an enemy position, but did not have the legs or the power to break out. Even when they did so, as at Cambrai, the lack of motor transport for troops meant tanks tended to be stranded without support.

The final word on the Somme might be afforded to someone who fought in it. There were certainly instances where failure of command sent men against the wrong obstacles in the wrong way. Far more common among the men was a sense of awe at the detail of the preparations made for the battle, summed up by one officer,

> If the success of any operation were entirely dependent on the preparations made before Zero Hour, then the Somme battle should have been a complete success.[28]

The 1917 Passchendaele offensive was a different story, and marked the nadir of Haig's fortunes as a commander. The reasons for launching it were sound enough, namely a dire need to take pressure off the French and an equal need to make a breakthrough before German reinforcements arrived from the Eastern Front. One is not aware nowadays of the widely-held conviction in government and army that the war was being lost in 1916–17. Haig could be seen as having bad luck with the weather, but any general who takes a massive gamble on the weather bears more comparison with King Canute than with Alexander the Great. The ground over which the offensive was launched was a quagmire. Misplaced loyalty saw too much reliance placed on weak commanders. The result was a bloody mess, a farce that should never have been started and should certainly have been stopped before it did so much harm. It is possible that Haig continued the offensive in the vain hope that it might allow British troops to capture the high ground that would aid them significantly in the future. If so, it was a mistaken dream.

Yet Passchendaele was not the whole story of Haig's command. The rearguard action supervised and controlled by him in 1914 was masterly. He was caught out by the German offensive of 1918 because his plan for defence in depth did not work, but he had the guts to tell his men the truth (his famous orders at the height of the British rout stated explicitly 'with our backs to the wall'). He undoubtedly suffered through those junior to him, but at the root of this weakness was the fact that he was prepared to delegate to the man on the spot and not dictate action to the man in the front line. He was in favour of tactical flexibility, and as early as 1909 was arguing against laying down too firm a set of orders for the man on the spot.[29] He was one of the few to foresee a long war in 1914:

> As regards meeting 'the storm' which we all foresee, it seems to me that it will take a long time, we'll win by wearing the enemy out, if we are only allowed three more years to prepare and organize the Empire.[30]

It cannot be stressed too heavily that all Haig's 'mistakes' were an attempt to make a breakthrough that would shorten the war and save lives. That breakthrough would, of course, make Haig the most famous general in British history: the two facts cannot be separated in any treatment of Haig, because to him they were identical. The war of attrition was his fall-back situation, his way of justifying the appalling loss of life in the offensives when the breakthrough failed to materialize. What no one has sought to deny Haig is the fact that in the final account the policy of attrition worked. Germany was worn down and exhausted, and the victory did go to those who held on longest. It was an unpalatable victory and one won at dreadful cost, but in military terms it was still a resounding and unequivocal victory.

As a society we demand of our generals that they win wars. Haig won the war. Before we damn him for doing so we ought perhaps to point out that no one made it a part of Haig's brief that he should win the war without offending people, do it nicely, and not lose lives in the process. We expect victory but not death. History seems to operate a strange alchemical process, whereby time changes the mixture that is war. The suffering, anguish and broken lives sink to the bottom of the jar and become invisible. The honour, the glory and the sweet taste of victory rise to the top, and are what is remembered. If Haig is a villain then we all share in that villainy. It is we who expect a general to win a war without losing life.

The so-called failure of command in the 1914–18 war is called into question by one very obvious fact. There was no serious mutiny among British troops for the duration of the war. As one man who served in the war pointed out,

> If they [the generals] really had been donkeys, their men would have refused to follow them: this was, of course, what happened in both the German and the Russian armies at the end of the war.[31]

69

The same author also commented,

> Haig's name, somehow, was not vilified [by serving soldiers],
> and if it had been, his army would not have survived to win the
> hard-fought Battle of the Hindenburg Line, the tactical blow
> that brought Germany to its knees, in September, 1918.[32]

We do not have to rely solely on the word of a public-school-
educated officer for evidence that the troops did not hate Haig.
His ability to worm his way into a corrupt establishment makes
him, by my own canon of beliefs, one of the most unpleasant men
I have ever researched. It was in that free and unbiased spirit that
I started delving into his career, expecting to find soldier after
soldier writing with the same intensity of mood, if not the same
skill, as Sassoon in 'The General'. The evidence for that view is
simply not there. Evidence for the alternative view is, and only a
few examples can be given here of the hundreds that exist. Basil
Farrer was a stretcher-bearer.

> Haig has been much criticized for what happened on the
> Somme, but you have to remember that he acted on advice from
> his staff and a long chain of advisers. I don't think he was a
> butcher, it was just that we were men up against modern
> machine guns. And although stated baldly it sounds mad to
> have walked across no man's land, arms aslant, remember that
> we thought the Germans had been knocked out and you can't
> run and dodge easily when you're carrying a rifle and masses of
> other gear.[33]

Another junior officer commented,

> It is nonsense too when you hear people saying that Field
> Marshal Haig sent thousands to their deaths. Do you think he
> wanted them to die? Something had to be done. Belgium had
> gone. France had nearly gone. We'd lost most of our regular
> army at Mons. We had to move at the Somme, even though it
> meant terrible losses. We had to attack. If we hadn't the French
> would have soon surrendered and the Kaiser would have over-
> run us.[34]

Haig failed to make the breakthrough he yearned for, at least until
1918, and the failure cost an appalling number of lives. But he
never failed to command the basic loyalty of his troops, which is
why there is so little contemporary evidence of any real hatred of

Haig and other 'top brass'. Of course, most officers and men never came within miles of Haig, and most saw, with him, that there was little alternative. Another infantryman partly supports this view:

> Historians say that Haig had the confidence of his men. I very much doubt whether this was strictly true. He had such a vast number of troops under his command and was so completely remote from the actual fighting that he was merely a name, a figurehead. In my view, it was not confidence in him that men had, but simply their ingrained sense of duty and obedience, in keeping with the times. They were wholly loyal to their own officers, and that was as far as their confidence went. It was trust and comradeship founded on the actual sharing of dangers together.[35]

It is perhaps hard for us to realize now how little interest the ordinary soldier had in the real top brass. It should be easier for us to realize that the average infantryman's sense of fair play and intelligence told him there was no better way of breaking the stalemate than that adopted by Haig.

Finally, Haig knew what he was fighting for. It was the same thing as every thinking man in the British army was fighting for, and the similarity of aims perhaps explains why the men in Haig's army never lost faith in him:

> The aim for which the war is being waged is the destruction of German militarism. Three years of war and the loss of one-tenth of the manhood of the nation is not too great a price to pay in so great a cause.[36]

Blunt, perhaps callous, and certainly wholly politically incorrect; yet, for all that, Haig merely wrote what many of his contemporaries thought.

Haig was only one man, and the myth of the callous and blundering brass hat had more than one source. The myth is a convenient one, as the discussion of Haig has shown, but it is generally unfair to both officers and men of the British Army. The key to understanding that army lies in the realization that it was essentially a colonial army. As a result,

> [The army] did not shackle itself to a theoretical system of war as the French and Germans had done. How could it? . . . the army might have to fight (and soon did) on the North-West

frontier of India, in the Middle East, the Sudan or Southern or central Africa.[37]

All wars show up weaknesses in armies. The difference for the British was that the Boer War showed up weaknesses which were ruthlessly reported on by Royal Commission and acted on by Haldane. Nor was the officer class obsessed by black bottles at dinner instead of beating the enemy:

> A new school of officers has arisen since the South African War, a thinking school of officers who desire to see the full efficiency which comes from a new organisation and no surplus energy running to waste.[38]

The massed frontal attack has been the bludgeon by which many commentators have damned high command in the Great War. There is overwhelming evidence to support the fact that alone among European armies the British had prior to the war realized the importance of avoiding close-order attacks. A German observer of British army manoeuvres in 1904 noted,

> Frontal attacks were entirely avoided. . . . No detachment was ever seen in close order within three thousand yards.[39]

A German officer fighting the real thing wrote,

> Stretched out across the broad expanse of meadows between us and the river was a long line of dots wide apart, and looking through these glasses one saw that these dots were infantry advancing, widely extended: English infantry, too, unmistakably. A field battery on our left had spotted them, and we watched their shrapnel bursting over the advancing line. Soon a second line of dots emerged from the willows along the river-bank, at least ten paces apart, and began to advance. More of our batteries came into action; but it was noticed that a shell, however well aimed, seldom killed more than one man, the lines being so well and widely extended. The front line had taken cover when the shelling began, running behind any hedges or buildings near by, but this second line kept steadily on, while a third and fourth line now appeared from the river-bank, each keeping about two hundred yards distance from the line in front. Our guns now fired like mad, but it did not stop the movement: a fifth and a sixth line came on, all with the same wide

72

intervals between men and the same distance apart. It was magnificently done.[40]

This was in 1914, with the old army. It took time to train a volunteer and conscript force up to the same standard, but trained eventually they were. A year before the end of the war the British Army was showing its American allies that it had not forgotten the lessons learned in close-order skirmishing in South Africa:

Our main item was a demonstration of a 'Platoon in the Attack', which we carried out strictly in accordance with the official pamphlet issued on the subject. At this period of the war the platoon was considered as the principle unit of the Army. It was self-contained, consisting of four sections. A Lewis gun section, with two guns. A section of rifle grenadiers who were also bombers, and two sections of rifle and bayonet men. An army in miniature, the Lewis guns supplying covering machine-gun fire, the rifle grenadiers acting as artillery; and the riflemen making the infantry assault.[41]

Self-sufficiency, individuality, initiative – these features were to mark the successful German offensive in 1918, but the British Army had never forgotten them. Unfortunately such features were a relative luxury that could come only in the second phase of training, after the rifleman had been taught to aim, fire and clean his weapon, and the bomber to know how to handle a bomb. A comment from a soldier in 1915 shows how far the army had to go to reach that stage of training with many of its recruits:

A box of bombs was placed in readiness to hold up any of the enemy that might chance to come along. I had not the faintest idea how to work a bomb, as I had never thrown one of them in my life.[42]

Even one of the great myths of the war, the presence of headquarters miles behind the front line, had considerable military validity:

When we attacked at Gheluvelt in October, 1917, our Divisional HQ lay on the Scherpenberg, as the crow flies near ten miles away, and more by road. Had they been nearer, they would not have been more useful: once an attack was mounted, it was impossible to control it. Its fate rested on the skill with which it

73

had been prepared; if the time-table went awry, there was no opportunity for sudden improvization.[43]

The top commanders in the First World War were far from perfect, but they were far from the blundering idiot described by Sassoon in 'The General'. In 1914 they were able to fight to a standstill the most professional and powerful army in Europe, and conduct one of the most successful fighting retreats in the history of warfare. They set up a system which for all its faults managed to recruit 5,704,416 men between 1914 and 1918 and train them sufficiently well for them to win the war. They led an army which fought massive and major battles in every year of the war, which never mutinied at the front and which came to terms with gas, aircraft and tanks as well as fighting a permanent battle against its own political leaders and allies in addition to the military battle. Relative to the number of people available for military service, the war they fought was no more wasteful of human life than Wellington's campaign a hundred years earlier.

That fact does not excuse the terrible waste of life that is war. It merely makes the point that a war is paid for in blood as well as money, and the First World War was no different from any other war in that respect. The post-war generation could not come to terms with this and blamed Haig and others for loss of life that was the fault of war, not the generals. They were a convenient scapegoat, though there is no evidence that they were any more or less bloody than their ancestors in warfare. The real turnaround in concepts of war came some twenty-seven years later, when an American president ordered the destruction of two whole cities of enemy civilians. His justification? To save the lives of soldiers and sailors, and bring a war to an end. In this light Haig's decision to launch the Somme offensive for exactly the same reasons, but risking the lives only of enlisted and volunteer soldiers, does not appear to be without some form of honour. Haig killed no babies and old men in 1916. His crime was to launch attacks that were wasteful of soldiers' lives and which, until 1918, did not bring victory; his real crime was to be seen not to care about these losses, and to be the agent whereby British society was brought to terms with the reality of modern warfare.

Notes

1 Manning, *Her Privates We*, p. 171
2 Coppard, *With a Machine Gun to Cambrai*, p. 115
3 *ibid.*, pp. 115–16
4 Quinn, *Tales of the Old Soldiers*, pp. 20–1
5 *ibid.*, p. 17
6 Edmonds, *A Subaltern's War*, p. 92
7 *ibid.*
8 see Prior & Wilson, *Command on the Western Front*
9 Chapman, *Vain Glory*, pp. 404–5
10 Marwick, *Deluge*, p. 41
11 Vaughan, *Desperate Glory*, p. 78
12 Vansittart, *Voices*, p. 23
13 Panichas, pp. 157–8
14 de Groot, *Haig*, p. 26
15 Winter, *Haig's Command*, p. 41
16 de Groot, p. 112
17 Chapman, *Vain Glory*, p. 451
18 de Groot, p. 300
19 Chapman, *Vain Glory*, p. 409
20 see Warner, *Haig*, p. 81
21 Carrington, quoted Warner, p. 194
22 Edmonds, p. 114
23 de Groot, p. 201
24 Winter, *Death's Men*, p. 118
25 *ibid.*, p. 179
26 Captain von Hentig, quoted Warner, p. 212
27 *ibid.*
28 Captain P. J. Trousdell, quoted Macdonald, *Voices and Images of the Great War*, p. 153
29 de Groot, p. 137
30 Haig, quoted de Groot, p. 324
31 Carrington, quoted Warner, p. 194
32 Carrington, *Promises of Greatness*, p. 160
33 Quinn, p. 142
34 R. Hawkins, quoted Quinn, p. 24
35 Coppard, p. 76
36 Haig, quoted de Groot, p. 242
37 Terraine, *White Heat*, p.30
38 Sommer, *Haldane of Cloan*, pp. 169–70
39 Terraine, p. 30

40 Chapman, *Vain Glory*, pp. 79–80
41 Captain A. Pollard, quoted Macdonald, p. 285
42 Stuart-Dolden, *Cannon Fodder*, p. 19
43 Chapman, *Passionate Prodigality*, p. 225

CHAPTER THREE

Enlisting

It was not an unthinking mass of men who marched to war in 1914. Nor were the famous war poets the only intelligent people who took part. One of the most intelligent, Vivian de Sola Pinto, fought side by side with Siegfried Sassoon and became a distinguished professor of English literature after the war. In the 1960s his attitude was unequivocal:

> I find it hard to understand how people whom I respect, like Bertrand Russell, can still argue that we could and should have stood aside from the European conflict in 1914. If the pacifist minority in the Liberal Government had had its way and we had failed to fulfill our legal obligation to Belgium and our moral obligation to France, the nation would certainly have been split from top to bottom. The Germans would, doubtless, have over-run Western Europe as they did in 1940; but in the meantime, I have no doubt that thousands of British volunteers without adequate arms or organisation would have streamed across the Channel to help the resistance, and the tragedy of the International Brigade in Spain in 1936–37 would have been anticipated on a much larger scale in France and Flanders. In the meantime, the German militarists controlling the resources of the whole Continent would have dictated their own terms to a divided and isolated Britain without a friend in the world, and the next victim would certainly have been the wealthy and, at that time, almost defenceless American democracy.[1]

It is hard to equate this comment from a sensitive and thoughtful man with the comment made by the author of one of the most influential modern books to have been written on the war:

> In the Great War eight million people were destroyed because
> two persons, the Archduke Francis Ferdinand and his consort,
> had been shot.[2]

Historically, this is hogwash. Eight million people died because
Germany was a lethal combination of militarism and expansion-
ism, without the saving virtues of wisdom or humility. Eight
million people died because Germany quite calmly decided to
invade two countries against whom it had no specific quarrel
(Belgium and France) for fear of ending up fighting a war on two
fronts. Eight million people died because the system of checks and
balances engineered by the great European powers was a disaster
waiting to happen, and because no one in government or the army,
with the possible exception of Kitchener, had the faintest idea of
what modern warfare would involve. To say that eight million
people died in the Great War because of an incident in Sarajevo is
to say that thousands of civilians were burnt to cinders in Coventry
in the Second World War because Herr Heinkel founded an aircraft company. It is to blame the explosion on the inventor of the
match. Yet it is typical of the way in which those who joined up
and fought in the Great War have been patronized by successive
generations of critics, all convinced of the fact that the 'senseless
slaughter' meant that those who died had very little sense, and
were shepherded to their deaths like sheep. It was simply not true,
as countless contemporary records show:

> I never meet an 'old sweat', as we liked to describe ourselves,
> who accepts or enjoys the figure in which we are now presented,
> though it is useless – undignified – to protest. Just smile and
> make an old soldier's wry joke when you see yourself on the tele-
> vision screen, agonised and woebegone, trudging from disaster
> to disaster, knee-deep in moral as well as physical mud, hesi-
> tant about your purpose, submissive to a harsh, irrelevant
> discipline, mistrustful of your commanders. Is it any use to
> assert that I was not like that, and my dead friends were not like
> that, and the old cronies that I meet at reunions are not
> like that?[3]

Where the 1930s in particular went wrong was in the attempt to
impose a view of the war on those who lived through it. Not for
the first time the wisdom of hindsight was allowed to give one
colour to events that at the time held all the shades of the rainbow.
There were as many reasons for fighting in the war as there were
soldiers in it. Of some joining up was expected, for others it was

necessary, and for some it was outwardly inexplicable. The myth of the war has us believe that men enlisted through blinkered or jingoistic patriotism: many did just that, many others had reasons as varied as needing the money or wishing to bring an end to German militarism. There were many who went to war because they were, by and large, the product of a culture with more simple imperatives than those which pertained post-1945. There were many who, through the introduction of conscription, were given no choice.

The myth of the war also has us believe that the Somme was the turning-point for Kitchener's volunteers, and that 1916 marked the onset of cynicism and disillusion among British soldiers: in fact the losses to the original British Expeditionary Force in 1914 were proportionately larger and potentially more of a death-blow to British skill at arms than the casualties suffered at the Somme, and anyone who fought at the Battle of Loos in 1915 would find the Somme held few surprises and little that was new. The myth of the war states that soldiers became cynical and embittered, whereas by and large fighting soldiers were still among the most patriotic of their countrymen in 1918. The myth of the war states that the fighting soldier despised the top brass and felt a bond of sympathy with his fellow-soldiers in German uniform. The written record of the war suggests that the ordinary soldier neither knew nor cared much about the top brass and was cheerfully homicidal in his attitude to the enemy, particularly if that same enemy had just killed a friend.

Joining Up: The Trench Poets

Outwardly, it seems hardly surprising that Rupert Brooke joined up. 'The Old Vicarage, Grantchester' enthuses about things English in general and East Anglian in particular, and his patriotic sonnets have become a symbol of the easy, self-worshipping patriotism with which many intelligent young men joined up in 1914. Yet prior to 1914 Brooke had been a savage critic of the British middle classes, a Fabian and opposed to any Establishment. Brooke was not a simple man. He was a symbol of the greatest irony of the Great War, the fact that young men from every background and walk of life would be prepared, against all logic and reason, to take a rifle in hand and plant a bullet through the head of an opposing German.

In Brooke's case, his reasons for joining up were more complex than many. He was by modern standards a very disturbed figure. A Freudian analyst would make hay of the frequency with which he addresses one of his greatest loves, Cathleen Nesbitt, as 'My sweet child', and what appears to be his tortured choice between homosexuality and heterosexuality. Regardless of his sexual preferences and his ability to undergo and inflict what would now be termed as nervous breakdowns, Brooke was a confused and perhaps deeply unhappy man in 1914. The war offered him simplicity and certainty. It offered him a cause which demanded total obedience and absorbed his whole being, so that for once he ceased to be responsible for the course his life took. The impression given by reading Brooke's letters is that the war allowed him to take a holiday from thought, which had more often than not led the highly intelligent, unstable and genuinely creative Brooke into dark alleyways of self-doubt and neurosis.

One of the classic Edwardian responses to the war is that of 'Swimmers into cleanness leaping'. The young men joining up to fight on the side of goodness dive from a muddy, diseased and dirty world into a cleansing simplicity, a purgatorial experience that will buy rejuvenation for society in exchange for the blood of some of its youth. This element in Brooke's mood is summed up by Charles Sorley in that most remarkable of poems, 'All the Hills and Vales Along': 'Cast away regret and rue/ Think what you are marching to'. Sorley knew what they were marching to, and no one has expressed it better than in his poem 'When You See Millions of the Mouthless Dead'. Brooke knew that joining up allowed him to cast away regret and rue, and many of his generation felt that in joining up they were casting off a dirty, shabby, grey overcoat and changing into bright new clothes in primary colours.

This is the intellectual, perhaps even literary-critical, argument for a fêted young Fabian appearing to welcome the war with open arms. There is a simpler reason why young men of liberal or socialist tendencies often joined up with what to us might appear unseemly haste. Germany's nightmare prior to 1914 had always been what it ended up doing in two world wars, fighting on two fronts. In both wars its answer was to deliver a hammer blow to the west before turning on the east. Unfortunately in 1914 this necessitated invading a neutral country, Belgium, without a declaration of war. The effect on the civilian population was small beer in comparison to what happened to the citizens of Hiroshima, Dresden and Coventry, but its effect on Brooke, brought up within a cocoon of decency and fair play, was almost beyond our imagining. This extract from one of Brooke's letters takes the reader closer to the heart of his support of the war than anything else I have read:

It hurts me, this war. Because I was fond of Germany. There are such good things in her, and I'd always hoped she'd get away from Prussia and the oligarchy in time. If it had been a mere war between us and them I'd have hated fighting. But I'm glad to be doing it for Belgium. That's what breaks the heart to see and hear of. I marched through Antwerp, deserted, shelled, and burning, one night, and saw ruined houses, dead men and horses: and railway trains with their lines taken up and twisted and flung down as if a child had been playing with a toy. And the whole heaven and earth was lit up by the glare from the great lakes and rivers of burning petrol, hills and spires of flame. That was like Hell, a Dantesque Hell, terrible. But there – and later – I saw what was a truer Hell. Hundreds of thousands of refugees, their goods on barrows and hand-carts and perambulators and wagons, moving with infinite slowness out into the night, two unending lines of them, the old men mostly weeping, the women with hard white drawn faces, the children playing or crying or sleeping. That's what Belgium is now: the country where three civilians have been killed to every one soldier. That damnable policy of 'frightfulness' succeeded for a time. When it was decided to evacuate Antwerp, all of that population of half a million, save a few thousands, fled. I don't think they really had any need to. The Germans have behaved fairly well in the big cities. But the policy of bullying has been carried out well. And half a million people preferred homelessness and the chance of starvation, to the certainty of German rule. It's queer to think one has been a witness of one of the greatest crimes of history. Has ever a nation been treated like that? And how can such a stain be wiped out?[4]

The answer to Brooke's question is that many, many nations had been treated like that in European and world history, and Brooke's horror is a symbol of a generation of middle-class Englishmen suddenly baptized into the reality of warfare. Despite his naivety, Brooke is eminently fair, acknowledging that Germany had stood for far more than Prussian militarism, and debunking the myth of wholesale German atrocities. Yet at the same time Brooke is the archetypal Englishman of his generation, brought to a sudden realization that war is not a gentleman's game fought between elegantly painted and accoutred lead figures on a baize table, but a matter of innocents being led to death and starvation, great cities burning to the ground. European peasantry, accustomed to having wars fought on and through their homes for centuries past, were less shocked, but this does not diminish Brooke's heroism. He had a pessimism about his own fortunes in war that was in part realism, in part the self-glorification which is so much a part of the patriotic sonnets and of being young. Yet Brooke was comparatively old when he joined up, and had clearly thought through the implications of being in uniform in a way that many of his contemporaries had not:

> When they told us at Dunkirk that we were all going to be killed in Antwerp, if not on the way there, I didn't think much (as I'd expected) what a damned fool I was not to have written more and done various things better and been less selfish. I merely thought 'What Hell it is that I shan't have any children – any sons.' I thought it over and over, quite furious, for some hours.[5]

This makes one realize that Brooke knew what he was losing by joining up. He was, at times, an idealist, but he was never an unthinking one. He did not join up because of 'poor Belgium', but rather because war was unavoidable and offered a way out. He continued to fight, and eventually die, because of it, and because of it hundreds of thousands of young men decided to join up. We know now that putting on a uniform, learning the rudiments of military discipline and going out to be slaughtered at Loos, the Somme or Passchendaele did not in any serious way affect either the fate of Belgium or the number of innocent civilians slaughtered, starved or rendered forever refugees in that and subsequent wars. We know that the sufferings of the inhabitants of Antwerp hardly bear comparison with those inflicted by both sides on the inhabitants of Vietnam. Brooke did not know it, and his generation was perhaps the last to believe in such numbers that an individual action could affect history, or be motivated by such a desire to influence it. It is hard not to condemn them for their folly, their simplicity and perhaps even their stupidity. At the same time it is hard not to feel an admiration for young men who, however puffed up they may have been by vainglory and self-worshipping adolescence, believed enough in a cause to risk their lives for it.

Charles Sorley has left no real explanation of why he joined up. He was in Germany when war was declared, spending a year there prior to going up to Oxford. He was imprisoned 'for eight-and-a-half hours' before being allowed to proceed home. Sorley had no hesitation in joining up, but the self-mocking irony of his letters gives only hints as to his reasons:

> But isn't all this bloody? I am full of mute and burning rage and annoyance and sulkiness about it. I could wager that out of

twelve million eventual combatants there aren't twelve who really want it. And 'serving one's country' is so unpicturesque and unheroic when it comes to the point. . . . Besides the Germans are so nice: but I suppose the best thing that could happen to them would be their defeat.[6]

Sorley had no time for patriotic fervour:

But, when everyone else is being so splendidly patriotic, that '*Wille zu Widerspruch*' or cussedness, which is chief among my (few) vices, is making me, since I cannot be actively pro-German, merely sulky.[7]

Sorley knew and loved Germany, yet his understanding never undercut his feeling that he was fighting on the right side:

So it seems to me that Germany's only fault . . . is a lack of real insight and sympathy with those who differ from her. We are not fighting a bully, but a bigot. They are a young nation and don't yet see what they consider is being done for the good of the world may be really being done for self-gratification. . . . I regard the war as one between sisters, between Martha and Mary, the efficient and the intolerant against the casual and sympathetic. Each side has a virtue for which it is fighting, and each that virtue's supplementary vice. And I hope that whatever the material result of the conflict, it will purge these two virtues of their vices, and efficiency and tolerance will no longer be incompatible.[8]

Sorley's final loyalty was for tolerance, perhaps comparable to the 'unofficial English rose' immortalized in Brooke's 'The Old Vicarage, Grantchester'. It was a loyalty torn out of him at times, as when he wrote that,

I am giving my body (by a refinement of cowardice) to fight against the most enterprising nation in the world.[9]

Sorley also managed to include, in an off-hand manner, a phrase that has always struck me as one of the great truths to be written about the First World War, 'What we are doing is casting out Satan by Satan.'[10] He was the author of what must stand at the same time as the most sympathetic, intelligent and damning comment on Brooke's patriotic sonnets:

He is far too obsessed with his own sacrifice, regarding the going to war of himself (and others) as a highly intense, remarkable and sacrificial exploit, whereas it is merely the conduct demanded of him (and others) by the turn of circumstances, where non-compliance with this demand would have made life intolerable. It was not that 'they' gave up anything of that list he gives in one sonnet: but that the essence of these things had been endangered by circumstances over which he had no control, and he must fight to recapture them. He has clothed his attitude in fine words: but he has taken the sentimental attitude.[11]

I am not aware of any more fair or shrewd comment on Brooke's sonnets. Sorley punctured the patriotic bubble of so many of his contemporaries with the lance of intelligence and common sense. He saw that Germany and Britain were simply variations on the same theme, saw in advance of many the total tragedy represented by the war (and its futility), but also recognized that he was caught in a wheel of history that would not cease revolving until it had ground down countless young men. For Sorley, and one suspects many of his generation, joining up was simply the lesser of two evils. It carried a risk, but not to do so carried a certainty of shame and punishment that made it no choice at all.

It is tempting to believe he was unique in saying at one and the same time that 'useless' sacrifice could have a meaning. He is unique in terms of the letters and poems that have come down to us, and unique in that his father was a member of the syndicate which ran the Cambridge University Press, and which therefore published both his poems and letters. It is a great pity that the Cambridge University Press have continued to ignore the wishes of the father and the work of the son, as the latter needs no excuse for reprinting. There is no way that Sorley's immensely complex reasons for joining up can be categorized, labelled or dismissed. But they stand for many thousands of intelligent young men who joined in 1914 to fight and died thereafter, men considerably patronized by succeeding literary and historical commentators who refused to believe that they knew what they were doing.

The issue is complicated further when looking at the life of Julian Grenfell, who bears comparison with Rupert Brooke. Both young men were through background, education and intelligence, clearly destined for great things in a normal peacetime existence; both wrote rather self-glorifying poetry that was brought to an early prominence by their deaths early in the war, at a time when it was comparatively rare for a bright, public school and Oxbridge-educated young man to die in uniform for his country.

There the similarity ends. It is hard to imagine any other war in which someone of Brooke's intellectual and even Bohemian background would have joined up; it is hard to imagine any war in which someone of Julian Grenfell's background would not have joined up. His father was a Conservative MP and landowner, knighted in Julian's lifetime. As an MP he was more or less a disaster, as a sportsman he was unsurpassed. He swam the pool beneath Niagara twice, rowed across the Channel and shot everything that moved. His mother was a famed society beauty of aristocratic lineage. Julian went to Eton and then to Balliol to read Greats. From there he joined the army in India in 1910; his early letters suggest that the activity he most enjoyed was pig-sticking. On the basis of that record, Grenfell was the archetypal English aristocrat, a member of a tribe who since the days of William the Conqueror had bartered their sons to military service in exchange for vast wealth and privilege. The fact that he seemed to enjoy the war is a final nail in his coffin as far as many critics have been concerned.

> I adore war. . . . It is like a big picnic without the objectlessness of a picnic. I've never been so well or so happy. No one grumbles at one for being dirty. I've only had my boots off once in the last ten days, and only washed twice.[12]

Reading a new entry in Grenfell's game book, coming after that for 105 partridges shot, listing '2 Pomeranians'[13] (he had gone on a daring solo raid into enemy trenches for which he was awarded the DSO) one's gorge begins to rise. Yet it would be wrong to categorize him as the unthinking aristocrat, the cavalry officer whose brains were in his backside or in that of his horse, for all that it is an easy assumption.

Grenfell was far more complex than the basic facts of his background and upbringing might suggest. For starters, he rode two horses for much of his time at Eton, and was editor of the official *Eton College Chronicle*. At the same time he founded and ran *The Outsider*, a rival paper designed to mock the Establishment journal. In his life he also showed one of the chronic dichotomies of the Edwardian period, the clash between a form of vibrant optimism based on a belief in the power of intellect and a dreadful pessimism that yearned for simplicity and even death. This clash was very visible in the life and work of Rupert Brooke, whom Grenfell admired, and was commented on by Grenfell's biographer:

This was characteristic of the age – an optimism allied insanely with an expectation of Armageddon.[14]

As with so many of his generation, Grenfell turned against his own kind, writing with contempt of:

> those who value for its own sake the wealth, the magnificence and the display; those whom conventionality forces to keep servants and whom competition forces to keep an army of servants; those who rate the worth of themselves and others by the amount of these things that they possess and the show that they make of them.[15]

In an unpublished manuscript, Grenfell damned the English convention of doing not what was right, but doing simply as others do:

> a man's point of view and a man's method of life are his own and if he is made to conform to a fixed point of view and a fixed method of life it will kill his soul.[16]

Nothing remarkable in that for the twenty-first century, but perhaps something very remarkable for a product of Eton and Balliol prior to 1914? Only if one believes what one reads . . . Grenfell, Sorley, Brooke, Graves, Sassoon: a compelling list of names, all the sons of upper-middle-class families fully embedded in the Establishment of the time, and all capable of taking an entirely individual and even anti-Establishment view. Most also went through serious mental crises, none more so than Brooke and Grenfell. The latter wrote about one of his breakdowns;

> I don't know what I am doing, now, I feel as if I had been smashed up into little bits and put together again very badly with half the bits missing. All Thursday I felt as if I had something inside my head which was just going to burst; and then it did burst, and I broke up, and didn't know what I was or what was going on, except that I had gone right out of myself and become something quite different; and the agony of it, just the pure physical agony was like being hammered to death without dying.[17]

Grenfell at one stage wanted to leave the army (his early love of overseas service soon died when he realized that a majority of the officers were blockheads), but his main reason for staying on, apart from pressure exerted by his mother, seems to have been the fact

86

that army service did at least get him out of England, with what he saw as its hypocrisies and animosities. Grenfell was trapped, as his biographer points out,

> It was when he had been in England for some time that the army did not seem too bad; it was when he was back in South Africa that he felt his situation there again to be hopeless.[18]

For Grenfell, and one suspects many others, the war was a vast inevitability. There was no avoiding it, and nowhere to run. Its total certainty acted as a balm to chronic self-torturing. Its removal of choice acted as a comfort, as a recidivist prisoner can be comforted by the choice-free ritual and routine of prison life.

Edward Thomas and Isaac Rosenberg were perhaps the most unlikely soldiers of any who achieved posthumous poetic fame. Thomas was a 'doomed hack', tied to a treadmill of sub-standard prose works on the English countryside, a treadmill that his wife and family inadvertently made him tread even harder. He was nearing forty, and as a family man of that age was not subject to popular pressure to join up. What is certain is that for Thomas, and perhaps also for Brooke, love of England was actually love of the English countryside. Brooke wrote that he was prepared to die for 'the actual earth of England'. As we have seen, he was heavily influenced by the plight of Belgium. Thomas was remarkably similar:

> All I can tell is it seemed to me that either I had never loved England, or I had loved it foolishly, aesthetically, like a slave, not having realised that it was not mine unless I were willing and prepared to die for it rather than leave it as Belgian women and old men and children had left their country. Something I had omitted. Something, I felt, had to be done before I could look again composedly at English landscape, at the elms and poplars about the houses, at the purple-headed wood-betony with two pairs of leaves on a stiff stem, who stood sentinel among the grasses and bracken by hedge-side or wood's edge.[19]

Thomas had three choices in 1915: go to America to join his friend, the poet Robert Frost, carry on as a civilian, or enlist. As with so many of his contemporaries there is an almost compulsive inevitability about his choice, which subtly became no choice at all. Going to America would leave his wife Helen and the children on their own, and there were no new commissions for books awaiting him. Despite that, there is no simple explanation for his enlistment. He shared the deep and sometimes savage melancholy of so many of his literary friends and contemporaries, and his letters show a strange contentment with army life that echoes sentiments expressed by Brooke, and perhaps sprang from the same source as both Brooke's and Grenfell's peace of mind: here was a cause demanding total obedience and commitment, with simple rules and simple yardsticks by which to judge success,

> I have conspired with God (I suppose) not to think about walks and walking sticks or 6 months or 6 years hence. I just think about when I shall first go on guard etc.[20]

Thomas in effect joined up twice. As a map instructor he could have remained in the UK, but volunteered instead in 1916 for a commission in the Royal Artillery. There can be little doubt that he knew the risk he was taking, and was offering his 'eyes and breath/For what would neither ask nor heed his death' – his country. At around this time he wrote 'The Gallows', a bleak description of the gamekeeper's traditional hanging of dead vermin. The weasel,

> Swings in the wind and the rain,
> In the sun and in the snow,
> Without pleasure, without pain,
> On the dead oak tree bough.

The mood of the poem and its vision of death is similar to those found in much of Sorley's poetry, where death is simply an end, not a beginning, a 'slate wiped clean'. One could be forgiven at times when reading critical works on the war for thinking that Wilfred Owen invented objectivity in First World War poetry. There are few more objective poems than Thomas's 'The Gallows' or Sorley's 'When You See Millions of the Mouthless Dead', both written by 1916 and before either poet had extensive front-line experience. The objectivity and detachment commanded by Sorley and Thomas may not owe a specific literary debt to the poetry of Thomas Hardy, but shares much of Hardy's power. Hardy's 'The Darkling Thrush' and 'The Blinded Bird' come firmly from the same natural world and countryside as was walked by Edward Thomas and run by Charles Sorley.

Thomas's poetry raises the issue of whether he did not merely welcome the certainty and simplicity of army life, but actively sought death. A yearning for oblivion is a common feature in the work of many young poets who enlisted. It can be dismissed as adolescent fantasizing, but whatever else they may have been these young men were intelligent and very much in touch with their emotions, albeit rarely in control of them. Thomas had the same willingness to meet death that one finds in Brooke and Sorley's poetry, and in Julian Grenfell when he quite cheerfully told those he met, in defiance of the outward evidence, that he would die from the head wound he had just received. Thomas's poetry suggests more than a fatalistic acceptance of death. 'Lights Out' has the superb gentleness of touch that marks out much of his poetry, but there can be no doubt that the light going out is the light of his life and the sleep is death.

> I have come to the borders of sleep,
> The unfathomable deep
> Forest where all must lose
> Their way, however straight,
> Or winding, soon or late;
> They cannot choose.

and,

> Here love ends,
> Despair, ambition ends;
> All pleasure and all trouble,
> Although most sweet or bitter,
> Here ends in sleep that is sweeter
> Than tasks most noble.

Thomas sought oblivion in the war. The fact that he was granted it is one of that war's greater tragedies.

Thomas was no conventional patriot, nor was he blinkered about Germany. He had serious rows with his father when he suggested that German soldiers were likely to be just as brave as English troops. It is a feature of many of these young poets that they had no jingoistic hatred of Germany and a sharp awareness of the hypocrisy, failures and shortcomings of English society. Nevertheless, they enlisted.

So, remarkably, did another author, Hector Hugh Munro, now best known for the short stories he wrote under the pen-name of 'Saki'. Saki lies somewhere between the wit of Oscar Wilde and the mischief of Joe Orton, and his unconventionality was nowhere better expressed than in the fact that he joined up immediately in 1914 at the age of forty-three, deciding to enlist as a private. He wrote no war poetry as that term is now understood, and only a few stories during the war, none of which refer directly to the fighting. He did produce one of the most unusual poetic offerings of the war,

> While shepherds watched their flocks by night,
> All seated on the ground,
> A high explosive shell came down,
> And mutton rained around.

He was of firmly upper-middle-class background, had attended Bedford School and was an established member of London journalistic life. A more unlikely recruit as a private is difficult to imagine, and it is as if Oscar Wilde had signed up as a fusilier. Undoubtedly the same mass movement that drew so many people into the war must have affected Munro, but as with Edward Thomas his age meant that he had a perfectly honourable claim to civilian life, particularly in 1914. One comparison is with T.E. Lawrence, who also exorcized some private ghost by joining up in the ranks, but my limited research in this field suggests there is a whole study to be written on the reasoning behind so many middle-class men joining up as privates. There were a large number, though just how many and how varied their reasons waits on a proper study of the topic.

One such was Oundle public schoolboy Robert Macfie, an Edinburgh BSc and Cambridge MA, chairman of a sugar-refining company and author of several small books. He had been colour quartermaster sergeant of a territorial battalion, and insisted on serving in the ranks throughout the war. He is one of many who has left no satisfactory explanation of why he chose to remain in the ranks, save for some rather vague statements that this was the best way he could steady the men. Presumably some of the other unlikely privates joined up because it was the only way into the war, which they thought might be over by Christmas. Rather more seem to have had more complex reasons for crossing a class divide that was an abyss in comparison with the present time.

Saki was homosexual, and this may have indirectly influenced his decision. The suggestion that he joined up as a private because it provided easy sexual pickings is silly. Munro appears to have had no problem finding partners before the war, and it would need someone a great deal more foolish than he to assume that life as a private soldier on active service gave either the authority to command compliance or the opportunity to consummate a relationship. Saki was a tortured soul, as were so many of his generation. The apparent ease with which he bore his homosexuality had to be in part a pretence in an age and culture which had destroyed Oscar Wilde.

There is at the heart of Saki's work an awareness of decadence, of pretence, and perhaps in the final count of the futility of it all. War was something cleansing and purifying, something totally absorbing, removing at a stroke self-doubt, questioning and uncertainty. For the homosexual to whom the phrase 'coming out' would have been a cruel joke, enlistment meant something else: a life lived among men, in which the word 'comradeship' allowed one to care passionately, albeit with a stiff upper lip, for the 'lads' with whom one shared one's life and one's death. It was not an answer to the problems of existence, but a holiday from them, with certainties dictated by external forces and decisions operating to clear-cut rules. To that extent Saki bears comparison with Brooke and Thomas. In addition, the First World War was bound to have a major appeal for a man whose writing suggests that he saw life in general as a joke in rather bad taste.

Robert Graves enlisted through a long-standing belief that bullies had to be resisted, because of the widespread horror of what was reported to be happening in Belgium and, no doubt, because of the widespread social pressure on public schoolboys to do their bit. It is also likely that Graves genuinely believed the war would be over in a few months, thus enlistment would simply release an experienced soldier for service in France whilst the raw recruit did garrison duty. The belief was common, and Graves was not unique in holding it. Nor were Graves's family unique in rather liking the change that enlistment brought to their son, for much the same reason that a proposal nowadays for a return to national service brings forth subterranean grunts of right-wing approval from any audience of suitable vintage. Graves's uncle wrote some verses for *Punch* commemorating the change; 'Eric' is Robert Graves:

> My gifted nephew Eric
>   Till just before the War
> Was steeped in esoteric
>   And antimonean lore,
> Now verging on the mystic
> Now darkly symbolistic
> Now frankly futuristic
>   And modern to the core . . .
>
> In all its multiplicity
> He worshipped eccentricity,
> And found his chief felicity

In aping the insane.
And yet this freak ink-slinger,
    When England called for men
Straight ceased to be a singer
    And threw away his pen . . .

Transformed by contact hourly
    With heroes simple-souled
He looks no longer sourly
    On men of normal mould,
But, purged of mental vanity
And erudite inanity,
The clay of his humanity
    Is turning fast to gold.[21]

It was not quite as simple as that, of course, outside the pages of *Punch*.

Isaac Rosenberg's decision to enlist remains one of the great mysteries of the war. Rosenberg's letters, in the instance below dated June, 1915, tell us why he did not want to join:

> I am thinking of enlisting if they will have me, though it is against all my principles of justice – though I would be doing the most criminal thing a man can do – I am so sure my mother would not stand the shock that I don't know what to do.[22]

In fact he was unable to tell his mother face to face that he had enlisted. As a comparison, Edward Thomas did not tell his wife when he went to enlist, and the first she knew about it was when he sent her a telegram after having signed up. The simplest reason for Rosenberg's enlistment is that he despaired of finding work that suited him and he needed the money: prosaic reasons that might stand for many other people. At least Rosenberg was true to the spirit of many of his Georgian contemporaries, with a large element of despair fuelling his resolve.

Wilfred Owen and Siegfried Sassoon represent two of the greatest enigmas of the war. Both wrote bitterly effective poetry condemning the war and, by implication, those who supported it. And both won the Military Cross in actions where there could be no compunction about taking German lives. Owen and Sassoon were walking dichotomies, contradictions defying logic. They were effective and efficient officers (even, in Sassoon's case, inspirational), willing and able to kill their enemy. At the same time they were bitterly opposed to the war. It is no wonder that

Owen declared himself a 'pacifist with a seared conscience'; there were too many German dead on his hands to leave his conscience in any other state. What kept Owen and Sassoon rooted to the war is far more complex than their respective reasons for joining in the first place. Wilfred Owen sounds what is by now a familiar note in 1915:

> I have not abandoned all ideas of enlisting, but it need be discussed before I get home. My present life does not, as Father points out, lead to anywhere in particular. . . . I have not struck out in any direction yet. I have made soundings in deep waters, and I have looked out from many observation towers; and I found the deep waters terrible, and nearly lost my breath there.[23]

Again, there is a feeling of inevitability. If one was the right age and gender, and lacking the most obvious manifestations of cowardice, it was quite hard not to join up in 1914–15, particularly as few had any realistic idea of what joining up might actually involve. For Owen enlistment offered another golden opportunity, the chance to be an officer. Owen's family were sufficiently near the abyss of working-class status for this to matter. His sense of his own importance was unlikely to make it less attractive. Officer status was entrenched in the English class system. Other routes – public school, university, the clergy – had been blocked off for Owen either by his family's finance and status, or, in the case of ordination, by himself. A desire to 'better himself' is conveyed strongly in his letters, and in his brother's recollections. It is difficult not to believe that officer status held attractions for Owen that would have been alien to Brooke, Sorley, Graves or Sassoon, all brought up to claim such status as their right rather than their privilege. It is far easier to explain why Owen enlisted than it is to explain why, afterwards, he did one thing and wrote another.

The experiences of the enlisting poets proves what is already known: there was a mass movement to enlist, like a giant net trawled through the sea, catching all shapes and sizes of fish and landing them at the same destination almost indiscriminately. Surprising features are the genuine horror occasioned by what was happening in Belgium, the lack of any real hatred for Germany, and the release from anguish that the war provided for some poets. Most surprising of all is the great individuality the poets brought to this mass movement. Sassoon represented one form of individuality, the essential selfishness of vision that was at the heart of Brooke's patriotic sonnets:

Somehow I knew that it was inevitable, and my one idea was to be first in the field. In fact, I made quite an impressive inward emotional experience out of it. It did not occur to me that everyone else would be rushing off to enlist next week. My gesture was, so to speak, an individual one, and I gloried in it.[24]

Other poets had more mature and reflective reasons, and few indeed were thoughtless sheep going passively to slaughter.

If one can generalize on the basis of the war poets' experience, the reasons for joining up were more complex than has sometimes been supposed. Having read those poets, I can no longer look at photographs of placid men lined up outside the recruiting offices without seeing each face as an individual quandary, an individual reason for becoming part of a mass action. Underpinning each man was the inevitability that Sorley described: 'non-compliance with this demand would have made life intolerable'. Yet one is left with the feeling that for each poet the ultimatum was written in very different words.

Joining Up: The Remainder

The vast majority of those who joined up were not destined to become major authors, nor do anything more than either be killed or survive to live lives of nondescript anonymity. But it would be wrong to assume that they lacked intelligence. We know some of their reasons for enlisting, but all historians are hampered by the fact that, despite the continents of paper left by those who fought, the vast majority left no letters or written record of their feelings. For many (perhaps those for whom Owen appointed himself spokesman) the greatest height to which their command of words might lead them was to reassure their wives or sweethearts that they were 'in the pink'.

We are fooled by the mountain of written records left behind after this war, and magnificent histories based on those records, most notably that by Lyn Macdonald. Vivid and accurate though those histories are, it is still history based on those who had the knowledge, intellect and ability to put down what they thought and felt in writing. The old soldiers interviewed by historians and researchers are those who lived long enough, those who joined the British Legion and were thus contactable, and those who were prepared to talk about their war. The written record is therefore based on the outpourings of the literate and educated middle class, the precocious working-class author or the random workings of chance.

A Marlburian who had joined up in the ranks (yet another one!) early in the war told me how he had spent three sides of notepaper trying to describe to his family what exactly was implied when one of his fellow soldiers, on a filthy November evening in the trenches when his platoon was being lashed by rain and bitter wind, looked towards the German lines, brought out a Woodbine, and spat into the trench thoughtfully before lighting it with a 'Cheers, mate!' to the friend who had the matches. In the end he gave up, tore up the letter and never mentioned the incident to his family. For all the thousands of millions of words that have been written on the First World War, we are mainly dependent for our vision of the poor bloody infantryman on the words and thoughts of those who were articulate. My own research, which comes nowhere near matching that of others in the field, has left me with a nagging doubt that even the best anthology gives an incomplete sense of the war: the book which comes closest to speaking for the unrepresented masses is Manning's *Her Privates We*.

So what do we have to go on for the reasoning that made so many men enlist? The answer is very little, at least in comparison with the records left by subsequently famous people. A simple patriotism, almost too simple for us to comprehend, affected many. It was based on a belief that Britain and her Empire were the most civilizing and beneficial force to have appeared on earth, and that there was in effect no contest between the virtues of German *Kultur* and British common sense.

Reading these transparently honest diaries is to enter a world it is difficult now to imagine. It is a world where patriotism, dedication to a cause, devotion to duty and service to one's fellows have not become tired clichés.[25]

'I don't think we can have peace now, sir,' he said. 'If we don't beat them properly we'll have to fight them again in a few years' time.'[26]

I thought the Country worth living in, was worth fighting for.[27]

Although it may seem strange today, at that time the idea of not trying to join up was almost unthinkable. It wasn't the fear of a white feather or the fear of being sent to Coventry, it was just that this was a time when everyone wanted to be as patriotic as he or she possibly could.[28]

95

Undoubtedly there was tremendous popular pressure to join up. The women with white feathers have had a bad press from post-war historians, but most of them only found out about the reality of the Somme after the war was finished. Naivety is not a criminal offence. That being said, it is hard to forgive Harold Begbie, author of one of the most revolting poems to have been written during the war. In Begbie's poem one does not join up because one loves one's country, or because one wishes to fight for Belgium, or because one's life had stalled at the closed end of a cul-de-sac. One joins up because other people will scorn you if you do not:

> What will you lack, sonny, what will you lack
> When the girls line up the street,
> Shouting their love to the lads come back
> From the foe they rushed to beat?
> Will you send a strangled cheer to the sky
> And grin till your cheeks are red?
> But what will you lack when your mate goes by
> With a girl who cuts you dead?

The poem illustrates the negative pressure applied to those who did not enlist, the fear of being mocked and humiliated. There were undoubtedly those whom Squire 'nagged and bullied', as in Sassoon's poem 'Memorial Tablet: Great War', but one suspects that the permanent servant crisis which seems to have affected middle and upper-class households prior to 1914 meant many rich people hoped enlistment was the last thing their men would consider. For many it was not a girlfriend's scorn nor a bullying master that drove them to enlist, but rather existing friendship:

> Although we lived in what was a fairly remote part of the country the talk everywhere was of the war and all the other lads were off immediately to join up. That was the reason I went. It was as simple as wanting to be with my friends and we were all caught up with the excitement and adventure of it.[29]

Perhaps the greatest tragedy of the First World War is that most men joined up for the same reason that most of us get caught up in major historical events: no one gives us much choice. A massive tide swept men along and deposited them at the recruiting stations. That tide had been building for years, in the shape of a war that most people believed would come, and this expectation goes some way to explaining the sense of relief felt by many when war became a certainty.

Notes

1 Panichas, p. 69
2 Fussell, *The Great War and Modern Memory*, p. 8
3 Carrington, quoted in Panichas, p. 157
4 Brooke, *Letters*, pp. 632–3
5 *ibid.*, p. 633
6 Sorley, *Letters*, pp. 220–1
7 *ibid.*, p. 221
8 pp. 231–2
9 p. 241
10 p. 262
11 pp. 262–3
12 Mosley, *Grenfell*, p. 239
13 *ibid.*, p. 243
14 p. 113
15 pp. 139–40
16 p. 149
17 p. 166
18 p. 217
19 Marsh, *Thomas*, p. 143
20 *ibid.*, p. 153
21 Graves, *Assault Heroic*, pp. 110–11
22 Rosenberg, *Collected Works*, p. 216
23 Owen, *Letters*, pp. 319–20
24 Fussell, *Sassoon's Long Journey*, p. 37
25 Moynihan, p. 43
26 *ibid.*, p. 52
27 Liddle, *A Soldier's War*, p. 16
28 Edwin Bigwood, quoted Quinn, p. 75
29 Andy Andrews, quoted *ibid.*, p. 113

CHAPTER FOUR

In the Pink

What was it like to serve on the Western Front as a junior officer or private? The Myth of the War has no doubts: it was hell. Contemporary records provide a very wide range of views. One very pithy vision of what it was like was coined by a serving officer whose correspondent complained of conditions at home:

> Console yourself with the reflection that it may be bloody in Britain but it's positively *fucking* in France.[1]

A contrasting view comes from Captain Henry Ogle, whose chronicler commented on his

> complete lack of bitterness at the loss of four years of his life and the death or maiming of so many of his friends and comrades.[2]

The myth has a simpler outlook. Chronologically, it states that hundreds of thousands of young men joined up in the spirit of naive innocence, believing that the war would be over by Christmas and with only the vaguest idea of what they were fighting for. If questioned they would say that England was the best country in the world and therefore what it did was right; if what it did was fight Germany, then every right-thinking Englishman had no option but to support it. The volunteer armies trained in blue uniforms with wooden rifles until they were hurled into the needless slaughter of the Somme, thereby turning hope into despair, idealism into disillusion. There was then much gritting of teeth and stiffening of upper lips, and amid a welter of cynicism, depression and conscription, the war was fought to a finish. In the course of this the generals proved themselves idiots, lions led by donkeys. Finally came mutual exhaustion, universal bitterness, and tired, weary men coming home to a land fit for profiteers and a vindictive peace.

Minor myths run alongside the major concept. The soldiers sympathized with their opposite numbers in the German trenches, and felt bonded to them by a universal horror of experience. The men hated the top brass, who were seen as malevolent and murderous incompetents. All women at home handed out white feathers to any man not in uniform, and parents cheerfully sent their sons out to die.

The war poets have played a major part in the establishment of these myths. Owen was not the only poet who stated that his task was to speak for those who could not speak for themselves. Yet a surprising number could and did speak for themselves.

> The First World War 'cut deep', as one historian has said, 'into the consciousness of modern man'; and the traumas it induced are both recorded and perpetuated by imaginative literature. That literature, however, has often been presented too selectively and too simplistically as expressing first of all a naive enthusiasm for war and then, after the shock of battle experience, an overwhelming sense of disillusion, anger and pity, culminating in pacifism and protest. . . . The clear diagrams drawn by some of the poets themselves and elaborated by a multitude of critics have tended to blind even more sophisticated readers to the fact that much of the finest literature of the war transcends the simplicities of protest to acknowledge a far greater complexity of response to disturbingly complex experience.[3]

Quite. The myth of the war is sometimes close to accuracy when it describes the reasons for men enlisting, although it tends to over-simplify and to patronize those who joined up knowing what they were risking. As for the experience of these men when they entered combat, disillusion certainly plays a part. There is no shortage of comments such as

> nothing now but distracted thoughts, prowling round the cage. . . . Filthy from lying on the dirty yard, overrun with lice, grimy through want of soap, unshaven and, I feel now, one of God's lowest of creatures. May God bring Peace to the world soon.[4]

The loss of most of one's friends over the course of a day, week or month, especially when those friends were part of a unit suffused with camaraderie and professionalism, was enough to bring a man near to despair. It is doubtful that despair of 1914–18 vintage was different in any significant way from the despair felt by any fighting soldier throughout history. But to my surprise, despair and disillusion are not the dominant features to emerge from an unbiased reading of contemporary records.

One feature emerging almost relentlessly from those records is the sense of excitement felt by many young men on joining up and throughout the war. There are two forms of this excitement. The minority one affected only a very small number of people, but people by and about whom a disproportionate amount has been written, part of what one might call the 'Brideshead' syndrome. Evelyn Waugh wrote *Brideshead Revisited* about the Second World War, but it is in many respects a marvellous evocation of the First World War. The novel's hero, Sebastian, seems to have everything: a glittering school career, an equally glittering and charismatic sojourn at Oxford, and all the charm and good looks necessary to sustain an idyllic life. Yet he also has an emotional cancer gnawing away at his stability, a cancer based on an emotional void. The glittering past leads to a diseased alcoholic dying unnoticed in an obscure country.

Sebastian's decline has been taken as a symbol of the decline of England after the First World War, but it reflects a pattern well in evidence long before war was declared, a pattern whereby Edwardian society offered everything it had to its young at school and university, and thereafter offered them less and less. The prime symbol of this is the 'Souls', a group of witty, elegant and upper-class men and women who lived in each other's pockets, and not infrequently each other's beds, at the turn of the century.

> The 'Souls' – men and women for the most part in their twenties and early thirties but the men already prominent in public life and the women renowned for intelligence as well as beauty. These friends had been nick-named by Lord Charles Beresford at a dinner party in 1888 – 'You all sit and talk about each other's souls, I shall call you the "Souls"' – a moderate joke . . . and one which was in any case misleading; because it suggested seriousness and intensity whereas what the Souls wanted to be above everything else was witty. [Julian Grenfell's parents] were original members of the Souls; others were . . . Arthur Balfour, George Curzon, George Wyndham, Evan Charteris, Margot Tennant, Hugo and Mary Elcho, Tommy and Charty Ribblesdale.[5]

Personal venom crept up on the group, personal animosities replaced personal warmth, and an air of seediness began to pervade what once had been so youthful and full of promise. Well before 1914 many of those society stars had degenerated into death, disease, bourgeoisie or plain boredom. The promise, wit and effervescence soon staled into flat beer under the pressure of life in the House of Commons, the Foreign Office or as an ambassador. Quite simply, the Souls became old, and their witty flippancy a debased coinage in a world that was having to realize that some things were serious. The link between *Brideshead Revisited* and the Souls might seem tenuous, but it is simple. The young and not-so-young of the Edwardian period had promised much, but in the normal run of everyday events found it far harder to deliver. They were, like Rupert Brooke, shooting stars who were starting to believe that they had reached their apogee, and all that remained for them was a plunge into disintegration and nothingness. The war was a reprieve, an event so vast and powerful that it could overcome even the most strenuous ennui.

The other form of excitement was less intellectual and, if anything, even more powerful. For the vast majority the release offered by the war was simple; war was exciting. They were young, with their naivety matched only by their energy and animal good spirits. Many of the new officers had spent their adolescence cooped up in all-male boarding institutions where one's friends were the ten or twelve people who joined the boarding house in one's own year. Female companionship was matron or one's dame, the housemaster's wife or the occasional turn of an eye from a 'skivvy' or school kitchen assistant. Sex was restricted to homosexuality, with 'tarts' or young boys the objects of lust. There might be an occasional opportunity to get drunk, but very rarely in post-Arnoldian days, and the nearest many public schoolboys came to drunkenness was the cider served with the house feast at Christmas. Excitement was winning Cock House at footer.

This was replaced by life as a young officer. The soldiers gazing bleary-eyed at him in the morning were quite likely to have spent the previous evening doing what would have resulted in immediate expulsion for a public schoolboy. He himself had money in his pocket, was in uniform, and was part of the greatest war the world had ever seen. He was a hero, fêted as such (something not restricted to the officers) and the centre of attention. He had taken up one of the greatest challenges ever offered to any generation, and if he did not believe this then he had read nothing in the popular press for years. He was no longer expected to refrain from women and strong liquor, but merely to take them in his stride and

not let them affect his job. Mummy, Nanny and Daddy were across the Channel, a world away. To go with the revelatory freedom he now enjoyed were all the joys of comradeship, and a feeling that life would never be lived again at such full stretch.

These young men were experiencing life at a force and strength of great magnitude. Their love of life was matched by their fear of death. The suffering, horror and pathos were part of the almost drug-like jolt this experience gave them, what nowadays we would call a 'high', or a plateau of experience that normal, everyday life simply could not match. A private commented about his time on active service, 'I have never before or since been so acutely aware of life.'[6]

Many of those who have talked to veterans of both World Wars have commented on the passionate yet almost dreamy manner of their reminiscences. For many of the old men I talked to between 1970 and 1980 nothing had come to match the intensity of what they had gone through in 1914–18. Everything after that was an anticlimax, and the older they became the more it was those memories that surfaced as the most important in their lives. I have long been amazed at the affectionate manner in which ex-public schoolboys recollect their time at school, when to an impartial observer it seems as if they must have been subjected to every humiliation known to man. The reason, I suspect, is not because they enjoyed being humiliated, but simply the intensity which boarding school life gave to the experience of living. It is there in the impassioned memories pupils have of such schools as Eton, and its avoidance was what sent Charles Sorley away from Marlborough before his time. If school could give such intensity, then war, when life itself was at stake, gave even more. Robert Graves explained, 'The trenches made us feel larger than life.'[7]

An officer who had fought through the Somme commented:

War was, of course, horrible, yet I could not help liking it because it was a great challenge. . . . War was hateful, but, if it had to be, the best place for a young unmarried man was in the front line.[8]

One ex-combatant wrote, 'Human beings draw their pride from their worst sufferings.'[9] Long after the Somme offensive another officer commented,

I remember that spring of 1917 as a time of warmhearted comradeship both with the men of my platoon and the other company officers, and although I naturally missed my books and the amenities of civilized life, I was a good deal happier than in the comfort of my 'nice' prewar bourgeois suburban home.[10]

A private says the same thing in different words: 'Nevertheless, like yourself, I would not have missed it – Hooray! Hooray!'[11] The sense of release, adventure and excitement was as strong, if not more so, for these ordinary infantrymen. Many had led lives of unrelieved drudgery and were children in all but name when they joined up. 'I was only seventeen remember and you think you can do anything and everything when you are seventeen.'[12] This was a young man's war, and those who fought it had the resilience as well as the energy of youth:

> I enjoyed the training, the comradeship – in fact, I enjoyed pretty much everything about army life. . . . I remember we covered some 150 miles on foot on that occasion. . . . Of course when you are young, as we were, this sort of thing is an adventure so we didn't mind.[13]

It would be simple enough to dismiss these comments if they dated from the first flush of excitement at joining up. The disturbing fact is that they are repeated throughout the war. War did not cease to be exciting after the Somme offensive, nor did it lose many of its other features. Posterity has tended to focus on the horrors of going 'over the top', but the horror formed only a part of the war experience:

> It wasn't all horror and gloom. It was more short bursts of tremendous activity when dozens would be killed and injured followed by long, sometimes boring bouts of inactivity.[14]

> The war produced odd bits of humour . . . because when we were in trenches our time was spent mostly being bored. Only now and then when there was a battle or shelling would we be terrified for what, I suppose, were really relatively short periods – short compared to the long periods of inactivity anyway.[15]

The horrors of the war were never understated by survivors, but nor were the joys of recuperation:

> If no man now . . . can guess the meaning of twenty-four hours' bombardment, nor has he any notion of the joy of ninety-six hours' rest.[16]

In one sense trench life enhanced awareness and appreciation of normality, and made even mundane things appear good,

> I think only those who have been in front line trenches can realise how delightful ordinary things are. What a blessed thing sleep is: the relief of not being shelled. And how nice it is to have clean hands and wrists. Periodic tours in trenches are necessary to keep one's appreciation of these things keen.[17]

Others describe a time in their lives which nothing afterwards could equal,

> The war years will stand out in the memory of vast numbers who fought as the happiest period in their lives.[18]

> I disliked war in principle but the war years were the best of my life. No sport can equal the excitement of war; no other occupation can be half as interesting.[19]

Such comments are an alternative truth to the vision of the war given by the trench poets; neither vision has a monopoly of truth, if only because time tends to make as many survivors see the war through rose-tinted spectacles as see it in shades of red. It is not surprising that the war seemed a good time for some of those thrown out of work in the 1920s, and with their families decimated by influenza.

There was excitement off the battlefield as well as on it. The new sexual freedom brought by the war was enjoyed to the full by many combatants,

> there was a pervasive feeling of sex in the air which quickened the senses. . . . In the yard of the restaurant the men queued up to have the waitresses, who charged nothing.[20]

In the area of sexuality the great poets of the war were not spokesmen for the majority. Sassoon and Owen were homosexual, the former at least revolted by crude heterosexual physicality. Graves may or may not have let his intense emotional attachments be consummated physically, but he was a prude and offended by sensuality. Rosenberg was in sexual terms totally without charisma, Edmund Blunden little more than a delicate boy when he joined up, and Sorley apparently far more interested in food. We have gained so much of our vision of war from the pens of these men that it is hardly surprising that the sexual history of the First

World War has yet to be written, and that what has been written has concentrated on the homosexual viewpoint of many of the major authors. The scenes of physical excess visible on Armistice night in 1918 were not something new, but an unsentimental celebration of a freedom that had been claimed rather than won since 1914. After the war there was an attempt to bring things back to normal:

> I wonder what happened to girls like Irene after the War. They disappeared as completely as the men who were killed. They were a soldier's true companions. The excitement, the adventure, the risk of living involved them also. There existed a ready-made sympathy between the two.[21]

More than sympathy existed between the two: the illegitimacy rate increased some thirty per cent between 1914 and 1918. The increasing availability of effective methods of contraception undoubtedly made sexual liaisons more likely, and the illegitimacy rate probably shows only a portion of the increased sexual activity. Above all there was the atmosphere of the time:

> Life was less than cheap; it was thrown away. The religious teaching that the body was the temple of the Holy Ghost could mean little or nothing to those who saw it mutilated and destroyed in millions by Christian nations engaged in war. All moral standards were held for a short moment and irretrievably lost. Little wonder that the old ideals of chastity and self-control in sex were, for many, also lost. . . . How and why refuse appeals, backed up by the hot beating of your heart, or what at the moment you thought to be your heart, which were put with passion and even pathos by a hero here today and gone tomorrow. . . . If these young men, alive today and dead tomorrow, if these young women who, as they read the casualty lists, felt fear in their hearts, did not seize experience at once, they knew that for many of them it would elude them for ever. Sex became both precious and unimportant: precious as a desired personal experience; unimportant because it had no implications – except to mothers of 'war' babies.[22]

Temptation was far from being restricted to officers. A private remembered:

> The thing that amazed me about that first march in France was the fact that all along the road young Frenchmen shouted at us,

'You gig-a-gig my sister for tin of bully!' I think they were rather hungry, poor devils. And there were prostitutes everywhere. It was a job to keep them out of the tents.[23]

Sexual opportunity runs like a thread through many recollections from the war:

A very kind old lady was dispensing coffee and rum from a jug and two very much younger girls were dispensing pills which they assured us would give extra power to our amorous exploits. Colonel Hayley Bell, father of Mary and grandfather of actress, Hayley Mills, took the opportunity to swallow two![24]

It was another world after my quiet life near Bristol. I suppose I was really rather innocent, having always lived at home. I remember on one occasion while we waited at Rouen a rather more worldly lad who was part of our little group suggested we have a night on the town. Four of us went, I remember, and what an eye-opener that was. I will never forget it. We went to what I quickly realised was a brothel, but we had no money and I suppose we just went to gawp at the girls wearing only a slip of lace. I just couldn't believe it, but I think all four of us were really rather terrified. We had a look round and left pretty quickly. We went on to what I think was called The Red Lamp. Another establishment with no concern to conceal its true function. Here I remember we pushed the door open only to be confronted by six naked girls who rushed up to us. We were so terrified we ran away![25]

Many soldiers quickly became used to these new experiences. It is also wise to treat recollections of sexual activity with more than a pinch of salt. The majority of the material available on this topic from contemporary sources falls into three categories: a rather wistful wasn't-it-fun-and-where-has-all-the-casual-sex-gone tone from middle-class authors, a revulsion against the coarseness and perceived bestiality of the men (again from middle-class writers), and a rather coy, 'Madamoiselle from Armentières' tone from soldiers themselves. One suspects that for many men, middle and working class, the sexual freedom led to nothing more than a rather seedy reckoning in a filthy room, the awful and mechanical coupling for money with a diseased partner that Nicholas Monsarrat shows the young sub-lieutenant going through in *The Cruel Sea*.

There were undoubtedly girls who slept with men out of compassion, or because when life was cheap experience had to be taken without time to season it. Perhaps scenes from 'Hello, Dolly!' were enacted in the brothels of the Western Front, and perhaps some were peopled with whores with hearts of gold. There was undoubtedly also rape, exploitation and girls driven to prostitution not through choice but through abject poverty and despair. There was also a huge increase in venereal disease, an illness which no one has yet made coy, wistful or romantic. The war made life, and sex, cheaper. What was bought and lost at the price was frequently not pretty. That lack of prettiness was reflected in the soldiers' marching songs, which so offended Wilfred Owen when he first heard them and led to his initial dismissal of the men as a form of animal:

> Tiddleywinks, old man,
> Find a woman if you can,
> If you can't find a woman,
> Do without, old man.
> When the Rock of Gibraltar
> Takes a flying leap at Malta,
> You'll never get your ballocks in a corn-beef can.

or,

> Do your balls hang low?
> Do they dangle to and fro?
> Can you tie them in a knot?
> Can you tie them in a bow?
>
> Do they rattle when you walk?
> Do they jingle when you talk?
>
> Do they itch when it's hot?
> Do you rest them in a pot?
>
> Can you sling them on your shoulder
> Like a lousy fucking soldier?
> DO YOUR BALLS HANG LOW?

The songs do not, of course, tell the whole story. They are probably best seen as the soldiers' grabbing at life, tearing their 'Pleasures with rough strife,/Through the Iron gates of Life'. As if to compensate for the brutality of some songs, others are wholly sentimental, a contrast which often bemused observers. Some are just very funny, giving a pithy and poignant view of the soldier's vision of just how much the war was worth,

> I don't want to be a soldier,
> I don't want to go to war.
> I'd rather stay at home,
> Around the streets to roam,
> And live on the earnings of a well-paid whore.
> I don't want a bayonet up my arse-hole,
> I don't want my ballocks shot away.
> I'd rather stay in England,
> In merry, merry England,
> And fuck my bloody life away.

Such was not a career option that featured in the curriculum of too many public schools, and in this song sex is neither romance nor rape, but merely a comfort. Alcohol was another great comfort, and sex shared with alcohol many of its features. It was exciting to think about, frequently anti-climactic when acquired and often unpleasant in its aftermath. Sex was simply one of the narcotics that some needed to survive the experience of war.

If one reads only Sassoon and Owen one might be forgiven for thinking that soldiers dreaded women, and that leave consisted of showing pictures of mutilated corpses to civilians to bring home to them the horror of war, or sitting in revolting music halls listening to putrid songs about tanks. In fact for many soldiers there was a lot to compensate for the horrors of the trenches, most notably the power and freedom that being a 'hero' brought:

> I felt quite the little hero in my war-stained uniform and cap with the shell-splinter hole through it.[26]

In June, 1917, the same soldier wrote from the front, 'It's a good life!'[27]

It was a good life for a mixture of reasons, some of which gave a frightening insight into the life of the average working-class man before 1914. No one can pretend that the bitter cold and wet of the trenches, expressed vividly in Owen's poem 'Exposure', continual fear of death from shell or bullet and the gut-wrenching fear of an attack were fun. Equally, it is horrific to realize how good conditions in the army were for many who joined up. In Leeds in 1904 fifty per cent of working-class children had rickets, and twenty per cent of babies in Cornwall died before their first birthday in 1914. Forty-one per cent of males were given the bottom health qualification in 1916 (C3), and only one-third were found to be fully fit. These figures go some way to expressing the unspeakable privations that were the lot of many working-class families in town and country.

An old lady in the Norfolk hamlet of Pockthorpe in the 1970s proudly kept a letter from the King commiserating with her mother on the death of her four sons in the army. At the same time one of her most vivid memories was of the happiness of those brothers in the army when faced with three meals a day, a rum ration and the money to buy cigarettes. Rural poverty was neither picturesque nor pleasant. Neither were conditions in the trenches, but the horror of the middle-class officer on facing them was sometimes not matched by his men, used to pre-war conditions that by middle-class standards were already hellish. Those from better backgrounds soon noticed the physical quality of the recruits, thereby helping to start a revolution in social awareness.

> Many men who went to France came from such poverty-stricken backgrounds that they were underdeveloped and undernourished even before the test of war began.[28]

A world of suffering is called up by a young private for whom a full stomach – almost regardless of what it was filled with – was a rare luxury:

> As it was all a bit of fun I was really rather enjoying myself and I was never hungry – there were army biscuits all over the place that you could eat at any time, even though they were a bit like dog biscuits.[29]

What united officers and men, and seems now to have been the single most important factor in making life in the trenches more than a waking hell, was comradeship. Denis Winter comments,

> Shared experience and shared awareness recall a time when a man's life was at its prime and when men experienced closer friendship for the duration than they were ever likely to enjoy in civilian life after the war.[30]

A survivor wrote:

> Some people say that you came to accept death, but I don't think any of us really did. It affects you terribly when a man dies, but we had some happy times because there was such a sense

of comradeship, which is something it is impossible to understand unless you have been part of it. We would all have done anything and everything to help another man.[31]

This comradeship was subjected to a strange alchemy at the hands of Wilfred Owen, transmuting it into the pity that has become the most famous and favoured response to the experience of that war. It was turned down a different channel by Sassoon, emerging as the burning hatred found in his satirical poems. In both cases the comradeship drew men inherently opposed to the war back to it as fighting soldiers, believing that by doing so they were ensuring their own deaths. Owen has been widely quoted when writing about his need to lead his men and tell the truth on their behalf:

> I came out in order to help these boys – directly by leading them as well as an officer can; indirectly, by watching their sufferings that I may speak of them as well as a pleader can.[32]

Stirring though these words are, they are the words of a poet. They are also very much the words of a young officer who had been accused in the past of cowardice, been hospitalized for neurasthenia, and just proved to himself and his regiment that he was not only as brave as the next man, but braver than most. One has to look elsewhere for archetypal expressions of comradeship and what it meant on the Western Front to the ordinary man:

> Of my memories of life in the trenches, the one thing I cherish more than anything else is the comradeship that grew up between us as a result of the way of life we were compelled to lead – living together under the open sky, night after day, fair weather and foul, witnessing death or injury, helping in matters of urgency, and above all, facing the enemy.[33]

Another young officer wrote a considerable while after the Somme:

> The battalion is moving as one man; very strong, very steady, with a sway in the shoulders and a lilt in the feet. We have regained our youth; we have recovered the innocence with which we came to France, an innocence not now of ignorance but of knowledge. We have forgotten whither we are marching; we do not greatly care what billets we find tonight. We are content to live in the moment.[34]

A clumsy but telling evocation of comradeship is found in a letter from John Mudd, a Cockney, to his wife:

> Out here dear we're all pals, what one hasn't got the other has, we try to share each others troubles, get each other out of danger. You wouldn't believe the Humanity between men out here. Poor little Shorty . . . I often think of him yet poor fellow I don't think he even has a grave but lies somewhere in the open. Still dear I don't want to make you sad but it just shows how we seem to stick together in trouble. It's a lovely thing is friendship out here.[35]

The comradeship was so strong that it drove men on leave back to the front before their time was up: 'I am sick of it [Paris] and want to get away back to the Front.'[36] That restless feeling of guilt, the desire to be back with one's friends and men, is found throughout the literature of the war, from the most famous and literary to the most obscure and illiterate. The better known and the obscure poetry of the war is littered with accounts of the pangs of guilt felt by soldiers home on leave, feeling that in some way they have betrayed their friends left in the line. In 'Sick Leave' Sassoon writes,

> Out of the gloom they gather round my bed.
>   They whisper to my heart; their thoughts are mine.
>   'Why are you here with all your watches ended?
>   From Ypres to Frise we sought you in the line.'

A less famous poet, E.A. Mackintosh, wrote in similar manner,

> So here I sit in a pleasant room
> By a comfortable fire,
> With every thing that a man could want,
> But not the heart's desire.
> So I sit thinking and dreaming still,
> A dream that won't come true,
> Of you in the German trench, my friends,
> And I not there with you.

The bond of comradeship that did not fade as the years went by is often recorded in more matter-of-fact tones:

> I also had to pay one pound for the privilege of joining the London Scottish Regiment. At the time I thought this rather

odd, but looking back over the years I realise that in view of the bond of comradeship created during the War, and which has continued ever since, that it was indeed a privilege to have belonged to such a regiment.[37]

The same writer refused a commission, something not at all uncommon when the offer might mean losing the comradeship that made war bearable:

> This decision I never regretted since it enabled me to remain with my comrades with whom I had served for so long, until the end of the war.[38]

The middle and upper-class officers joining the new army were often shocked by the coarseness and foul language of their men. It rarely took them long to perceive that more sterling virtues lay underneath the unpromising exterior. One public-school educated officer watched his platoon doing gym. At school the pathetic boy who failed to vault the horse would be mocked and derided, teased into eternity for his failure. In the army, all the men joined in cheering him on and supporting him, his eventual victory over the horse being treated as a victory for the whole platoon and a cause for celebration. Another young officer commented:

> I was overwhelmed by the simplicity of all these men, with the comely innocence which in spite of the obscenity and profanity breaking from harsh throats, was borne above them like a banner.[39]

Praise for the men from their officers was genuine and unpatronizing:

> They were unselfish and generous, as quick to go to the aid of a wounded enemy as a wounded friend. They had one supreme quality – a capacity to endure without flinching.[40]

> I shall never think of the lower classes again in quite the same way after the war.[41]

British officers were quick to change their attitude to their men; the warmth was surprisingly mutual. Frederick Manning's upper-middle-class private speaks at length about comradeship and friendship in the trenches. Bourne is being asked by the padre about his life with 'the men'. The padre supposes that one such as

Bourne cannot have a friend among them, because of the class difference:

> 'No,' he said finally, 'I don't suppose I have anyone, whom I can call a friend. I like the men, on the whole, and I think they like me. They're a very decent generous lot, and they have helped me a great deal. I have one or two particular chums, of course; and in some ways, you know, good comradeship takes the place of friendship. It is different: it has its own loyalties and affections; and I am not so sure that it does not rise on occasion to an intensity of feeling which friendship never touches.'[42]

The contrast here is between the padre's middle-class concept of friendship and Bourne's acquired feeling of comradeship. His evident confusion arises because there is little or no common ground between himself and the padre, and he stumbles to explain precisely what it is among the easy relationships of 'the men' that makes it so different and special.

A majority of those who fought in the war believed they were fighting for something worthwhile, but more than that they believed in their friends and comrades, and in the final analysis perhaps fought more for them than for their country:

> if there is any one message to be gleaned from this book it is the unquenchable spirit and will displayed by the Poor Bloody Infantrymen in the unspeakable horror which surrounded the war in the Western Front. The loyalties to cap badge and comrades were strengthened rather than weakened as danger increased, and such were the bonds formed, that over sixty years later, with another world war and so many other momentous events which have passed in between, they have not loosened.[43]

Such loyalty was also a potential weakness. What if the unit to which a soldier had given his heart and soul was wiped out? One officer came near to describing that feeling, writing after a few brief days of action had killed most of his friends and the men he commanded:

> It seemed the ruin and decay of the life in which I had revelled and with my face against the wet mud I lay choking and gurgling, and longed for the hateful sun to go and take away the memories of similar bright days now lost for ever.[44]

Yet, as one survivor commented, 'The legend of disenchantment is false.'[45] If it is so it is partly because of the tremendous resilience of the human animal, its almost incredible capacity to recover from adversity and hardship. After a major action in 1916, when only two officers and forty men out of the 130 who went into battle are unharmed, their sergeant writes:

> They are queer chaps: you will imagine our camp plunged in gloom. Not a bit of it! After a good sleep and a good meal the men at once recovered their spirits, and are peacocking about in German helmets taken with their own hands, and proudly showing their souvenirs, and the rents in their clothing, and recounting how they bayonetted Huns, or how they had narrow escapes.[46]

There is ample evidence that the fighting soldiers continued to believe in the ideals for which they fought, partly through the power of comradeship and partly because only if those ideals were valid could their sufferings be justified.[47] In Manning's *Her Privates We* a man whose company has just fought a savage battle with terrible losses comments:

> 'They can say what they bloody well like,' he said appreciatively, 'but we're a fuckin' fine mob.'[48]

Support for the war continued right through to the end:

> Lieutenant Drummond told us to crouch on the fire-step – the raised platform at the front of the trench – with our backs to the trench wall, drawing up our knees to our chins and covering our face with our arms. 'Now,' he said, 'you have covered your vital parts and there is nothing else to be done but to stick it out until Jerry stops shelling, and,' he said, 'if any of you do stop one, well, what better way to die than in the front line for your King and Country.' That was a spirit which appealed very strongly to the men of eighteen in those critical days in the spring of 1918. We were fortunate in having such good officers.[49]

One historian whose work is based on contemporary material was stung to comment:

> it remains something of a mystery as to why a strange mixture of patronising disdain and sheer ignorance . . . should have been successful in obscuring that which was readily verifiable.[50]

The 'mystery' was the support for the war from serving soldiers, support which continued long after the Somme. The same historian compares the sentiments expressed in Sassoon's poem 'Does It Matter?' with those expressed by eight survivors from across the social spectrum. All eight were maimed by the war. None showed any deep-rooted resentment, none had any concept of being rejected by society.[51] There is a remarkable lack of rancour in many memoirs, diaries and letters: 'The loss of my leg never really interfered with the rest of my life.'[52] Another commentator writes of a mangled regiment, 'and from the village came curious throngs of men with a steely light shining in their eyes.'[53] Shattered comradeship was a terrible ordeal, but comradeship could be and was rebuilt.

One of the myths that has grown up about the war says British and German soldiers saw each other as allies in suffering, reserving their hatred for those at home and the top generals. The average soldier undoubtedly felt venomous towards some at home, most notably journalists and those seen as making a profit out of the war, and it is true that in the early stages there was fraternization among the troops, particularly at Christmas, but also where a quiet sector had trenches close to each other:

> At about lunchtime, however, a message came down the line to say that Germans had sent across to say that their General was coming along in the afternoon, so we had better keep down, as they might have to do a little shooting to make things look right!!!![54]

There is little evidence that the British soldier or officer had any great affection for his German opposite number; respect, perhaps, for a professional job well done when it applied, but no great love or even fellow feeling. It was difficult to feel affection for an enemy when one's best friend was coughing up his lungs after a gas attack, or his brains had been spattered over one's own face. George Coppard, a machine gunner, summed up the spirit of Christmas for the majority of British troops, writing about an attack in which his machine gun had killed twenty German soldiers,

> Many years later, an American Jew named Ben Hecht said he had 'a happy holiday in his heart' every time a British soldier was killed in Palestine. That about sums up what we felt like towards Jerry on that Christmas night many years ago.[55]

Speaking for my companions and myself, I can categorically state that we were in no mood for any joviality with Jerry. In fact, after what he had been through at Loos, we hated his bloody guts. We were bent on his destruction at each and every opportunity for all the miseries and privations which were our lot. Our greatest wish was to be granted an enemy target worthy of our Vickers gun.[56]

A similar sentiment was offered by an officer:

We all knew that the Germans were anxious to kill as many of us as possible; that every individual was animated by the same idea; that Germany had her tail up; and we all to a man felt we should ourselves kill as many Germans as we could in return.[57]

One gunner showed his delight at the enemy getting 'plastered':

All those not engaged in working the guns mounted the slope in front to get a good view of Vimy Ridge in the distance being inundated by a storm of shells from twelve-inch to eighteen-pounders. This was much more to our liking.[58]

At times simple personal hatred took over. A private who had recently lost his brother wrote:

I settle my rifle in an easy position and start to shoot them down. This was the only time in the war that was mine and mine alone.[59]

Yet the irony of war is such that shortly after combat British troops could be seen giving cigarettes to captured German soldiers; once battle itself was over hatred could dissipate in a wash of simple humanity. It could also lead to prisoners being shot more or less out of hand on their way to a holding position.

One part of the myth of the war which is quite hard to disentangle is the amount of time spent under fire by the officers and men. The television series *Blackadder* is a brilliant summary of many of the myths of the war, and the impression it gives of the officer condemned to life in his dug-out until killed in an attack is one probably shared by many people. Some officers spent more time in the trenches than others, inevitable when there were 'good' and 'bad' regiments, and when the exigencies of active service meant that planned reliefs could not come up.

The phrase 'time in the trenches' is also suspect. Some trench lines saw as much action as Hyde Park on a Sunday morning, others were under a continual deluge of shells more or less from the first months of the lines being established. Prior to its holocaust in 1916 the Somme was a peaceful and neglected area of the front. However, there is no reason to believe that Charles Carrington's experience as a junior officer in 1916 was unusual. Culled from his war diary he worked out that he spent 101 days 'under fire' in 1916 – sixty-five days in front-line trenches and thirty-six days in support. Beyond that 120 days were spent in reserve; seventy-three days in rest; twenty-one days in schools of instruction; ten days in hospital with German measles (!); seventeen days on leave; nine days at base camp; and fourteen days travelling.[60] Spending a third of the year in the front line at the Western Front was no joke by anyone's standards, but it is far less of a load than might be assumed from many books and films about the war.

The infantryman's life was more difficult, though exact figures are almost impossible to come by. Despite the vast and often cruel demands made on soldiers of the time, it is sometimes overlooked that it did not make military sense to expose soldiers to continuous danger, because when that happened, in Owen's words,

> Courage leaked, as sand
> From the best sandbags after years of rain.

One of the most reliable estimates of time spent in the trenches comes from Denis Winter:

> Individuals served in this trench system relatively rarely. Of the 20,000 in a division, only 2,000 were in the front line at any moment. . . . Few men fought for long periods. Noakes reckoned a typical month as four days in the front line, four in support, eight in reserve and the remainder in rest.[61]

Taking over a trench system was often more a matter of the filth left behind by one's predecessors than immediate threat from the enemy. A.P. Herbert served with the Royal Naval Division, which took over a section of trenches from Portuguese units, notorious for their lack of hygiene. The Portuguese had left solid evidence of their presence behind, and the trenches were inspected by Major-General C.D. Shute, who complained about the filth. Lyn Macdonald, in *Somme*, records one of the forgotten classics of the war, a poem written by Herbert to mark the occasion.

The General inspecting the trenches
Exclaimed with a horrified shout,
'I refuse to command a Division
Which leaves its excreta about.'

But nobody took any notice
No one was prepared to refute,
That the presence of shit was congenial
Compared with the presence of Shute.

And certain responsible critics
Made haste to reply to his words
Observing that his Staff advisers
Consisted entirely of turds.

For shit may be shot at odd corners
And paper supplied there to suit,
But a shit would be shot without mourners
If somebody shot that shit Shute.

This poem demonstrates something else which made life bearable
for the front-line soldier: humour.

The tactics adopted during the war have come in for a great deal
of criticism, much of it from literary specialists who have accepted
as gospel a vision of the war not authenticated by military historians. One exception is Denis Winter, who has no hesitation in
damning the training offered to infantrymen:

> The basic training which provided the civilians with their mili-
> tary skills had an air of unreality . . . the unreality related to what
> was taught. One-third of the time for a start was given to drill
> alone – 'we sloped, ordered, presented, trailed, reversed, piled
> arms and did everything possible with them except fire them,'
> wrote Noakes. 'With rifles we marched, counter-marched,
> wheeled right and left, inclined and formed squads and about
> turned until we were streaming with sweat and weak in the
> knees with exhaustion.' It was hard to relate any of this to the
> needs of a soldier in battle, particularly since the platoon train-
> ing which was fundamental in this region entered the schedule
> only in the tenth and final week.[62]

Winter goes on to complain that the leap-frogging style of advance
(where a group of soldiers rushed for a vantage point, stopped to
regroup and scout out the terrain, and then made another rush

forward) was outdated but still taught, and that bayonet practice and the importance placed on it was a waste of time and effort.

Nothing could be further from the truth than to say that this training was irrelevant. It had a multiplicity of aims. Winter's Noakes complained about tiredness. The majority of enlisted and conscripted men were dreadfully unfit even if they were not medically ill. The purpose of such drill was to make them fit, essential for any decent soldier, and no one has invented a way of making unfit men fit without some pain. The drill had far more important aims even than that. It was an attempt to get men used to obeying orders instantly and without the questioning, thought and evaluation that is the privilege of the civilian. It was an attempt to get men used to working together as a group and, when it was done well, it was a vital element in producing the comradeship and pride which was the driving force behind the dedication which kept the British Army in the war. Its effectiveness can be judged by the effect marching had on a very unlikely recruit, a Bohemian Jew from the East End of London apparently hopelessly unsuited for military life. Isaac Rosenberg wrote,

> My eyes catch ruddy necks
> Sturdily pressed back –
> All flaming pendulums, hands
> Swing across the Khaki –
> Mustard-coloured Khaki –
> To the automatic feet
> We husband the ancient glory
> In these bared necks and hands.

It is difficult to see where Winter draws his objection to the leap-frogging style of advance. It was obviously preferable to men advancing in line together at walking pace, because its objective was to keep advancing whilst never offering a large, block target to the enemy (see Chapter 2). Its absence at Loos and the Somme was simply the result of lack of time to train raw recruits in the art of offensive tactics, a credible belief that relatively untrained men would panic if split from their fellows or officers, and an exaggerated belief in the power of the artillery shell. Winter misses the basic point of training in such tactics: it was not the actual style of advance that mattered so much, more the fact that, in leap-frogging, men had to think for themselves and take responsibilty for what they did and where they did it. The spirit behind that training was summed up in a lecture given to officers of the Third Battalion, the London Regiment (Royal Fusiliers) in mid-1915:

Up to the present we have being doing close order drill by Battalion, Company and Squad, to teach the men to act and move together on the word of command *almost without thinking*. We are now going to start Company Training.

Company Training is the work of teaching each man *individually* the real work of a soldier in the field. *To teach the man that he has now to think and act for himself.*

This does not by any means mean that a man is to be taught to act without orders. He should be taught that when given an order, say, to advance when in the firing line, he should be able to take advantage of the ground in his line of advance. Teach him what is cover and see that he understands the use and abuse of cover. Teach him to be observant of what is going on around him and to note it and to draw his own deductions from his observations.

You will all get stupid men to deal with. As far as you can keep your own temper, and in dealing with a stupid man, don't bully or rag him – take extra pains with him. On no account be *sarcastic* and don't hold *any* man up to the ridicule of his comrades. It disheartens the man and often makes him sulky to be the butt of a parade of the whole Company. Take it step by step. Do not leave any exercise until you have got the whole company to carry it out correctly and *intelligently*. The successful Company trainer is the one who brings his whole section, half-Company and Company up to a certain mark of proficiency – not the one who has twenty very sharp men and eighty dull half-trained men.[63]

Nor is it true that tactics remained cast in concrete throughout the war:

Later in the war, by the time my lot went over, we did it in single file – that way we were much less of a target.[64]

The changes that took place were far greater than a reversion to attack by column. At the start of the war the British soldier was deprived of two weapons that were to prove essential. The first was the trench mortar, a simple gun that could lob an explosive charge high up in the air and drop it down into an opposing trench, or, for that matter, an advancing enemy. These weapons did not exist at the start of the war, and the story of their invention by the renowned Mr Stokes is one of the great cameos of the war. Nor did the soldiers have effective hand grenades in 1914, another essential item for trench warfare.

Weapons, tactics and the ability of the average soldier to carry out those tactics changed dramatically over the course of the war. Commentators have ignored material proving this – sensible, intelligent and above all practical material issued by the army and clear proof that tactics and thinking did change in the light of experience – and this has alienated some war survivors from the literary and historical establishment, those who have written that the army could only blaspheme obscenities at a man and drive him unthinkingly to slaughter. You do not get an army to survive nearly five years of war when the majority of men never dreamed of active service prior to enlistment or conscription if that is your approach, as the French found out after Verdun. Of course not all training was like this; of course there was gross coarseness, humiliation and bullying in the training, but there was also much else. Some of that has not been seen by literary critics of the war, who watched lines of men in uniform and assumed they were trained soldiers, and took the views of professional poets who were amateur soldiers as their guideline and sole authority.

We return to the same point. Everything written by the famous war poets and many of the prose memoirs were true for some people at least some of the time. We have tended to assume that it was true for all the people all the time. The First World War must be the first major conflict since Troy where poets have been so active in writing history.

The major First World War poets were better poets than historians. However, as the next chapter suggests, some of the minor poets may have been better historians than they were poets.

Notes

1 Captain Fleming, quoted in Brown, *Western Front*, p. 33
2 Ogle, *Battle Line*, p. 1
3 Rutherford, *Literature of War*, p. 65
4 Brown, *First World War*, p. 260
5 Mosley, pp. 14–15
6 Frederick Hodges, quotes Quinn, p. 53
7 Graves, quoted Panichas, p. 10
8 Brenan, quoted *ibid.*, pp. 46–8
9 Jacques Meyer, quoted *ibid.*, p. 65
10 *ibid.*, p. 75
11 Coppard, *Machine Gun to Cambrai*, np (appendix)

12 Andy Andrews, quoted Quinn, p. 115
13 Clarrie Jarman, quoted *ibid.*, pp. 2–3
14 Frederick Hodges, quoted *ibid.*, p. 53
15 Edwin Bigwood, quoted *ibid.*, p. 79
16 Edmonds, p. 195
17 Edward Chapman, quoted Brown, *First World War*, p. 68
18 S. Rogerson, quoted Winter, *Death's Men*, p. 55
19 Winter, p. 224
20 Brenan, quoted Panichas, p. 42
21 Carroll Carstairs, quoted Chapman, *Vain Glory*, p. 258
22 Marwick, *Deluge*, pp. 108–9
23 Clarrie Jarman, quoted Quinn, p. 4
24 Fred Dixon, quoted *ibid.*, p. 33
25 Edwin Bigwood, quoted *ibid.*, pp. 76–7
26 Tennant, *Saturday Soldier's*, p. 28
27 *ibid.*, p. 87
28 Fred Dixon, quoted Quinn, p. 36
29 Andy Andrews, quoted *ibid.*, p. 115
30 Winter, *Death's Men*, p. 21
31 Tom Broach, quoted Quinn, p. 130
32 Stallworthy, *Owen*, p. 278
33 Coppard, pp. 172–3
34 Chapman, *Passionate Prodigality*, p. 122
35 Brown, *First World War*, p. 71
36 Moynihan, p. 35
37 Dolden, p. 11
38 *ibid.*, pp. 91–2
39 Chapman, *Passionate Prodigality*, p. 22
40 quoted Winter, *Death's Men*, p. 229
41 Carrington, quoted Winter, p. 62
42 Manning, *Her Privates We*, p. 87
43 Messenger, *Terriers*, p. 135
44 Vaughan, *Some Desperate Glory*, p. 209
45 Carrington, quoted Hynes, *War Imagined.*, p. 450
46 Robert Macfie, quoted Brown, *First World War*, p. 60
47 see Hynes, p. 119
48 Manning, p. 6 taken from *The Middle Parts of Fortune*, Buchan & Enright, 1986
49 Frederick Hodges, quoted Quinn, p. 57
50 Liddle, *Somme*, p. 7
51 *ibid.*, p. 10
52 Clarrie Jarman, quoted Quinn, p. 14
53 Private letter in possession of author
54 Macdonald, p. 52

55 Coppard, p. 61
56 *ibid.*, p. 59
57 Chapman, *Vain Glory*, p. 144
58 Tennant, p. 81
59 Moynihan, p. 100
60 Edmonds, p. 120
61 Winter, *Death's Men*, p. 81
62 *ibid.*, *Death's Men*, p. 39
63 Macdonald, pp. 56–7
64 Tom Broach, quoted Quinn, p. 125

CHAPTER FIVE

Literature, Combat and Minor Verse

It is not conventional to use poetry as source material for history, but it is interesting. Large numbers of people were writing poetry in 1914, perhaps more than ever before in our history. Poetry was a popular medium. People turned to it naturally, even if much of what was written now qualifies only as doggerel. The next chapter looks at this minor verse as literature; here I would like to look at it, and other popular and populist writing, in an historical context.

One could be forgiven for thinking that it was the post-war period which spotted the gap between the idealism of pre-war Imperialist poetry and the reality of war. Yet from the outset those fighting in the thick of it showed an instinctive tendency to parody the great works of poetry they had imbibed in school. A marvellous source of such parodies is *The Wipers Times*, a 'trench' newspaper published from the front line by Lieutenant-Colonel F.J. Roberts, MC, from February, 1916, until the end of the war. Among many others, Kipling suffers from its affectionate humour,

> If you can drink the beer the Belgians sell you,
> And pay the price they ask with ne'er a grouse,
> If you believe the tales that some will tell you,
> And live in mud with ground sheet for a house,
> If you can live on bully and a biscuit,
> And thank your stars that you've a tot of rum,
> Dodge whizzbangs with a grin, and as you risk it
> Talk glibly of the pretty way they hum.

A poem such as this brings us close to a truth of war. It is a lesser truth than that shown in the work of Owen, Sassoon and Rosenberg, because many soldiers worked and thought on a lesser level. It is not that what Owen and Sassoon wrote was in any way wrong or misguided, simply that their concern with the higher issues of pity, morality and command were not shared by many lesser mortals. A tot of rum, the price of beer, keeping a good face on things while scared – these issues come up time and again in the lesser poetry of the war.

Some of that poetry undoubtedly keeps the horror of the war at arm's length, almost as an act of survival, whilst the poetry of Owen, Sassoon and Rosenberg seeks to place its stench under our nostrils. Owen may well be doing the correct thing morally, and no one can doubt his intense artistic power, but it is wrong to assume that his view was typical, or that it represented the average fighting man's vision of the war. Sometimes the simple parody of *The Wipers Times* comes surprisingly close to telling us major truths about the war. The key is that the narrator in the parody does not see himself as special, or in any way marked out from other men. Owen, Sassoon and Rosenberg were all artists, with an enhanced self-belief and a vision of themselves as having something special to say. Owen admits as much when in 'Strange Meeting' he writes,

> For by my glee might many men have laughed,
> And of my weeping something had been left,
> Which must die now . . .

> Then, when much blood had clogged their chariot-wheels,
> I would go up and wash them from sweet wells,
> Even with truths that lie too deep for taint.

Owen has a mission. There is none of this sense of artistic purpose in *The Wipers Times*, but simply a battle for practical survival. The anonymous poet paints a simple and strangely moving picture of a fight not only against an enemy and death, but also for self-respect and dignity, a fight restricted not to high ideals but to the absolute basics of human existence on the Western Front. Thus in the way of all good parodies the poem finishes not by mocking the values of the original but rather restating them,

> If you can crawl through wire and crump holes reeking
> With feet of liquid mud, and keep your head
> Turned always to the place which you are seeking,
> Through dread of crying you will laugh instead,
> If you can fight a week in Hell's own image,
> And at the end just throw you down and grin,
> When every bone you've got starts on a scrimmage,

And for a sleep you'd sell your soul within,
If you can clamber up with pick and shovel,
And turn your filthy crump hole to a trench,
When all inside you makes you itch to grovel,
And all you've had to feed on is a stench,
If you can hang on just because you're thinking
You haven't got one chance in ten to live,
So you will see it through, no use in blinking
And you're not going to take more than you give,
If you can grin at last when handing over,
And finish well what you have well begun,
And think a muddy ditch a bed of clover,
You'll be a soldier one day, then, my son.

The Wipers Times was not the only 'local' journal produced in the war. Indeed, a large number of regimental museums contain similar offerings, produced for long or short periods, depending on casualties and the availability of editors. One of the most interesting and representative is *The Fifth Gloster Gazette*. Appearing first as a brief newsletter for the Fifth Battalion of the Gloucestershire Regiment, it soon had a circulation of over 1,500 copies, and can claim to be the first of its kind as well as one of the most successful. For much of the war it was printed in Amiens by a printer who knew no English, under the instructions of an editor who knew no French. It gives results of the battalion's endless fixtures in soccer, rugby, running and anything else inventive officers could find to compete at on a sports field or in a gym. It also lists awards, promotions and the general minutiae of battalion life, though after a few issues it was not allowed to produce casualty lists for security reasons. It still managed to print some moving tributes to some of its casualties. Much of it is gossip – one regular section is entitled 'Things we would like to know', and a typical entry is, 'Who is the NCO who said, "Extend a bit more, one of you is all in a bunch?"'[1] It also contained cartoons, sketches, news and poems.

How seriously should one take the mood and spirit of such a magazine? It was produced with the blessing of the battalion 'establishment', and started life as a means of raising the troops' morale. As such it is easy to view it as propaganda, and critics at least have tended either to ignore or deride such publications for the same reasons they have ignored the wartime editions of *Punch*. Both were seen as 'populist', a dirty word in the literary establishment after the 1930s, and fell prey to the general belief that anything funny about the war must be immediately dismissed as wrong-headed. It has been fashionable to go to left-wing magazines and journals produced at home, but to ignore the offerings of the front itself.

Perhaps this dismissive attitude to *The Wipers Times* and *The Gazette*, and others of their kind, is misguided. Firstly, they were read in large numbers, and were wildly popular with the troops. It is unlikely that this would be the case if they had not struck a chord with those who knew most closely what war was like. Secondly, they were held in far higher regard than newspapers of the time, and indeed often included straightforward satire of home-based newspapers in general and journalists in particular, who were seen as writing hopelessly inaccurate material about the war. Thirdly, there is a surprising and rewarding range of humour and comment in these magazines. They give a flavour of the war which is as true for some people as the tone of Owen's savage 'Dulce et Decorum Est' is for others.

Humour was as important as rum, cigarettes and tea for the average soldier. *The Gazette* takes a delight in mocking the idiocy of army life, whilst never losing faith with it. The fun is affectionate and only very rarely malicious. As with so much of the neglected war literature, the real criticism is aimed at those who are 'not doing their bit', which usually means not the generals, but staff officers and all those seen as having 'cushy' jobs. A mock play in *The Gazette* has the RTO (Regimental Transport Officer) interviewing 'AS', or Ancient Soldier. The humour is maniac, what might at one time have been called 'zany' or even Pythonesque. It takes a standard and familiar situation and by excess and exaggeration makes the normal abnormal.

> *RTO*: These papers are in order. You will leave by the 2.15 train, report here at 3.45.
> [*AS remains*] Is is quite clear; well, what are you waiting for?
> *AS*: I'm very sorry [*breaking down*], but I have been on the RE dump and got no rations, so I ate my iron rations.
> *Pink:* Blimy, you're for it.
> *RTO: (thunderstruck) [Goes over to table and produces red volume – Manual of Military Law]*: Ah, I feared it. Here are the very words. [*Reads.*] As iron rations are liable to deteriorate rapidly when unprotected damp, it is important that only such as are required for immediate use should be uncovered. Maximum penalty – death.
>
> [*Hands revolver to Pink, bought in Padua, 80 lire, specially made to carry without inconvenience on a Sam Brown.*] Take him away, orderly, you know your duty.

[*Exit Pink and AS. Six shots are heard in rapid succession. Pink reports each shot. No. 1 fired, sir. No. 2 fired, etc.*]

Pink (re-entering): Good Lord, sir, I've missed 'im, but I've got a rabbit [sic].²

A small poem tucked away at the end of the last issue of *The Gazette* is typical of many such to be found elsewhere, and is based on the fictional and comic 'Lieutenant Shellback, RNR', of *Punch*. 'Lieutenant Shellfire, TF' reveals an immense pride in the fact that ordinary men could be enlisted, turned into soldiers and win their war. The poem, comic with a very serious undertone, does not seek to condone the heady optimism of 1914, or hide the horrors of trench warfare. It seems to believe that the young man in question is a better man for doing what he did.

> Now he wasn't a husky born and bred,
> 'Twas a different life to the one he'd lead –
> Seven years in a nursery, ten at school,
> The rest on a soft-seated office stool;
> Nurtured in comfort, sleeping on feathers,
> Changing his clothes with the changing weathers;
> Never went hungry nor yet lacked a bed –
> That's the pre-war sort of life that he'd led.
> But on August 4th, one nine one four,
> When the roughs and the toughs were wanted for war,
> And Belgium was falling and things at their worst –
> About-town Shellfire was there with the first.
>
> They gave him khaki and boots and a gun,
> And told him that was the best of fun –
> September would see him booting the Boche!
> November would end it! – and such-like tosh.
> Pushed in a train and sent to the coast
> He soon found he knew a lot less than most.
> But strength of spirit faltered no trifle,
> Linked to a flesh that could not slope a rifle.
> It was drills, and parades, and hellish marches,
> Sore feet, galled back, and throat that parches,
> With nothing to drink – and it's dusty and hot—
> But Private Shellfire he went thro' the lot.
>
> He learnt the ways of the army at war,
> To shoot, and march, and a good deal more;

Muscled like whipcord, and browned by the tan,
He soon looked the right sort of soldier man.

Private Shellfire gains a commission when he takes an enemy post:

Yes, he's learnt the ways of the men on land,
Who live, fight and die on that foreign strand;
Body-dog weary and senses areel,
With bullet and bomb and the keen, cold steel . . .

And there isn't a sector of line in France
Where Hell plays the music of Death's own dance,
In the roofless hall where the floor is mud –
And the walls are fire and the drink is blood –
And all is red with the cups aspill –
But Lieutenant Shellfire has drunk his fill.

A similar sense of pride is shown at the end of *The Song of Tiadatha*:

So I leave him and salute him
Back in his beloved London,
Knowing that the war has one thing
(If no others) to its credit –
It has made a nut a soldier,
Made a man of Tiadatha
And made men of hundreds like him.
And the world has cause to thank us
For that band of so-called filberts,
For those products of St James's,
Light of heart and much enduring,
Straight and debonair and dauntless,
Grousing at their small discomforts,
Smiling in the face of danger,
Who have faced their great adventure,
Crossed through No Man's Land to meet it,
Lightly as they'd cross St James's,
Eyes and heart still full of laughter,
Till the world had cause to wonder,
Till the world had cause to thank us
For the likes of Tiadatha.

The feeling of a job well done was very common at the end of the war, but does not find its way into either the work of the major war poets or the myth of the war as a whole. It may, of course, be just wishful thinking, impressing on literature the hope that it has been worthwhile in defiance of the reality. Comments in *The Gazette* on the Armistice are typical of many others in similar magazines:

> All of us received letters stating what a jolly time we must have had on Armistice Day. The feeling was far too deep for that, and the sense of our own preservation, and the loss of many of our comrades, produced nothing but a deep feeling of thankfulness that the end that all had fought for had been attained at last.[3]

There is a dignity in some of these contemporary writings that does not scale the heights of the great writers in poetry or prose, but which nevertheless has a powerful attraction and an ability to move. Sadness is there in plenty, but little sign of bitterness, and I suspect this was a feeling far more common than the bitter regrets that began to be published in the 1920s, when the myth of the war was established. *The Wipers Times* said a great deal in a few words when it retitled itself, as it had done several times before, after the Armistice. The new title? *Better Times*.

The scorn of the average soldier for journalists at home was often expressed in *The Gazette* by quite sophisticated satire. The cynical author of 'Politics and Peace' was casting his mind back after the Armistice to the lead-up to war given by the press, and adopts the simple tactic of substituting 'peace' for 'war'; it is alarming how well the article reads.

> Once again we feel forced, in the national interest, to protest against the action – or rather inaction – of the present Government. For years we have warned the people, and we have urged to our uttermost this same Government, that sooner or later peace must be declared. And what heed have they paid? Absolutely none, and yet today Peace is upon us. The enormity of their offence cannot be too strongly reiterated. Whilst they have been occupied with their political bickerings, we have, in spite of all obstacles, been slowly winning the war and drifting towards Peace. Germany knew it – Germany recognised it. For twenty years they have been preparing for this Peace, and have been turning every factory to the manufacture of the Munitions of Peace, and now – as usual – they have caught us absolutely unprepared.[4]

This is a complex piece of writing. It satirizes the holier-than-thou, know-it-all declamatory tone of many leading newspapers before and during the war, and the huge authority adopted by those who had not fought. It also has a deeper level, suggesting the soldiers' fear that peace would not be prepared for or handled correctly.

There is an interesting contrast with the more literary war poets in the anonymous 'A Perfect Nightmare'. Robert Graves's poem 'A Dead Boche' seeks to illustrate the thesis that war is hell:

> . . . he scowled and stunk
>   With clothes and face a sodden green,
> Big-bellied, spectacled, crop-haired,
>   Dribbling black blood from nose and beard.

The Gazette's attitude to German corpses is rather different:

> When you come to the end of a long, long trench,
>   And you walk into no-man's-land;
> If your nose is assailed by a bad, bad stench,
>   Why, then you will understand
> It's a dead, dead Bosch, and you better strive
>   To break fresh ground instead,
> For the Bosch has an evil smell alive,
> But a damn sight worse when dead.

The dead German is an object of horror and pity to Graves. To the author of the poem in *The Gazette* he is a dead enemy, an object of loathing rather than pity. Pity dominates the work of many of the famous war poets, and many of the novels, films and plays that have been written about the war. It is far less common in those who did not have a pre-existing literary background. Pity is the uniform adopted by many of the writers who enlisted; many others from different backgrounds chose to wear a different uniform, and one altogether more brutal.

The staff officer is fair game; one 'story' in *The Gazette* can stand for many:

> An Officer was recently appointed to the Staff as Super-intendent of Musketry Training. When he came to tea arrayed in his new attire, his little daughter, aged 8, greeted him with these words: 'Will they all hate you now, Daddy?'[5]

The Gazette was for all ranks. Despite that, it took delight in parodying the letters sent and received by the infantry. In the hands of Wilfred Owen, the stumbling, incoherent phrases of the ordinary soldier become a focus for pity and the senseless sacrifice of the war:

> With B.E.F. June 10. Dear Wife,
> (Oh blast this pencil. 'Ere, Bill, lend's a knife.)
> I'm in the pink at present, dear.
> I think the war will end this year.

The Gazette takes a far more robust line. It parodies soldiers' letters, and also reprints a letter which may or may not in reality have been sent to the War Office:

Respected Sir, Dear Sir,

Though I take this liberty as it leaves me at present I beg to ask you if you will kindly be kind enough to let me know where is my husbin through he is not my legible husbin as he a wife though he says she is ded but I do not think he knows for sure but we are not married though I am getting my allotment reglar which is no fault of Mr Loy george who would stop it if he could and Mr Makena but if you know where he is belong to the Royal Naval Fling Corps for ever since he joined in jan when he was sacked from his work for talking back to his Bos which was a woman at the laundry where he worked I have not had any money from him since he joined though he told Mrs Harris what lives on the ground floor that he was a pretty ossifer for six shillings a week and loots of underclose in for the bad weather and I have three children what he has been the father of them though he say it was my fault. Hoping that you will write to me soon and you are quite well as it leaves me at present I must close now hoping you are well.

Mrs Jane Jenkins.[6]

To modern taste such satire can seem cruel and heartless, yet much of this humour – complaints against staff officers, sergeants pocketing the rum ration, endless form-filling, the very stuff of which *The Gazette* is made – is not First World War humour, but the rough and ready humour associated with army life since the dawn of time. *The Gazette* gives us a soldier's response to war. Owen and Sassoon gave us a response of outraged middle-class protest against war in general, and the First World War in particular.

Another authentic note is struck by some of the poetry of

'Woodbine Willie', now largely neglected. His poem 'The Spirit' acts as an accurate checklist of the concerns of many infantrymen: women, mail, cigarettes, rum, food, cold, wounds and death of friends. It is not, I suspect, great poetry; it is, though, a very good picture of the spirit of the times, even down to the morale-boosting last few lines:

> When there ain't no gal to kiss you,
> And the postman seems to miss you,
> And the fags have skipped an issue,
>   Carry on.
>
> When ye've got an empty belly,
> And the bulley's rotten smelly,
> And you're shivering like a jelly,
>   Carry on.
>
> When the Boche has done your chum in,
> And the sergeant's done the rum in,
> And there ain't no rations comin',
>   Carry on.
>
> When the world is red and reeking,
> And the shrapnel shells are shrieking,
> And your blood is slowly leaking,
>   Carry on.
>
> When the broken battered trenches,
> Are like the bloody butchers' benches,
> And the air is thick with stenches,
>   Carry on.
>
> Carry on,
>   Though your pals are pale and wan,
>   And the hope of life is gone,
>   Carry on.
>   For to do more than you can
>   Is to be a British man,
>   Not a rotten 'also ran',
>   Carry on.

There is no shortage of minor poetry that faces up to the full horror of the war from an early stage. At times one could be forgiven when reading conventional accounts of war literature for believing that

133

poetry moved from Brooke's patriotic sonnets to Sassoon's vicious satire in one sickening leap. The difference between much of the minor verse and that, say, of Sassoon is that the former may hate the war but rarely loses faith with it or condemns it.

Woodbine Willie confirms several impressions left by reading a mass of minor poetry. Officers and 'top brass' come in for very little criticism, upholding the view of Carrington and others that they were by and large trusted by the men, or simply ignored as beings from another planet. Ivor Gurney went some way towards summing this up in entitling a poem 'I Saw French Once'; Gurney served as a private, and it is hard not to repunctuate the title as 'I Saw French – Once'. The sergeant does come in for criticism, and a common theme in the lesser verse is the ability of non-commissioned officers to fiddle the rum and other rations. Woodbine Willie believes that the only thing which keeps soldiers buckled down to their job is cigarettes, Woodbines in particular. He does not like the Germans or feel them to be fellow sufferers in a universal tragedy. Sassoon blamed those at home for extending the war; many front-line soldiers blamed the Germans for starting it and keeping it going. In the words of *The Wipers Times*,

> H for the Hun who lives over the way:
>   His future is black and his present is grey;
>   Yet a Hun is a Hun, and as such he must pay
>   For making us live in the trenches.

Anonymous minor versifiers can be appallingly sentimental:

> Good-bye Nellie,
> I'm going across the main
> Farewell, Nellie,
> This parting gives me pain.
> I shall always love you
> As true as the stars above.
> I'm going to do my duty
> For the girl I love.

and also quite moving:

> I've lost my rifle and bayonet,
> I've lost my pull-through too,
> I've lost the socks that you sent me
> That lasted the whole winter through,
> I've lost the razor that shaved me,

I've lost my four-by-two,
I've lost my hold-all and now I've got damn all
Since I lost you.

As earlier examples showed, he can also be thoroughly obscene.
He is very wary of any grand abstractions or theorizing. Rats and
lice feature heavily in his productions, one of the few examples of
a content cross-over between greater and lesser war poets.
Rosenberg wrote two poems about lice, 'The Immortals' and
'Louse Hunting'. He served as a private, and this is perhaps one
of the few areas where his non-officer status can be seen. E. J.
Garston's 'To the Rats' has no particular vision or objectivity, but
it gives a vivid impression of an ordinary soldier's revulsion:

There is a thing which I could never pen,
The horror with which I regard your race,
For how can I describe my feelings when
I wake and find you sitting on my face.

In other respects Rosenberg is untypical, in particular because of
the complete absence of any mention of comradeship in his poetry
and letters. He complains about anti-Semitism and gives the
impression of being much put upon by fellow soldiers and those
in authority over him. Reading between the lines one can also see
that Rosenberg might well have been a liability as a soldier, absent-
minded, impractical and sometimes plain obtuse; in a world where
one's life could depend on a fellow-soldier's skill, Rosenberg might
well have lost friends for reasons other than his race and religion.
    What does come over time and again from reading the minor
verse is the all-embracing power of comradeship, and the respect
engendered in men by bravery. In the words of Patrick MacGill's
poem 'Matey'.

The bullet went through your head, matey,
But Gawd! it went through my 'eart.

Not great poetry by any academic standards, but for all that these
are words with the power to move and to flick a picture at full
intensity across the brain. The minor poetry reaffirms the letters
and diaries: comradeship was for the majority of soldiers the most
important single thing, outside life and death, encountered on
active service. Comradeship is at the same time almost a passive
emotion. Owen adds to it a power of fierce questioning which
transmutes it into pity. In its pure form, comradeship does not ask

questions; it simply is. Acceptance, simple pleasures, intermingled fear and boredom, homesickness, humour, irritation at the army: these are the staples of the minor writing of the war. They leave out vast tracts of experience the heights and depths of which were mapped by the likes of Owen and Sassoon, but what they do present is in its own way as vivid, honest and truthful as the findings of the great authors.

Notes

1 *The Fifth Gloster Gazette*, p. 267
2 *ibid.*, p. 279
3 p. 275
4 p. 267
5 p. 95
6 p. 91

CHAPTER SIX

What Passing Bells?

There is a story that the roof-space of Burghley House, near Stamford, is crammed to the eaves with unread Elizabethan and Jacobean documents, and that perhaps somewhere buried among them might even be the original manuscript of one of Shakespeare's plays. There is less mystery about the mountain of paper left by the First World War, but several major pinnacles of that mountain are composed of paper with poetry written on it, and the contents of the average modern anthology represent only a tiny percentage of what was being written between 1914 and 1918. It is possible, very roughly, to divide that poetry into several categories.

At the summit of achievement are the famous poets of the war – Owen, Rosenberg, Sassoon, Brooke, Graves, Thomas and Blunden. At the other extreme there is the poetry (or perhaps more often doggerel) found in the various magazines produced by soldiers in the trenches. One level up from this is the wealth of poetry printed in daily newspapers and popular magazines of the time, such as *Punch* and G.K. Chesterton's *The New Witness*. There is then a vast library of 'slim volumes', poetry published during or after the war, often written by young officers who had been killed or the occasional upstart private. Following this is a significant number of volumes written by relatively well-known non-combatants whose poetry touches on the war in one way or another: J.C. Squire, a leading literary figure of the day, and Harold Monro, founder of the Poetry Bookshop, are examples. There is a whole tranche of poetry written by famous poets who were too old to see service: the obvious examples are Thomas Hardy and Rudyard Kipling. Then there are poems about the war written by authors who later achieved fame in other fields, or writing about different subjects; A.P. Herbert and A.A. Milne are two examples.

Weaving in and out of these various categories are poets and poems that have missed the spotlight but which cry out for attention. Most obvious is the seriously impressive body of poetry written by women. There is Sidney Walter Powell's epic poem 'Gallipoli', published as a result of a deception in the 1930s and now forgotten, but which brilliantly foreshadows the work of Keith Douglas in the Second World War. 'Gallipoli' has died a death because it was a poem for the Second World War written by someone who fought and served in the First. A more famous, but similar, poem is David Jones's *In Parenthesis*. Then there is Charles Sorley, too shrewd and honest to write poems in the vein of Brooke and Grenfell, and killed too early to write enough to earn the fame of Owen. Owen Rutter wrote a comic parody of *Hiawatha* and, in common with most great comedy, used it to isolate nuggets of high seriousness. There is the work of Jeffery Day, the poet of the air war, at times chillingly distanced from the war.

As with the reported attics in Burghley House, a confused jumble of paper lies there for the taking. If those attics exist, most of the paper is probably no more exciting than the laundry bill of a junior chamberlain. In the attics of First World War poetry there are a surprising number of gems buried among the litter. Unfortunately, there is no undiscovered poetic genius lurking in the debris, with the exception perhaps of some of the women poets. None of the minor war poets can match the intensity and greatness of Owen, Sassoon or Rosenberg, and none achieves the consistency of the former two. Minor though the minor poets may be, they can nevertheless be very rewarding and of much more than mere academic interest.

Woodbine Willie, John Oxenham and Robert Service

'Woodbine Willie' (1883–1929), John Oxenham (1852–1941) and Robert Service (1874–1958) were all immensely popular poets during the war, but faded out of the public eye from the mid-1920s onwards. Robert Service is still known as a minor voice of the great outdoors, and 'Woodbine Willie' is known as a phrase, but all three have more or less died a literary death since their peak of popularity. As a measure of that popularity, I am looking as I write at John Oxenham's '*All's Well*', first published in November, 1915. The book proudly announces that by July, 1916, it had sold a staggering *seventy-five thousand copies*. His *The King's High Way*, published in 1918, contains this information about Oxenham's verse (he also wrote a large number of novels):

Verse:
Bees in Amber *228th Thousand*
'All's Well!' *203rd Thousand*
The King's High Way *120th Thousand*
The Vision Splendid *100th Thousand*
The Fiery Cross *65th Thousand*
High Altars (partly verse) *40th Thousand*
Hymn for the Men at the Front *7th Million*

Instead of the modern 'Second Impression', publishers in 1914 and for some while thereafter tended to tell the reader how many copies had been sold by giving the number of copies, to the nearest thousand, published up to the time of that particular edition. Admittedly, Oxenham's books were small, hardly more than pamphlets costing a shilling or so, but the sales figures are still staggering.

One reason for his success is simple. He offered comfort within the confines of a Christian vision of the war. The sub-title of *'All's Well!'* is 'Some helpful verse for these dark days of war'. Enough said, one might think, and turn to something more interesting. Yet Oxenham's work is almost but not quite the simplistic, easy evangelizing of horror into something more worthwhile than one might expect. There is plenty of pap, for sure, including the old stalwart of a poem exclaiming in wonder at Oxenham's son reporting that in a ruined church all three crucifixes were miraculously left standing. It was stories like this that most angered serving soldiers, leading to the oft-reported episode of a sergeant taking firing practice ordering the platoon to aim at a wayside crucifix, 'Bloke on cross: five round rapid; FIRE!'

What makes Oxenham's work more rewarding than sucked sugar stick is the bleak reality sitting beside the sometimes facile expressions of market-stall Christian hope. The refrain of 'Watchman! What of the Night' might be, 'I SEE THE MORNING LIGHT!' but before we get to the light we pass through a Slough of Despond:

> – The Ways are dark;
> Faith folds her wings; and Hope, in piteous
>   plight,
> Has dimmed her radiant lamp to feeblest
>   spark.
> Love bleeding lies –

The dead in Oxenham's work are not killed on a crest of courage with a neat and miraculously blood-free hole through a socially-acceptable part of their body. Rather they are those who

> Weak and broken lie,
> In weariness and agony.

Oxenham's son was at the front. Sometimes, in a simple, almost crude manner, he touches what must have been a chord for untold thousands of parents,

> Where are you sleeping to-night, My Lad,
>   Above ground – or below?
> The last we heard you were up at the front,
> Holding a trench and bearing the brunt; –
>   But – that was a week ago.
>
> Ay! – that was a week ago, Dear Lad,
>   And a week is a long, long time,
> When a second's enough, in the thick of the strife,
> To sever the thread of the bravest life,
>   And end it in its prime.

This is not great poetry by any conventional definition, but at times it has a sincerity that I personally find both surprising and appealing. All my preconditioning led me to believe that in Oxenham I would find the worst type of 'professional' writer, the man who wrote not from conviction but for the market. His remorseless sales figures created the impression of a poetic equivalent of Horatio Bottomley, the journalist who milked the war for all it was worth and set himself up as the voice of the people, to the disgust of the troops at the front. In practice Oxenham keeps a sufficient grip on reality to produce fits and starts of grim vision. His work is designed to reassure and console, but the occasional bitter almond stings the tongue with more force because it is buried in so much sugar. Oxenham tells his readers that their son died when, 'God was with him, and he did not blench' and that God has called him to a higher service; nothing new in that, except before the comfort Oxenham tells the truth, '*He died unnoticed in the muddy trench.*'

What distinguishes Oxenham from many others, and possibly what made him so popular, is that he does not duck the horror of war. He does not seek to offer comfort by ignoring the reality of combat, but offers that comfort despite it. Occasionally there are

moments of stark clarity in his work, and in particular a realization
that the war marked an end to a way of life and a way of looking
at life.

> The World is in the Melting-Pot,
> What *was* is passing away,
> And what will remain, when it cools again,
> No man may safely say.

> But of this we may be certain, –
> The Old Things have gone for aye;
> The wood, and the hay, and the stubble, they
> Have passed in the heat of the fray.

Apocalypse now: it may be no accident that Oxenham uses the
imagery of rural England for what has passed away. As happens
rather too often in his verse, he destroys this promising and interesting opening by standard images of cleansing and purifying, and
by the statement that if we build on God then we will build secure.
It is a perfectly acceptable sentiment, and there is no doubt of its
sincerity: Oxenham's suffering and faith come over too strongly to
be other than genuine. Unfortunately, it does not make for great
poetry.

Oxenham cannot do what George Herbert does so magnificently, namely resolve doubt but still leave the memory of the
doubt fresh in the mind of the reader. The resolution of an
Oxenham poem is so overwhelming, so certain, that it swamps the
doubt which gives the poems their credibility. W.B. Yeats argued
that out of conflict with others comes rhetoric, but that out of conflict within ourselves comes art. Oxenham's poetry defeats his own
inner conflict, and usually ends on a note of total certainty and
rhetoric which gave massive comfort to many hundreds of thousands of people; but that comfort has no literary value. It must
have a value in human terms. I have no measure to test its value,
any more than one can measure in finite terms the comfort offered
by the paramedic cradling the dying victim of a road accident.

A hardened cynic might argue that Oxenham's comfort
extended the war by consoling those at home who could bring it
to an end if its full horror was made clear to them. I wonder if such
a view does not patronize the home populace, reading the vast
casualty lists day in, day out, seeing minuscule advances and
retreats on the map, and every one of them close to someone who
died or was injured in the war. In fact towards the end of the war
there are times when the fabric of Oxenham's belief begins to crack

and shiver. One poem in particular seems to predict a revolution, a terrible price to be paid for the war. In an imaginary telephone message the receiver of the call is warned that terrible trouble is coming,

> *What trouble?*
> Every trouble, – everywhere,
> Every wildest kind of nightmare
> That has ridden you is there,
> In the air.
> And it's coming like a whirlwind,
> Like a wild beast mad with hunger,
> To rend and wrench and tear.

In a way Oxenham's work is similar to H.G. Wells's novel *The Invisible Man*. Both are stories of wasted opportunity. Wells has the chance to make serious points about science, its amorality, and the frightening power for good or evil it gives to the individual who can command it. He also has a major theme concerning humanity's reaction to the outsider. These themes are taken a certain distance – and then dropped in favour of the cheap options: slapstick, fisticuffs and backing away from serious issues. So with Oxenham's poetry, which promises much in parts, sometimes almost gets there, but in the end subverts everything to the need (or perhaps the irresistible desire) to feel that in truth 'all's well!'. Yet Oxenham's poetry is also fascinating because of its weaknesses. He writes for the ordinary men and women who underwent the experience of the First World War, and because he does not have the artistry to cover up he reveals the feelings of those men and women in sometimes surprising clarity.

Oxenham was a businessman before he became a full-time writer, whereas 'Woodbine Willie' (the Reverend G.A. Studdert Kennedy) was the pen-name of a clergyman, self-styled 'Chaplain to the Forces'. Studdert Kennedy was a powerful and impassioned preacher with the habit of upsetting the Anglican Establishment. He earned his nickname by his habit of handing out Woodbine cigarettes to the troops at the front; at his funeral in 1929 (he died of influenza while on a mission to Liverpool) a working man forced his way through the crowds to lay a packet of Woodbines on his coffin.

In the days when I believed I really was going to find the answers to the various enigmas that go to make up the First World War, I approached Woodbine Willie in the true spirit of condescension that is the hallmark of the only-just-a-postgraduate student. For starters, I had only heard about his poetry through an accidental meeting with an ex-serviceman, and the fact that it did not appear on any recognized reading list made me dismiss his work. Secondly, anyone who called themselves 'Chaplain to the Forces' was discredited before they started, and such an author was clearly going to be merely another arm of the Establishment and its continual efforts to persuade decent men to partake in an indecent war. I had not at the time come to the realization that Woodbine Willie was far from worshipping the god of power. Studdert Kennedy was a man whose saviour preached pacifism. Yet as his disciple Studdert Kennedy never did so. On a minor level he is a torn figure, as were, for very different reasons, Owen and Sassoon.

Oxenham and Woodbine Willie share several features. Both base many of their poems round God, and both tell their reader that Christ offers salvation. One difference is that Woodbine Willie's Christ is in agony on the Cross as often as he is in Heaven with his Father, whereas Oxenham's Christ suffers less pain and is more angel than human. Another difference is that Woodbine Willie had seen what he described, whilst Oxenham merely imagined it. Woodbine Willie's poetry has some sharply observed moments. Sassoon claimed credit for being the first poet to introduce the word 'syphilitic' into the diction of English poesy. Woodbine Willie, if not the first, is one of the first to acknowledge the pain of childbirth. His infantryman gives powerful expression to the idiocy and waste of war by the simple mechanism of having him grouse out loud in a type of verbal letter to his wife. It is not the wife who is the focus of the message, rather their child.

> Damn the blasted war to 'ell, lass.
>   It's just bloody rotten waste,
> Them as gas on war and glory
>   Oughter come and 'ave a taste.
> Yes, I larned what women suffers
>   When I seed you stand the test,
> But you knowed as it were worth it
>   When 'e felt to find your breast.

A major theme of this poem, 'What's the Good?', is the contrast between the appalling labour of giving birth and bringing up a child and the ease with which a father turns to killing other people's children. Simple stuff, and horrendously sentimental to modern taste, particularly as its hidden agenda is the common pre-war theme (found also in the poetry of Wilfrid Gibson) that the answer to any troublesome woman is to make her have a baby. It is also powerful, honest and in its bluntness and sentimentality not far from some degree of reality concerning the private soldier.

Woodbine Willie adopts in many poems the same pattern as Oxenham – a bleak vision followed by reassurance. It is often predictable stuff, but still has the capacity to surprise the reader:

> I know. It is not easy to explain
> Why should there be such agony to bear?
> Why should the whole wide world be full of pain?
> But then, why should her hair
> Be like the sudden sunshine after rain?

Woodbine Willie expresses the metamorphosis that overcame so many middle-class officers during the war, namely the realization that underneath the coarseness, bad language and outwardly foul manner of the ordinary soldier there lay virtues of decency, humanity and human sympathy that were equal, and sometimes superior, to those espoused by the educated classes. It is an irony that the war most often held up by the intellectual left wing as a total condemnation of Establishment values did more to establish among the Establishment a realization of common human values across the class divide than any other. Studdert Kennedy was a clergyman who had met the 'working class' before the war, and his poetry does little more than carry on the basic respect for that class he had formed then. In his poem 'A Gal of the Streets' a common whore refuses a 'client' when he tells her, almost by accident, of the death of 'Ted':

> She stood there and swayed like a drunken man,
> And 'er face went green where 'er paint began,
> Then she muttered, 'My Gawd, I carn't'; and ran –
>   She were a gal on the streets.

Or, in other words, the whore has feelings too. Poetry such as this could not have been written by an English clergyman if the path had not been blazed by the Georgians in general, and Wilfrid Gibson and W.H. Davies in particular.

Studdert Kennedy's Christ died on a cross in a violent world that was grossly unfair; no wonder he could write with authority on the First World War. His Christ dealt with the same world as that faced by the soldier of 1914–18, as is shown in his poem 'My Peace I Leave With You':

Man's Via Crucis never ends,
  Earth's Calvaries increase,
The World is full of spears and nails,
  But where is Peace?

Take up Thy Cross and follow Me,
  I am the Way, my son,
Via Crucis, Via Pacis,
  Meet and are one.

Colloquial language was used by Oxenham, Woodbine Willie and Robert Service. Sassoon and Owen were to adopt the use of colloquial language, as were a number of the more minor but 'serious' war poets, such as Robert Nichols and Wilfrid Gibson. Owen and Sassoon's use of colloquial language has not, to my knowledge, been given any significant critical attention in terms of ascertaining its roots, unlike Owen's use of pararhyme or Sassoon's adoption of satire. In *The Old Century* Sassoon comments that his great friend 'Wirgie' suggested he adopt an 'everyday' mode of writing, which Sassoon acknowledges as being something of a revelation. John Masefield was a pioneer in the use of colloquial language, and leaders among the Georgians were W.H. Davies and Wilfrid Gibson. It is possible that Owen and Sassoon were tipped off to the technique by the work of populist poets such as Oxenham and Woodbine Willie; given their popularity it would have been difficult for either man to be ignorant of their work, particularly if as officers they were living and working side by side with the men who read these poems, usually sent from home. Both my copies of Woodbine Willie's work were presents, both were owned and read in the trenches by privates; they are much-used volumes.

High or low, all the authors who used colloquial language soon found its limitations. Owen was introduced to poetic reality by Sassoon, but his colloquial poems ('The Letter', 'The Chances') soon take the medium as far as it will go, which often is not very far. Use of colloquial language demands the adoption of a poetic persona or speaking voice, and from that moment the vision of the poem is restricted, if realism is to be observed, to the likely vision of the speaker. In the form of a private soldier, this limits what can be said and shown quite dramatically. The temptation is to break out from the voice of the speaker and into the voice of the poet. All writers who use the colloquial mode fall prey to this. At the end of 'What's the Good' Woodbine Willie suddenly stops speaking

and the poet takes over, with no warning and something of a jar-
ring shock:

> Women pity soldiers' sorrow,
> That can bring no son to birth,
> Only death and devastation,
> Darkness over all the earth.

Then the 'h's' start being dropped again and Woodbine Willie
returns after his temporary absence. Wilfred Owen's wounded
officer in 'A Terre' suddenly launches into complex half-rhyme
and entirely Owenesque diction, to a stage where Owen hardly
bothers to restore dramatic credibility to the poem.

Robert Service was a banker, war correspondent and novelist.
He travelled widely in Canada and despite his age (he was born in
1874) served for two years as an ambulance driver on the Western
Front. His Canadian poetry was immensely popular, earning him
the title 'The Man with the Ice in His Voice'. It was treated, on
the other hand, with some hilarity by the London literary establishment, and Edmund Blunden castigated him in *Undertones of
War*, describing his 'cantering rhetoric about huskies and hoboes
on icy trails'. Service cultivated the image of the hobo, but he was
essentially middle class in background and something of a
watered-down harbinger (can you water down a harbinger?) for
Hemingway.

He differs from Oxenham and Woodbine Willie in that
Christianity plays no great part in his verse. Instead he interests
himself in the common man and the common soldier, in conscious
or unconscious imitation of Kipling. Service's feel for accent and
dialect is not as sure as Woodbine Willie's, but the poems can gain
power by their concentration on one speaker, and their descriptions have the authority of a writer who had seen and experienced
both fear and the reality of the front line. There is a stark contrast
between the work of all three of these popular writers and the colloquial poems of Owen and Sassoon. In the latter the ordinary
soldier is always shown as victim, almost the emblem of the passive suffering which Yeats so criticized in war poetry. Oxenham,
Woodbine Willie and Service show the ordinary soldier as far more
in control of himself and his destiny.

Service's poem 'The Volunteer' gives a rather vivid picture of a
working man's progress from cynic to enlisted soldier. All the
reasons for not joining up are listed – hatred of politicians and
'empire-grabbers', concern over who brings up the children – ending with the fact that the man 'gotta go'. Service manages to catch

a mood in this poem that is borne out by countless contemporary records detailing why people joined up, and he isolates the tide of inevitability that caught up so many thousands in its waves.

Owen and Sassoon show the ordinary soldier as suffering in flesh and spirit, an object of vast pity or an equal source of great anger against those who caused or prolonged the war. The lesser poets show him as having character, determination and far more control over events. Perhaps for this reason the old soldiers I met remembered and liked Oxenham, Woodbine Willie and Service far more than Owen and Sassoon: the former gave the ordinary soldier more respect for himself and placed him on an equal footing to the poet. At the same time they allowed his womanizing, swearing and unerring instinct for finding strong liquor to creep into their verse. The middle-class view of the infantryman that stands at the centre of Owen's and Sassoon's poetry is compromised by the vulgarity and occasional awfulness of the enlisted man, so these features rarely appear in their work; indeed, both poets are happier describing the suffering of their fellow officers or rather incredibly innocent-looking 'lads'.

Owen and Sassoon confirm us in our modern vision of warfare, and played a considerable part in forming that vision, but many who fought in the war did not wish to be seen as cattle going to slaughter, or told that what they were fighting for was a senseless exercise in waste. Nor did the rather laundered vision of the front-line soldier appeal to them, partly because it seemed unreal and partly because Owen, Sassoon and Rosenberg tend to leave out the acts of heroism, the courage that so many old soldiers remembered. This omission is perfectly justifiable in poetic terms, and in human terms Owen and Sassoon both felt heroism to be a de-valued currency, not an excuse for the senseless waste of war but in many ways something which made that waste even more poignant and obvious. However justifiable, what Owen and Sassoon left out of their verse often left them out of the favoured reading of survivors, at least from the ranks.

In their different ways Oxenham and Woodbine Willie told those who read them that this was a war for decency and peace, and that suffering and salvation had ever been allied in the form of a young man nailed to a cross. Service told them that to fight was both the decent and the manly thing to do, and brought a sense of humour to telling the tale. It is not difficult to see why the soldiers, and many at home who had lost those they loved most or daily feared to hear they had done so, preferred Oxenham to Owen. It is difficult not to sympathize with them, though by any standards of literary judgment they were clearly wrong, and to prefer Oxenham to Owen is to prefer the penny whistle to the symphony orchestra. Still, there is a time to tell a driver who has smashed his car that he is a bloody fool and deserves to be locked up; doing so when he is nursing broken limbs and has just been told that he has killed his wife is not it, any more than 1918 was the time to tell an emotionally raped nation what had been done in its name.

Major Owen Rutter and 'The Song of Tiadatha'

The Song of Tiadatha is a curio, a poem that has no right to exist and one which to my knowledge has no direct equivalent. Major Owen Rutter (1889–1944) was a soldier who became a writer and traveller after the war. *The Song of Tiadatha* was invented when Rutter was serving in Macedonia during the war and found a copy of Longfellow's *The Song of Hiawatha* in a dug-out. He adapted the form to a narrative poem about an imaginary young officer, Tiadatha, basing the character on a composite of all the officers he had known. Much of the poem was completed in the line in Rutter's various wartime postings. Published after the war it was an immediate success, and eventually a collected edition of *The Song of Tiadatha* and its sequel, *The Travels of Tiadatha*, was published in 1935, after which the book seems to have sunk without trace, a victim of the increasingly cynical and unforgiving attitude to the war that came in the late 1920s and early 1930s. It was also a time when war was brewing again in Europe, and the tone of *The Song of Tiadatha* was a total mismatch for the mood growing in a nation that dreaded war with as much strength as it had welcomed it in 1914.

Tiadatha is a 'filbert', or young man about town:

> You could see him any morning
> In July of 1914,
> Strolling slowly down St James's
> From his little flat in Duke Street.
> Little recked he of in those days
> Save of socks and ties and hair wash,
> Girls and motor-cars and suppers;
> Little suppers at the Carlton,
> Little teas at Rumplemayer's . . .

Rutter's version of how Tiadatha comes to join up is as succinct
(and possibly as accurate for many young men) as one can get:

> Then came war, and Tiadatha
> Read his papers every morning,
> Read the posters on the hoardings,
> Read 'Your King and Country want you,'
> 'I must go,' said Tiadatha,
> Toying with his devilled kidneys,
> 'Do my bit and join the Army'.

Larkin summarized the mood of that stanza in his poem '1914',
commenting on the lines queueing up for the recruiting office
with the refrain 'Never such innocence again'. Is it Rutter's poem
that makes me aware of the appalling and tragic innocence of
many of those who joined up in 1914, or is it the wisdom born of
hindsight operating on a rather flippant and superficial treatment
of those who enlisted? I simply do not know, but I suspect it is
something intrinsic in Rutter's style. Rutter is expert at placing
one-line ironic pointers in the verse, as when 'Toying with his dev-
illed kidneys' implies the naive ignorance with which Tiadatha
takes a crucial step. Having joined up, Tiadatha goes on the most
immense shopping spree, acquiring every accoutrement that
could possibly be required for modern warfare as an officer in the
'Dudshires':

> All day boys with loads were streaming
> To and from the flat in Duke Street,
> Like a chain of ants hard at it
> Storing rations for the winter.

When Tiadatha eventually arrives at the front it is as a huge mountain of kit with legs just visible beneath it. In the interim comes one
of the strange moments of descriptive pathos that Rutter manages
to inject:

> There was not a band or bugle,
> Not a single watcher waving,
> Not a single soldier singing
> On the night that Tiadatha
> Sailed for France upon his troopship.
> Silently they left the station,
> Silently embarked at midnight,

No one talking, no one smoking,
Not a sound except the tramping
Of the men along the gangway,
And the gurgling water bottles,
And the rattle of equipment.

Or 'Down the close darkening lanes they sang', as Owen wrote: different intensity, different style, same message. Kindly officers soon persuade Tiadatha to leave most of his kit behind, and after a brief period in the trenches the Dudshires are moved to Salonica, finding their fill of trench warfare in that campaign. The tone is often light, as it is in the regimental and battalion journals of the day; serving soldiers were used to reading between the lines in the clipped, official reports of actions, which is why so many officers writing about the war use what is almost a form of shorthand, unconsciously assuming a knowledge of the deeper truth in their readers. Thus when a French officer shows Tiadatha the wire beyond their trenches he falls into his own wire, swears loudly and thereby starts the war all over again; the story of a 'scare' whose like was repeated day in and day out all along the Western Front:

Thereupon a Bulgar sentry,
Wakened from his pleasant slumbers,
Feeling rather bored about it,
Heaved a bomb at Captain Siomme,
Heaved a bomb at Tiadatha,
As a householder in London,
Wakened from his pleasant slumber
By a tomcat on the house tiles,
Opens wide his bedroom window,
Heaves a bootjack at the noises.
Then a zealous Dudshire sentry
Swiftly flung a bomb in answer,
Followed it with five rounds rapid,
Thinking that there was a war on.
Then the Bulgars sent a light up,
And another and another,
Made the darkness light as Bond Street
On an afternoon in winter.
Siomme and my Tiadatha
Lay and grovelled on their tummies,
Still as any startled tortoise.
After that the German gunners
Put a dozen salvoes over,

And the English field-guns opened,
Feeling sure there was a war on.
Bits of bomb and crump and shrapnel
Made the autumn evening hideous,
Groups stood to, machine-guns rattled,
All the telephones got busy,
And supports turned out in dudgeon.

As a prairie fire is started
By a match or cigarette end,
So a mighty strafe was started
All because the gallant Siomme
Fell into his own defences.

The comparison between a sentry hurling a bomb and a householder a bootjack is typical of the poem. Rutter is the only war poet
who compares a German 'crump' with a chorus girl – great fun
and rather exciting when you first meet them, boring and rather
dangerous after the third or fourth time. To that extent *The Song
of Tiadatha* is a masterpiece in a particularly English vein of comic
writing, relying on understatement and gentle use of irony, but
understating horror at the same time. Despite this the poem can
drop into moods of sudden seriousness:

Had you been there when the dawn broke
Had you looked out from the trenches,
You'd have seen that Serbian hillside,
Seen the aftermath of battle;
Seen the scattered picks and shovels,
Seen the scraps of stray equipment,
Here and there a lonely rifle,
Or a Lewis gun all twisted;
Seen the little heaps of khaki
Lying huddled on the hillside,
Huddled by the Bulgar trenches,
Very still and very silent;
Nothing stirring, nothing moving,
Save a very gallant doctor
And his band of stretcher bearers
Working fearlessly in the open,
Giving water to the dying,
Bringing in those broken soldiers,
You'd have seen the sunlight streaming,
Down upon that stricken country,

And perhaps you would have wondered
How the sun could still be shining,
How the birds could still be singing,
While so many British soldiers
Lay so still upon the hillside.

Tiadatha survives his war and marries his Phyllis; the poem's conclusion is free of the cynicism and bitterness that marks the work
of the major trench poets. Rutter's poem has shrewdness, wit and
humour, and a neat, unobtrusive and affectionate irony. It is above
all brilliantly observed. The sequel, *The Travels of Tiadatha*, gives
a vivid picture of the restlessness that affected so many old soldiers,
unable to settle back into the old ways when they and the world
that had produced them had both changed so drastically, and so
many of the people they had known and loved were dead. *The Song
of Tiadatha* deserves to be rescued from obscurity. It may only be
Gilbert and Sullivan to the war's Ring Cycle, but there should be
room on the stage for both.

Wilfrid Gibson and A.P. Herbert

Wilfrid Gibson was a key figure in the Georgian poetry movement,
and one of the poets who took up residence near Dymock before
the war. He was a close friend of Rupert Brooke, who referred to
him as 'Wibson', and as one of the three legatees of Brooke's will
(the Georgian poets John Drinkwater and Walter de la Mare were
the others) Gibson was able to live a relatively easy life after the
war. He tried to enlist but was turned down, until he finally managed to join the Army Service Corps in 1917. There is uncertainty
over whether he actually saw service in the front line. He flickers
in and out of anthologies. It is not a question of always the brides-
maid, never the bride: rather he is the figure caught by the camera
on the edge of the frame, waiting by the gate to watch the wedding
party go by.

The remarkable thing about Gibson's poetry is the way that it
touches on almost every style adopted by the major and minor war
poets: his poems act as a guided tour through the contortions of
form and content undergone by the war poets in trying to come to
terms with new experience. Dominic Hibberd gives credit to
Gibson for more or less inventing the short, realistic, colloquial
war poem. Gibson's fondness for running within one poem parallel
pictures of the countryman at home in peacetime and the same
man at war in uniform is reminiscent of some of Blunden's work.

Gibson, Blunden and Edward Thomas were the three poets

most loth to leave behind the nature poetry they had written before the war when they found themselves writing during the conflict. Blunden's farm worker is jerked out of his reverie and plunged back into being a soldier in 'The Guard's Mistake', when the arrival of the general in a motorcade sends the soldier scurrying back for his 'bundook and spike', or rifle and bayonet. 'Bundook' was one of the many corruptions of native Indian words used in the British Army, a sign of its origins as a colonial force. Gibson's farm worker is not so much worried by whether or not he will be shot, but more by the fact that if he dies he will never know 'if the old cow died or not?' Both poets make the point that the outer man can be changed by giving him a uniform, but little happens to change the inner man. Blunden and Gibson share a willingness to write poems that exist both in the rural world at home and at the front, but Gibson does more than echo Blunden; he echoes almost every other poet who wrote on the war. Sassoon's poem 'The Bayonet' and Graves's 'A Dead Boche' are both attempts to shock. Gibson's 'The Bayonet' bears direct comparison.

> This bloody steel
> Has killed a man.
> I heard him squeal
> As on I ran . . .
>
> Though clean and clear
> I've wiped the steel,
> I still can hear
> That dying squeal.

Gibson was no stranger to such attempts to shock. He saw himself, in common with the other Georgian poet and supertramp, W.H. Davies, as the spokesman of the common man. Neither poet idealized their subject, and the work of both is full of decrepit old women, prostitutes and violence. Graves's mixture of fact and fantasy in 'Over the Brazier' is echoed in Gibson's 'In the Ambulance', with its crazed refrain, and in 'Mad'.

Owen's and Sassoon's colloquial verse can be compared with numerous poems in which Gibson talks in or uses the voice of the ordinary soldier, a technique which derives from Rudyard Kipling and John Masefield. Gibson takes the technique one stage further in 'Breakfast':

> We ate our breakfast lying on our backs
> Because the shells were screeching overhead.
> I bet a rasher to a loaf of bread

That Hull United would beat Halifax
When Jimmy Stainthorpe played full-back instead
of Billy Bradford. Ginger raised his head
And cursed, and took the bet, and dropt back dead.
We ate our breakfast lying on our backs
Because the shells were screeching overhead.

I think this is a rather neglected poem. Colloquial language is replaced with the most mundane of references to soccer, and the point made that death is almost a casual event. The ease or inevitability with which it is accepted is the greatest sign of its horror, and the repetition of the first two lines at the end of the poem suggests that death is cyclical and commonplace, marking the changed pattern of normality for all those who served in the trenches. Owen and Sassoon can rarely resist the urge in their poems of protest to place a marker at the end of the poem, just to ensure the reader gets the point. By using instead a simple repetition, Gibson conveys strongly the total difference between the world of the soldier and the world of the civilian, a difference emphasized rather than diminished by the use of so many 'civilian' words, not least of all the title of the poem.

Another neglected poem is 'Lament':

We who are left, how shall we look again
Happily on the sun or feel the rain,
Without remembering how they who went
Ungrudgingly, and spent
Their all for us, loved too the sun and rain?

A bird among the rain-wet lilac sings . . .

As with all Gibson's best work, this is sincere, simple and memorable. Its wistful tone concentrates the sense of grief and loss on those who have died, not, as is so often the case with poems on a similar theme by others, on the poet; we lament the dead, not the author.

Gibson's war poetry ranges far and wide, managing to touch on almost every topic and theme covered by other war poets. His 'The Dancers' has 'the dainty dancing demoiselles' of 'peacock dragonflies' dancing through an artillery bombardment, a reminder of Crosbie Garstin's poem about butterflies. 'Chemin des Dames'. Gibson has a shrewd eye for irony. In *Casualties* he wrote a series of short poems, each about or linked to a dead friend or acquaintance killed in the war. 'Donald Fraser', whose job was to polish granite tombstones, is now lying

> In a vast moundless grave, unnamed, unknown,
> Nor marked at head or foot by stock or stone.

'Peter Proudfoot' is a three-line poem, wholly self-explanatory:

> He cleaned out middens for his daily bread;
> War took him overseas and in a bed
> Of lilies-of-the-valley dropt him dead.

A personal favourite of mine, because of its simplicity, is 'Ralph Straker':

> Softly out of the dove-grey sky
> Drift the snowflakes fine and dry
> Till braeside and bottom are all heaped high.

> Remembering how he would love to go
> Over the crisp and creaking snow,
> I wonder that now he can lie below

> If softly out of the Flanders sky
> Drift the snowflakes fine and dry
> Till crater and shell-hole are all heaped high.

'The Conscript' is reminiscent of Sassoon in its vicious satire of a medical board passing soldiers fit for service:

> And the chairman, as his monocle falls again,
> Pronounces each doom with easy indifferent breath.

It finishes with the familiar comparison of the conscript with Christ. Sassoon's hatred of music-hall treatment of the war, as seen in 'Blighters', finds an echo in Gibson's 'Ragtime'.

Gibson's work contains specific front-line description, collo-quial language and satire, and as such the temptation is to rank him with Sassoon, Rosenberg and Owen as regards type if not quality. It is probably fairer to rank him with a different group, most notably Brooke, Edward Thomas and Edmund Blunden. Two different strands were visible almost from the outset in the development of First World War poetry. One was the poets who were deeply rooted to a tradition of nature poetry going back to

Wordsworth, and who never really left the fields and meadows of home. Rosenberg was never a part of that strand, and whilst Owen and Sassoon started the war with at least a partial allegiance to it, both were diverted down a different route based around tenderness, compassion and outrage. Brooke, Thomas, Blunden and Gibson acknowledged the war and wrote about it in a radically different way from the poets of pity and protest. Their offerings have tended to be submerged beneath the work of Owen, Sassoon and Rosenberg, which was both generally stronger and more in tune with the post-war mood and attitudes to the war.

Just as one suspects that some poets were judged post-1923 (when Eliot's *The Waste Land* was first published) not simply by how good they were but also by how close they came to being like T.S. Eliot, so any poet not immediately comparable to Owen or Sassoon has had to work twice as hard for recognition. One of the problems with Robert Graves's poetry, and one reason why he has never really established a reputation for himself as a 'war poet', is that his poetry has never sided with either camp, and sits awkwardly trying to straddle a pastoral sensibility and a more 'modern' one closer to Sassoon's drive for realism and banishment of artifice.

Gibson appears a better poet if he is judged by the standards of relatively simple English pastoral and brought out from under Owen's long shadow. His work can have a surprising strength, surprising because his reputation in general is not high and he has been too often dismissed as a lacklustre Georgian.

Another surprise is the poetry of A.P. Herbert, who became Sir Alan Patrick Herbert. Herbert wrote regularly for *Punch*, and the poetry published there has a lightness of touch typical of the magazine, but which has not recommended itself to subsequent generations. At times Herbert can be very, very funny, as in the poem quoted earlier on General Shute. That impromptu is not typical of his published work, which is usually more restrained, though rarely without a touch of humour. Generals feature largely, and they are rarely complimented. In 'After the Battle' 'the beaming general, and the soapy praise' are dismissed, not stridently nor even violently, but rather with the tired, exhausted exasperation of the officer drained after an offensive:

> We only want to take our wounds away
>   To some warm village where the tumult ends,
> And drowsing in the sunshine many a day,
>   Forget our aches, forget that we had friends.

Weary we are of blood and noise and pain;
    This was a week we shall not soon forget;
And if, indeed, we have to fight again,
    We little wish to think about it yet.

We have done well; we like to hear it said,
    Say it, and then, for God's sake, say no more.
Fight, if you must, fresh battles far ahead,
    But keep them dark behind your château door!

There is authenticity in the tone of this poem. Herbert is not frightened of the horror of trench warfare, but manages to integrate the horror into poems that can talk of other things, thereby recreating for us the real horror of the war, the normality of the abnormal. In 'A Song of the Spade' he writes,

        Dig – dig – dig,
      But turn some other sod.
  Leave him asleep where the maggots creep
    And an Army's feet have trod;
        But Oh, the awful smell!
        To think a thing so vile
    Went forth to war with a soldier's smile
      And wore the form of God!

Compassion and a dry, ironic humour are the mainstay of Herbert's poetry. In 'Cold Feet' Herbert listens to 'young blades' reporting that someone had got 'cold feet'. Almost idly, Herbert wonders if he too does not have cold feet, launching into a sequence of stanzas that describe, casually and without rancour, the horrors of trench life, its sapping boredom, its tension:

Or if it means that blood is in his dreams,
    And shattered jaws and heads precisely holed,
And quiet midnights shot with sudden screams,
    And snatched field dressings, ne'er to be unrolled,
      Or that at times he wakes in tears
      With 'Stretcher Bearers!' in his ears,
    And knows those stretchers will be biers, –
    Ah me, my feet are cold.

Herbert was twenty-four when he joined up, born in the same year as Isaac Rosenberg. Despite the fact that he was relatively young, his poetry has a quality of mature reflection that is absent from much other mature poetry, and reminiscent of poetry by some of the older poets in the war, such as Edward Thomas. Part of that maturity is the image he purveys of the old stager, particularly audible in 'Open Warfare'. In the great days of 1918 open battle was the order of the day, welcomed as marking the end of the stalemate of trench warfare, and perhaps the end of the war. Typically, Herbert has his doubts.

> I like a trench, I have no lives to spare;
> And in those catacombs, however cramping,
> You did at least know vaguely where you were . . .

> And say once more, while I have no objection
> To other men proceeding to Berlin,
> Give me a trench, a nice revetted section,
> And let me stay there till the Boche gives in!

This is classic *Punch* humour, but it makes Herbert one of the few poets who seeks to make near-cowardice both acceptable and amusing. He has an acute eye for detail and mood, noting soldiers encamped in an area where 'we' fought savage actions. To the soldiers camping the ground means nothing. To Herbert,

> We only walk with reverence this sullen mile of mud;
> The shell-holes hold our history, and half of them our blood.

Unfortunately, Herbert cannot sustain the note of elegiac intensity, and too many of his poems fade out gently, or retreat into self-effacing flippancy. Offsetting that weakness is the strength of his observation, which can show a strong fellow-feeling for German soldiers, as in 'The Swan-Song of the Bavarians'. It is surprising that Herbert's work has not been more fêted, because despite its strong individual flavour it does echo the more famous poets in two areas, dislike of the generals and a strong sense of pity, and one imagines that Herbert would have been seen by 1930s' criticism in the manner of a reserve to the first team.

The Establishment: Rudyard Kipling, J.C. Squire and G.K. Chesterton

The use of the word 'Establishment' here is potentially misleading. In general terms the Establishment usually means the almost unconscious association of respectable and conventional leaders of society. Respectability and conventionality have never been hallmarks of the literary world, and my use of the word Establishment with regard to Kipling, Squire and Chesterton has a slightly different slant. It is intended to imply simply that these were senior, established and respected writers, albeit not always conventional.

Rudyard Kipling is an enigma. He and T.H. White share the glory of having books turned into Walt Disney cartoons *(The Jungle Book* and *The Sword in the Stone)*, and Kipling is probably still best known for the Mowgli/*Jungle Book* stories and as an extreme right-wing Imperialist. My own rather limited academic career has been hampered by a tendency to pick from library shelves the book with the most dust on it, rather than the Important and Significant book I went to find. Thus in the Brotherton library at the University of Leeds I unearthed a tattered and coverless book of poems stuffed behind volumes of T.S. Eliot. The first page was Kipling's 'Epitaphs of War'. There may have been intentional irony in the placing: Eliot was a lifelong supporter of Kipling's work. If I had realized it was Kipling I would not have bothered to read the poems. As it was, I did so, and when I discovered who I had been reading I underwent a serious culture shock. The little I knew about Kipling suggested that he had forced his under-age and half-blind son, John, into the Irish Guards because the great publicist of the war could afford to do little else, that John's death had created in Kipling a furious and mindless hatred of all things German, and that he was the epitome of the hang 'em, shoot 'em and flog 'em brigade. The poems were a surprise, and I found them more complex and disturbing than ever I had imagined.

Kiplings's war poetry has to be dug out of his *Collected Poems*, where it tends to be buried in the vast amount he wrote. Kipling can be a brilliant technician, and it has been said that his later verse suffers from being all technique and no content. Whatever the truth of that, his technique allows him to make something forceful out of fairly simple ideas. One example is the 'Epitaph' 'Hindu Sepoy In France':

> This man in his own country prayed we know not to what
>   Powers.
> We pray Them to reward him for his bravery in ours.

There is some rather predictable poetry, like the 'Epitaph' 'Ex-Clerk', where the army gives a timid ex-clerk 'Strength of body, will and mind', not to mention 'Mirth, Companionship and Love'. If the poetry of Oxenham and Service can be compared to a bog-standard Ford, then this Kipling poetry is the GTI version: more flashy bodywork, but basically the same engine and chassis. If it stopped there Kipling would only be a footnote in the war. Yet some of his war poetry has a quality that I can only describe as resonance, a capacity to echo in the mind. There are similarities, if in one sense alone, with the best work of Thomas and Sorley, where an apparent simplicity of setting and diction belies a really rather complex and textured emotional effect. One example, which for some reason I remembered for over twenty years after reading it only once, is the 'Epitaph' 'A Son',

> My son was killed while laughing at some jest. I would I knew
> What it was, and it might serve me in a time when jests are
> few.

John Kipling runs through his father's war verse as an often unstated but extremely strong theme. His death (he was shot through the head and his body never found) crippled Kipling. It did not help that numbers of people wrote to him gloating over the death as the just reward for a man who had pushed the cause of militarism so vociferously before the war. The death provoked viciously jingoistic poetry, but also some complex writing. 'A Death Bed' is a remarkable technical *tour de force*, blending the voice of doctors commenting on a dying patient, the voice of the patient, the voice of the Establishment and an omniscient narrator:

> 'This is the State above the Law
>   The State exists for the State alone.'
> *(This is a gland at the back of the jaw,*
>   *And an answering lump by the collar bone.)*
>
> Some die shouting in gas or fire;
>   Some die silent, by shell and shot.
> Some die desperate, caught on the wire;
>   Some die suddenly. This will not.

As with some of the best verse written in or about the war, this uses the war rather than being solely about the war. The poem is about death, and is a complex and disturbing statement on that theme.

The surprise in Kipling's verse is the absence of rhetoric and the almost overwhelming sense of bitterness and guilt. 'Mesopotamia' is typical:

> They shall not return to us, the resolute, the young,
>   The eager and whole-hearted whom we gave:
> But the men who left them thriftily to die in their own dung,
>   Shall they come with years and honour to the grave?

In 'The Children' Kipling writes,

> They believed us and perished for it. Our statecraft, our learning
> Delivered them bound to the Pit and alive to the burning . . .
>   But who shall return us our children?

One of his simplest and most compelling statements is in 'Common Form':

> If any question why we died,
> Tell them, because our fathers lied.

In his letters Kipling suggested that he could accept the death of his son. Writing to the school friend who was the original of Stalky, he stated:

> I'm sorry that all the years' work ended in that one afternoon but lots of people are in our position – and it's something to have bred a man.[2]

He says the same thing in verse form, acknowledging that with no surviving sons or cousins the Kipling name had come to an end:

> Death favoured me from the first, well knowing I could not
>   endure
>   To wait on him day by day. He quitted my betters and came
> Whistling over the fields, and, when he had made all sure,
>   'Thy line is at an end,' he said, 'but at least I have saved its
>   name.'

Yet other poetry shows a deep well of bitterness, sadness and regret:

> I have slain none except my mother. She
> (Blessing her slayer) died of grief for me.

Kipling's guilt is understandable, and some of his best war poetry is produced from the tension between that guilt and his essentially right-wing attitude to the war. His verse also gives the lie to the vision of the older generation in Sassoon's and Owen's poetry, summed up in Owen's 'The Parable of the Old Man and the Young'. There were undoubtedly many stay-at-homes who supported the war from armchairs and delivered the young up to death, but there were also many like Kipling who suffered by proxy. Owen and Sassoon wrote from the viewpoint of young, childless men, understanding what it was to lose one's own life and the life of a friend or comrade, but failing to understand what it meant to lose a child.

Kipling's war poetry also confirms the findings of a book such as Hynes's *A War Imagined* that those at home became disillusioned with the war and it was the soldiers at the front who remained patriotic, if only as a means of making themselves believe that what they were going through was justified. Kipling's poetry does not condemn the war in the manner of some of the younger and famous poets, but often can condone it only by implication. It does not pull its punches in describing physical horrors, and while it sometimes seeks to console in the manner of Oxenham it is also laden with guilt, a violence at times on the surface and at times suppressed and suffused with a dark and rather terrible emotional sub-text. At times Kipling becomes war, rather than merely writing about it. Its violence holds a fascination for him, as if violence is an end in itself, a power that simply is and cannot be denied.

Kipling's vision of the war was more complex than his reputation as a belligerent militarist might suggest. J. C. Squire occupied a different corner of the ring reserved for the literary Establishment, but as with Kipling there are many reasons why one might expect him to be an unthinking supporter of the war, an armchair commentator of the type pilloried so mercilessly by Owen and Sassoon. Squire was a magazine editor who achieved a dominant position in the latter, declining years of the Georgian movement, taking over the mantle from Edward Marsh, so much so that the more traditional and rather lacklustre Georgians became known as the Squirearchy. He was knighted in 1933.

Some of Squire's poetry is remarkably bland. His contributions to the Georgian anthologies tend to favour rather pretty verse with foreign maidens doing not-very-alarming things in a pleasant metre to the accompaniment of moonlight; one of the reasons why in post-war years the Georgians were categorized as writing about moonlight and little else. It is becoming rather tedious to say yet again that a certain poet's work contains surprises, but in Squire's case it is true. The quantity and quality of the surprise depends, of course, on what the reader is expecting. I first came to Squire after ploughing through what still strikes me as quite the most irritating and banal poem I have ever read, 'Cuckoo Wood' by Edmund Beale Sargent, after which anything appears good. Three poems by Squire illustrate the nature of the surprise he can offer.

'Homoeopathy' is a satirical attack on popular newspaper coverage aimed at whipping up mass hysteria against the Germans. A group of men in a pub decide to loot and steal from German-owned shops, using the excuse that what they are doing is an attack on 'Prussian *Kultur*':

> Yes, even the coppers themselves took a part,
> With a cutlet apiece from Sid 'Awkins's cart,
> As a positive proof that they shared in our feeling,
> And did not confuse moral protest with stealing.

This poem was published in 1916, proving if further proof were needed that the use of colloquial language was well established long before Sassoon adopted it. No jingoism here, no unthinking patriotism, but a strong distaste for the hypocrisy bred by war. 'The Survival of the Fittest' is dedicated to two men known to Squire who died on active service, and prefaced by an extract from a newspaper dated 30 March, 1915, in which a certain Mr Tompkins announced that without war 'the race would degenerate'. Squire's response is stinging. He gives a list of reasons why the two men he knew joined up, and then dismisses the reasons:

> Romance and rhetoric! Yet with such nonsense nourished,
>   They faced the guns and the dead and the rats and the rains,
> And all in a month, as summer waned, they perished;
>   And they had clear eyes, strong bodies, and some brains.

His point is that the men are worth far more than Tomkins, and the poem is remarkable for its accurate and detached observation of the motivation of so many young men when enlisting, for its wholly unglamorous view of war, and for the fierce emotion it reflects. Taken together, the two poems reveal an intelligent and sensitive man highly aware of both the horror and the cost of war, and driven to great anger by the way in which popular culture responds to it. Squire was writing in 1915, before the full reality of the war had been brought home to the general public, and he had no particular military links, unlike Edward Marsh. Marsh was in high government office, but chose not to speak of what he must have known about the true nature of the war. Squire spoke out: it was a brave act from a man of considerable integrity who has been too easily dismissed by post-Second World War opinion.

The appeal of his poem 'To a Bulldog' is unashamedly sentimental, though I have to say that I have yet to show this poem to anyone who has owned a dog and found them unmoved by it. The basis is simple: Willy, an artist, joins up and leaves his wife and their bulldog behind. The speaker is Willy's wife, musing by the fireside:

> We shan't see Willy any more, Mamie,
>   He won't be coming any more:
> He came back once, and again and again,
>   But he won't get leave any more.
>
> We looked from the window and there was his cab,
>   And we ran downstairs like a streak,
> And he said 'Hullo, you bad dog', and you crouched to the floor,
>   Paralysed to hear him speak,

A number of stanzas follow harking back to old and happy times, until:

> And though you run expectant as you always do
>   To the uniforms we meet,
> You'll never find Willy among all the soldiers
>   In even the longest street,
>
> Nor in any crowd; yet, strange and bitter thought,
>   Even now were the old words said,
> If I tried the old trick and said 'Where's Willy?'
>   You would quiver and lift your head,
>
> And your brown eyes would look to ask if I were serious,
>   And wait for the word to spring.
> Sleep undisturbed: I shan't say that again,
>   You innocent old thing.
>
> I must sit, not speaking, on the sofa,
>   While you lie asleep on the floor;
> For he's suffered a thing that dogs couldn't dream of,
>   And he won't be coming here any more.

The manuscript of this book has been read by a number of people, and one of them, a highly intelligent critic, pointed out that at times I appeared homophobic, which I am not, and that at others a strong feeling of fairly desperate paranoia crept into this work. The latter accusation is undoubtedly true, and springs in large part from having spent so long preaching (or at least feeling) some politically very incorrect views. Among them is the fact that I like 'To a Bulldog'. I realized that such poems can arouse strong feelings when I started to deliver a lecture containing some of the finest and most moving poetry of the war (Owen's 'Futility' and 'Spring Offensive', Sassoon's 'To Any Dead Officer') plus lighter pieces such as 'To a Bulldog' and the scurrilous RFC version of the twenty-first Psalm. This created no problem with non-academic audiences, but some university audiences responded as if The Rolling Stones had been booked as the support act for Pavarotti. Squire's poem was 'sentimental' I was told (now there is a word to damn a poem with in the 1980s), 'far too lightweight' and 'sentimental rubbish'. It probably is, but it retains power to move me many years on from my first reading of it, and as such it must be worth something.

There is a danger that a sector of the academic Establishment closes down vast tracts of our taste-buds as far as the First World War is concerned, feeding us only the fantastic and rich creations of the great chefs, and forgetting sometimes that even the best gourmet can enjoy well-cooked fish and chips, or even a bacon sandwich. Squire's poem is neither, of course: more a farmhouse shepherd's pie, but like that pie, very good at what it sets out to do and blessed with no pretensions to do more.

Squire was a conventional figure, but he and Kipling both bit back at the war. G.K. Chesterton, best remembered for his Father Brown stories, was always more inclined to tilt at windmills, as well as some genuine enemies. A very talented artist and writer, he became a journalist and wrote widely as a thinker and humorist. He conducted well publicized controversies with, among others, Kipling, Shaw and H.G. Wells, and though Chesterton was never a member of anyone's party, except perhaps the Catholic Church after his conversion in 1922, his crossing swords with those famous figures and his situation at the centre of literary London made him in his own way a member of the Establishment.

Chesterton is typical of many well-known writers who were too old or ill to fight. He feels that the war is too important a subject not to write on, but is uncertain about the tone and manner to adopt. All too often the result is rather convoluted poetry, skilled in technique but unclear in its aims. Chesterton does share the guilt and loathing that feature both in Kipling's and Squire's work. 'To Captain Fryatt' he concludes:

> Why should you wake for a realm that is rotten,
> Stuffed with their bribes and as dead to their debts?
> Sleep and forget us, as we have forgotten:
> For Flanders remembers, and England forgets.

Bitterness at the older generation is as marked in Chesterton's poetry as it is in Kipling's and Squire's, as in 'Elegy in a Country Churchyard':

> And they that rule in England,
> In stately conclave met,
> Alas, alas for England
> They have no graves as yet.

The 1914–18 period was not a time to be old in England, reviled by young soldiers and by leading spokesmen of one's own age. I had not realized until beginning the research for this book that the bitterness shown by Owen and Sassoon to the older generation was mirrored by many of those who stayed at home. In literary terms the fact is worth nothing. In historical terms, it reinforces the impression that we have underestimated the knowledge, horror and guilt felt towards the war by the civilian population. I wonder if the reason for that underestimate is our glib assumption that all knowledge comes from the media, rigidly controlled between 1914 and 1918. With every village and hamlet having at least one man serving in the army, with published casualty lists and with common sense the general public were, I suspect, far less reliant on newspaper coverage than we in our age are on newspaper, radio and television news.

Chesterton can produce memorable two or four-line extracts, as when he writes of the 'simple' English soldiers,

> How small a shrivelled laurel leaf lies crumpled here and curled:
> They died to save their country and they only saved the world.

Chesterton has a command of rhythm that only Kipling and Sorley can equal, a skill which sometimes makes poems sound more convincing than they read.

Kipling, Squire and Chesterton were only three of the literary Establishment who wrote war poetry. Other established, highly respected and non-combatant poets who made at least some attempt to write about the war were Thomas Hardy, A.E. Housman, Henry Newbolt, John Masefield and W.B. Yeats. Even Hardy and Yeats can struggle to find the right voice with which to deal with the subject, and their war poetry confirms the impression that there is no substitute for direct experience. Or perhaps so much was written by those who actually fought that poetry relying on imagination of the experience lacks the authenticity we have come to associate with 'good' war poetry, and breaks with the variety of accepted house styles.

Hidden Voices

The First World War has more than its fair share of poets who became known or associated with one particular poem only. Alan Seeger's 'Rendezvous', Laurence Binyon's 'For the Fallen', Julian Grenfell's 'Into Battle', Cameron Wilson's 'Magpies in Picardy', Crosbie Garstin's 'Chemin des Dames', John McCrae's 'In Flanders Field' and Herbert Asquith's 'The Volunteer' are some examples.

Edgell Rickword is probably another such, his poem 'Winter Warfare' appearing in most anthologies. It deserves its fame. There are only five other poems in the war section in Rickword's *Collected Poems*. Each one is as impressive as 'Colonel Cold'. 'The Soldier Addresses his Body' has great scarcity value. There is a peculiar quality of prurience to much war poetry; no worry about detailed descriptions of wounds or the stench of rotting bodies, but a different value scale is used when anything sexual or even sensual is raised, this being the cue to transfer the poem into imagery that is purely emotional, or which uses coded language to suggest sexuality. Gibson, Davies and Sassoon are willing to run to a mention of syphilis, but while they are happy to dwell on the disease even they baulk at mentioning in any detail the process of acquiring it. Rickword's 'The Soldier Addresses his Body' is, I think unique. A young soldier addresses his body in easy, familiar terms, as if it were (as indeed it is) an old, tried and trusty companion. The poem's easy acceptance of heterosexuality and sensuality are refreshing after a diet of the intense male bonding that features in so many other poems:

> I shall be mad if you get smashed about,
> we've had good times together, you and I;
> although you groused a bit when luck was out,
> say a girl turned us down, or we went dry.

The following stanzas move into an apparently relaxed but actually tightly-structured vision of really rather innocent 'things we haven't done', before returning in the final stanza to the mood of the opening, at the same time gently dismissive of too much intellectual activity in the trenches:

> Yes, there's a world of things we've never done,
> but it's a sweat to knock them into rhyme,
> let's have a drink, and give the cards a run
> and leave dull verse to the dull peaceful time.

'Advice to a Girl from the War' sums itself up in the first stanza:

> Weep for me half a day,
> then dry your eyes.
> Think! is a mess of clay
> worth a girl's sighs?

Rickword has Sorley's ability to dismiss his own importance and place the war within a scheme of things rather than see it as a cancer that transforms and changes everything it touches. I find his 'Trench Poets' a remarkable poem. Here again, part of that attraction may be ill-founded and based not on a particular strength in the poem, but rather on the fact that it is so markedly different from so many others. Owen's 'Strange Meeting' states that, had he lived, the poet would have washed clean the chariot wheels; to Owen, following in the steps of Shelley, the poet can make a difference. Graves, Sassoon and Brooke were all very conscious of being poets, relatively young, and perhaps as a result touchingly committed to the concept of the artist as an actor rather than observer in life's drama. Rickword's poem stabs such an idea as neatly as a collector pins a butterfly to a display cabinet. Rickword's chum dies, so, macabrely, he reads him poetry to rouse him:

> I knew a man, he was my chum,
> but he grew darker day by day,
> and would not brush the flies away . . .
>   . . . I used to read,
> to rouse him, random things from Donne.

There is an intense black humour in the choice of poems and poets, and of course the poetry readings have no effect. Eventually,

> He stank so badly, though we were great chums
> I had to leave him; then rats ate his thumbs.

Poetry, Rickword tells us, is fine for the armchair but not for the front. If this poem were a racehorse its ancestry might be described as out of Saki by Edgar Allan Poe. It is self-mocking, and mocks literary concepts of war. It is also dark and brutal, ramming home with a cynical smile the callousness of war, the selfishness of survival, and the thin veneer that separates civilized man from a primitive lump of decomposing tissue.

'War and Peace' is notable for the lines,

> and seeing cool nurses move on tireless feet
> to do abominable things with grace,

and for the quiet bitterness of its vision of what will happen in old age to men who fought the war. 'Moonrise over Battlefield' is a glorious and vicious finale to the pre-war Georgian obsession with moonlight, possibly intentionally so. Standing watching the moon,

> Then I thought, standing in the ruined trench,
> (all round, dead Boche white-shirted slumped like sheep),
> 'Why does this damned entrancing bitch
> choose all her lovers among them that sleep?'

Rickword is a case of genuine neglect, and his blend of power, variety and ironic humour makes him an author who goes some way to bridging the gap between the essentially simple, narrative verse of the First World War and the far more intense, complex poetry of the Second. He is another member of a small band of authors (Graves, Blunden and Edward Thomas among them) who either took the war in their stride, or worked heavily to pretend that was what they were doing. Their verse is less dramatic than the more conventional, documentary poetry which sees the war as the only subject in a world which it is ruining, but in some instances its wider perspective gives it, as poetry, longer legs.

E.A. Mackintosh, Jeffery Day and Sidney Walter Powell

If this chapter were instead a whole book there would be several more authors whose work would repay closer examination. John Buchan, A.A. Milne, John Galsworthy, Osbert Sitwell, Robert Frost, A.E. Housman, Harold Monro and Alec Waugh all wrote interestingly on or about the war, and this list is by no means exhaustive. A host of authors produced at least a handful of effective war poems whose worth has hardly been recognized, including Arthur Graeme West, Wilfrid Halliday, Paul Bewsher, Rex Freston, Geoffrey Smith (a friend of J.R.R. Tolkien), Patrick Shaw-Stewart, Sidney Walter Powell and C. Blackall. From what is a very long list I have chosen three poets: Ewart Mackintosh, Jeffery Day and Walter Powell.

The choice of Ewart Mackintosh is the result in part of a far more famous figure. John Buchan (later Lord 'Tweedsmuir, and author of *The Thirty-Nine Steps*) wrote some very powerful poetry with a bias towards a Scottish outlook on the war. If it sounds strange to talk of a Scottish outlook (why not a Welsh or an Irish outlook, or even a Cornish or Lancashire outlook?) it is worth turning to the considerable number of poets of Scottish extraction who wrote on the war. Some of this poetry is very powerful, partly because Scotland is a nation with a strong military tradition, both of Scots fighting each other (I speak as the son of a Buchan loon and son-in-law of a man who fought the Second World War with the Scots Guards) and of sending a wholly disproportionate number of men to fight for English armies.

That Scottish military tradition is a peculiarly proud one, and different in type from that found with the English regiments. The difference is reflected in the poetry written by the Scottish soldiers, of whom by descent if not by regiment Charles Sorley could claim to be one. Charles Scott Moncrieff, Neil Munro, Ewart Mackintosh, George Menzies, Dugald MacColl, Joseph Lee, Violet Jacob and Hugh McDiarmid are only some of the authors who wrote with great variety and power about the war, and all with a recognizable Scottish strand in their verse. One part of Scottish culture is the existence of the 'extended family', where a form of parental responsibility extends beyond the nuclear family. The Scottish war poets show a tendency to treat their men as an extended family, something which can perhaps even be seen as a throwback to the clan system.

Of these authors, there is something particularly impressive about Ewart Mackintosh. Born in 1893, he won a scholarship from Brighton College to St Paul's, and went on to Christ Church,

Oxford. He joined the Seaforth Highlanders in 1915, won the MC and was killed in 1917. Despite being brought up in the south he was Scottish to the core, and the fact that he learned Gaelic and how to play the pipes recommended him greatly to the men when he joined up. Mackintosh won his MC when he carried Private David Sutherland a hundred yards through German trenches while being pursued by the enemy. Sutherland later died, and Mackintosh (known in the trenches as 'Tosh', and hugely popular with his men) wrote 'In Memoriam'. Its simplicity is intensely moving, and unlike so many of the young poets Mackintosh is seared to the heart by what it means to a father to lose a son. The poem is also typical of many of those written by Scots in that it places the casualty at home as well as on the front, increasing the sense of loss by seeing the dead man as not just another grey corpse on a battlefield, but a loss to a home and hillsides that will never be replaced.

> So you were David's father,
> And he was your only son,
> And the new-cut peats are rotting
> And the work is left undone,
> Because of an old man weeping,
> Just an old man in pain,
> For David, his son David,
> That will not come again.

In the manner of opposites in poetry, and just as Sorley and Sassoon can increase a sense of pain by being almost unemotional, the dismissive tone adopted to the father, 'Just an old man in pain', adds to the pathos.

Many poets would be content to leave it there. Mackintosh deceives his readers: his aim is to point to the bond that exists between (good) officers and their men. Mackintosh neither denies nor ignores the love between father and son; instead, he states that for all its strength the bond between officer and men is simply stronger. It is both an outrageous and an impertinent assertion, yet in Mackintosh's hands we can be made if not to agree with it then at least to understand why he makes the claim,

> Oh, never will I forget you,
> My men that trusted me,
> More my sons than your fathers'.
> For they could only see
> The little helpless babies

And the young men in their pride.
They could not see you dying,
And hold you while you died.

The Scottish poets inherit a strong military tradition, and also reflect an essentially feudal culture that nevertheless allows for strong bonding between, for example, farm worker and farm owner. The class difference existed, but it was an easy thing, had large areas where it did not apply and was based on a degree of respect. In stumbling to explain what I perceive as a major cultural difference between the English and the Scottish I am struggling to understand my own mixed cultural inheritance; perhaps I am seeing the past through tinted spectacles, but time after time there is a note in the Scottish poetry that sees the dead private as an equal, a note I fail to find in much equivalent English verse. One other very marked difference is a sense of history, a knowledge that victory and defeat, life and death, are eternal parts of war and in their basic form are no different from Waterloo to the Somme. Mackintosh may be torn by death and defeat,

By the unseen death that caught us
By the bullets' raging hail
Broken, broken, broken
Is the pride of the Gael.

But both are placed in the context of a warring nation and a pride in warfare. To modern minds this can perhaps be distasteful. Mackintosh comes near to providing another original against which a Wilfred Owen might write another 'Dulce et Decorum Est':

And our children dreaming,
Shall see your bayonets gleaming,
Scotland's warriors streaming
Forward evermore.

Yet it would be wrong to dismiss Mackintosh as a glorifier of war, and wrong to the tradition that helped form his vision. He had a deep hatred for 'fat civilians' who sent young men out to die. His response to a recruiting poster, 'Lads, you're wanted, go and help', stuck over a railway carriage wall was to write 'Recruiting':

Go and help to swell the names
In the casualty lists.
Help to make a column's stuff
For the blasted journalists.

Mackintosh felt the bond of comradeship with savage intensity. Like Sassoon he feels he is betraying his friends and comrades if he is not with them:

Filth and honour, and pain, and dying –
Dead friends of mine, oh, cease your crying,
    For I come back to you.

His poem 'The Dead Men' is a neglected masterpiece, too long to print here not because of the number of lines but because it is an integrated, finely-woven poem that falls into shreds if carved up for extracts. It concerns a moment when the poet hears 'The dead man talk with living men', but as it proceeds the reader loses track of who is dead and who is living, a faint echo of Owen's 'Strange Meeting' but even more marked than that poem by a 'charnel scent/Drifting across the argument'.

There is pride in Mackintosh's writing, but not at the price of horror. His skill is to combine the two in a way that is rare, and which suggests a remarkable maturity from a young man:

This is our Earth baptised
With the red wine of War.
Horror and courage hand in hand
Shall brood upon the stricken land
In silence evermore.

No bugles here: the silence that Mackintosh sees greeting his death is, like Sorley's rain, a symbol of an awareness of how very small man is in the scheme of things.

Another side to Mackintosh's output, left out here for reasons of space, is gloriously funny verse, often scurrilous, which he appears to have written for his men. It would probably be in very bad taste to publish a volume of Comic First World War Poetry; it would not be hard to fill it with good poetry, and Mackintosh's would rank highly.

Jeffery Day wrote only a handful of mature poems, perhaps not even half a dozen. He has achieved minor fame as 'the poet of the air': he was a brilliant fighter pilot who met his death when taking on six German aircraft. 'On the Wings of the Morning' is a much anthologized piece which actually has little to do with the war, but is rather a young man's cry of exultation at the sheer joy of flying. 'The Call of the Air', 'Coming Down' and 'The Joys of Flying' are variations on the same theme. The war does appear in his flying poetry, in two poems in particular. 'North Sea' is a vivid evocation of dreary, soul-destroying missions over a grey sea:

> Day on the drear North Sea! –
> wearisome, drab, and relentless.
> The low clouds swiftly flee;
> bitter the sky, and relentless.
> Nothing at all in sight
> save the mast of a sunken trawler,
> fighting her long, last fight
> with the waves that mouth and maul her.

'Dawn' is a poem that rests on its opening stanzas:

> 'Machines will raid at dawn,' they say
> It's always dawn, or just before:
> why choose this wretched time of day
>   for making war?

After a chill portrayal of combat flying, the poem descends into silliness and unconvincing flippancy. My interest in Day came not so much from his flying poems, but from glancing through the pitifully thin volume of his work, *Poems and Rhyme*, published after his death. And again, it was a surprise. 'An Airman's Dream' is not really an airman's dream at all; it is the dream of home of a well-educated and reasonably well-off English public schoolboy. There is a hint of 'The Old Vicarage, Grantchester', though without Brooke's ironic wit:

> And other things I'll have are these,
> large breakfasts and enormous teas,
> honey and homemade bread, still hot,
> and butter from an earthen pot,
> with new laid eggs and clotted cream.
> Oh Lord! – to think it's all a dream!

There is also an example of the best type of Georgian writing: simple, personal observation, lyric intensity and genuine passion without stridency. 'To My Brother' is an extended lament, but one of the most effective of its type that I have read. It is another poem that suffers when quoted in extract, but a taste is

> And when one day the aching blow did fall
> for many days I did not live at all,
> but, dazed and halting, made my endless way
> painfully through a tangled growth of grey
> and clinging thorns, dismal, towards belief,
> and uncontrollable, heart-racking grief.

Day has an easy, accomplished way with rhyme and metre; both are handled and driven with the same effortless ease with which he seems to have handled an aircraft. There is none of the clashing, crunching twist of syntax that a number of younger Georgians were reduced to when a convenient rhyme did not present itself, nor much use of the swaying, sleepy rhythms of pre-war poets using conventional form. There is facing up to grief, very sensitive and colourful use of nature imagery, and a disingenuous honesty that is never precocious or self-obsessed. So many 'in memoriam' poems are unbearably worthy, stilted and seeking to give stature to the dead person by the use of elevated and often archaic diction. Not so with Day, who manages that most difficult of things, to write simply and honestly of an overwhelmingly complex emotion.

'Leave' is a remarkable poem. Home on leave, an airman walks through fields and woods, then lies down to sleep in a favourite glade. All very familiar stuff, the mainstay of every imitator of the Georgian poets, but it is well done and makes one regret that the much-abused word 'charming' can no longer be applied to a poem without damning it – all until the last line:

> So soft and peaceful was the sound,
> so pure was everything around,
> so cool and fresh the friendly ground,
> that I dreamed there was no war.

The tendency in verse of the time was to use nature as a retreat from war and suggest that nature was the reality, war the aberration. By his last line Day shows up the preceding pastoral wander as what it is: a dream, and a dream confounded by the reality and presence of war. The reality is war, nature the dream.

One of the great clichés of war poetry is the 'if only he had lived' approach. The tragic but logical nature of war meant that, not surprisingly, very many poets did not live, and inevitably did not have time to produce a large body of work. It has always seemed to me that there has been too great a tendency to judge war poets by quantity as well as quality. I cannot believe that Charles Sorley is not a great poet, for all that he wrote only a handful of poems of lasting merit. A compromise answer would be a new anthology consisting entirely of the best work of those of whom it has most often been said 'if only they had lived to write more poetry . . .'. I would be more than happy to keep by my bedside a book containing the acknowledged work of Charles Sorley, Rupert Brooke, Jeffery Day, Julian Grenfell, Ewart Mackintosh and Arthur Graeme West, with five or six other names that could very easily be added. Prospective publishers please write to the address below . . .

It was not an early death that bothered Sidney Walter Powell, who was born in 1878 and died in 1952. His epic poem 'Gallipoli' had to wait until 1933 to be published, and then only made it by means of deception. Powell submitted it to a competition for poets under forty years of age; then aged fifty-four, Powell won, much to the annoyance of the competition's judge, John Masefield. Powell returned the prize money, but did get his poem printed in the *Poetry Review* a year later. Buchan & Enright published his book *Adventures of a Wanderer* in 1986, with the full text of the poem. The easiest comparison is with David Jones's *In Parenthesis*. 'Gallipoli' is a poem clearly written, or at least finished, long after the event. Its style owes more to T.S. Eliot than to Shelley or Wordsworth, and after reading it one is more aware of Keith Douglas, arguably the best poet of the Second World War, than of Wilfred Owen. The emotion is implied rather than stated. At times it has a cold, clipped objectivity that suggests the poet using the techniques of verse to distance himself from pain and memory. The imagery is sharp and frequently memorable:

> There goes another boat.
> This shuts up like a jack-knife, the blade upon the handle,
> And disrupts, leaving a dark molecular bobbing residue.

The knife image is violent yet almost surgically clean, like the deaths of men observed from afar. Powell's imagery has a callous edge, as when he describes the soldiers reaching the beach and racing up it from the boats:

> We do not pause. We stoop low and rush.
> They are the goal. We are the ball.
> Propelled, we go.

Soldiers as the ball in a game of rugby or soccer is a compelling image. The ball is insentient, or deemed such by those who command it, kicked and treated with the utmost violence by teams who are competing for nothing terribly important. Powell captures the insensitivity of war, and most of all the feeling of being pinned to the wheel, powerless in oneself and yet threatened by so much overwhelming power.

Women's Poetry of the First World War

To entitle a section 'Women's poetry of the First World War' is to patronize it, suggesting a neat, tidy little patch that has to be examined to give the ladies their small due measure of credit, but which must after all take second place to the great games played by the boys. If that is the impression given here it is wholly unintentional, and the discovery that women had written as powerfully about the war as men was one of the greatest revelations both of my doctoral thesis and of the work that went into preparing an anthology of war poetry.

Near where I was brought up in Yorkshire there lived a man and his two sisters. The man, an old Marlburian, had joined up in the ranks when war broke out. His two sisters both lost their fiancés in the war, and never married. They were, in one sense, the fortunate ones, with independent means and the freedom to carve out a life for themselves after the war. Yet it was quite clear that both had been devastated by their loss, recognizing that something good was gone forever from their lives, and that both knew things they had viewed as part of their human inheritance – love, marriage, children – would now no longer be theirs. They were not people to complain. One of them played golf for Yorkshire ladies well into her sixties and drove ferociously large Jaguars at daredevil speed round the country roads west of Sheffield. They came from a generation which saw grief as a private act, and seeing their courage I have never been able to bring to the phrase 'stiff upper lip' quite the regulation amount of derision.

But they *were* the lucky ones. The world after 1918 had a long way to go before it allowed women independence. War widows, single parents and those for whom there simply was no partner in their age range were given a life sentence. It is hard sometimes not to believe that their men had the better deal. One might argue, like Owen's officer in 'A Terre', that life is good at any price, but many of those who died did so in the instant obliteration of an artillery shell or a bullet through the head or heart, and on the way to death they had comradeship, the romance of uniform and the appalling excitement of war. Some women did, of course, have the equivalent excitement: for all the danger and horror of the munitions factory it was good work for good money to many girls, enjoying for the first time regular employment, comparatively high income and increasing social possibilities in the relaxed wartime atmosphere. Others became nurses, or took on jobs that before the war had been reserved for men.

To counterbalance that excitement there was the drear fact that society allowed women very little positive action, casting them in the role of waiters, watchers and carers. For many that meant trying not to think about what was happening to father, brother, husband or lover in France, dreading the ring on the door or the frantic call at work. For those who lost someone (and there were hardly any spared from contact with that fate in one form or another) there was the struggle to bring up children on a meagre pension in a world which had little to offer the single parent but sympathy, and sometimes not even that. Comradeship supported the men in the trenches and helped to make the unbearable bearable. There was friendship for the women at home, and support, but also a dreadful loneliness that very few soldiers on active service ever experienced, and sometimes a dreadful frustration at the burden of so much watching and waiting with no cause for action. All this is revealed in the poetry written by women in the First World War, and it is a remarkable record in social as well poetic terms.

For obvious reasons women could not share the experience of front-line service. Comparatively few women attempt to write directly about combat, though in the first year or so there is little difference between the women who try to recreate the actual fighting and the stay-at-home men who did the same thing: both live in a world of armour and lances and outmoded concepts of chivalry. However, some women poets can capture the horror of trench warfare, as does Ruth Comfort Mitchell in 'He Went for a Soldier'.

There he lies now, like a ghoulish score of him,
    Left on the field for dead:
The ground all around is smeared with the gore of him –
    Even the leaves are red.
The thing that was Billy lies a-dying there,
Writhing and a-twisting and a-crying there;
    A sickening sun grins down on him –
    Billy, the Soldier Boy!

Helen Hamilton's 'The Romancing Poet' deals in short order with poets who seek to make war glorious, revealing a keen, intuitive feeling for the reality of war shared by many who were not directly involved in fighting:

> The blood, the filth, the horrors,
> Suffering on such a scale,
> That you and I, try as we may,
>   Can only faintly vision it.
> Don't make a pretty song about it!
>   It is an insult to the men,
> Doomed to be crucified each day,
> For us at home!

The women poets may often have had an intuitive sense of war's horror, but none that I know of have any comprehension or apparent awareness of comradeship, the intense bonding between groups of men and the sanctifying power of friendship between 'pals' at the front. In women's poetry the relationships are one-to-one, usually between the woman and a single soldier, a woman and her child, or the nurse and her patient. There is the same tendency one sees in the poetry of Owen and Sassoon to isolate one single figure for compassion and tenderness, and avoid the large canvas or even broad generalization. There is a deal of writing along conventional lines on honour, glory and sacrifice, but precious little exultation in the work of the women writers, unlike, for example, Rosenberg's 'Flame Out You Glorious Skies'. On my limited reading very few women indeed saw the war as cleansing or purifying.

There are some remarkable poems for which there is simply no equal in tone or subject among the men's writing. One of the most remarkable is by Helen Mackay, who sadly finds no place in Catherine Reilly's excellent anthology of women's war poetry, *Scars Upon My Heart*. Her poem 'Train' shows an officer waiting for the train to start to take him back to France. His three children are there with their nurse to say goodbye; their mother is presumed dead. For some reason the train will not start, and the awful moment of parting is extended until it seems as if the onlooker will be torn apart by the agony of the waiting. The poem is punctuated by a tearing refrain,

> Will the train never start?
> God, make the train start!

By the time we reach the end of the poem we would be willing to push it with our bare hands. The officer and his daughter stare at each other silently, she from the platform, he from the train,

> They hold each other's hands
> across the window ledge.
> And look and look,
> and know that they may never look again.

with the last line forming another intermittent refrain. Sentimental? Yes, perhaps, in the manner of Squire's 'To a Bulldog', but also based on simple observation of an immediately recognizable scene, and presented in fairly bare terms for us to reach our own conclusions as much as to share the poet's vision. This is a poem built from the simplest of materials. It freezes a moment in time, and to me at least has more genuine anguish than a hundred descriptions of exploding shells and dismembered bodies.

If Helen Mackay's poem is helped by skilful use of repetition, Jessie Pope takes a leaf out of Walter de la Mare's and Wilfrid Gibson's book and uses a refrain whose very normality makes it almost manic. Pope produced three volumes of war poetry, one of which apparently inspired Owen to write '*Dulce et Decorum Est*', but the impression given by that fact is slightly at odds with the tenor of at least some of her writing. One poem is another illustration of how extremely powerful poetry can be made out of simple ingredients: a woman is sitting knitting socks, trying not to think. As her mind leads her inexorably to conclusions she does not wish to reach, the knitting pattern intervenes and returns her to sanity – '*Purl the seam-stitch, purl and slip./Knit two, catch two, knit one, turn.*'

There seems to be less outright anger and bitterness in women's poetry than in comparable work by men, but there are many more poems expressing a deep, lasting sorrow or loneliness. Margaret Postgate Cole comments on the life sentence imposed on many women by the loss they suffered in the war:

> But we are young, and our friends are dead
> Suddenly, and our quick love is torn in two;
> So our memories are only hopes that came to nothing.
> We are left alone like old men; we should be dead
> – But there are years and years in which we shall still be young.

The prevailing impression left after reading collections of women's verse is not of pity, nor even protest, though large numbers of

poems express both, but of pain and loss. Mary Wedderburn
Cannan's 'Lamplight' is representative of many:

> We planned to shake the world together, you and I
> Being young, and very wise.

Youth and the past are recreated, the 'great dreams of our future'
and the fact that the man asked simply of fame,

> . . . crossed swords in the Army List,
> My Dear, against your name.

The final stanza faces the present and future:

> We shall never shake the world together, you and I,
> For you gave your life away;
> And I think my heart was broken by the war . . .
> There's a scarlet cross on your breast, my Dear,
> And a torn cross with your name.

This sense of finality, loss and poignancy is subtly different from
anything I have found in male writing. It is not simply that the
women did not fight, rather that many of the female poets had to
face up to carrying on living, whereas the men simply had to face
up to dying.
   A number of poems express fury at the passive role enforced
upon women:

> . . . O, damn the shibboleth
> Of sex! God knows we've equal personality.
> Why should the men face the dark while women stay
> To live and laugh and meet the sun each day.

Rose Macaulay treats the same theme in lighter style:

> Oh, it's you that have the luck, out there in the blood and muck:
>   You were born beneath a kindly star;
> All we dreamt, I and you, you can really go and do,
>   And I can't, the way things are.
> In a trench you are sitting, while I am knitting
>   A hopeless sock that never gets done.
> Well, here's luck, my dear – and you've got it, no fear:
>   But for me . . . a war is poor fun.

I have never known how ironic this poem is intended to be. Perhaps, like Sassoon's 'The Kiss', it can be read both ways.

Social conventions of the time dictated that a number of men and women would write poems about the corruption of nature implicit in women making munitions of death, whereas their true role in life was, of course, to be mothers and offer nurture. There are some unintentionally comic poems where comparisons between nipples meant to give milk to babies and shell caps meant to sow destruction on the heads of men could lead to serious confusion for anyone not reasonably well informed about the details of female anatomy.

There is also a marvellous willingness in the poetry written by women to kick out at Establishment views. Women poets seem less likely to blame Germany, but have an acute eye for cant and humbug. Perhaps this was a self-selecting exercise, where only women of strong views and personality felt able to rouse themselves to the effort of writing poetry and getting it published in what was still firmly a man's world. Certainly there were some glorious eccentrics among the leading women writers of the time, such as Edith Sitwell with her lifelong commitment to rebellion and decision to wear medieval dress, Rose Macaulay, whose zest for life would have consumed whole regiments, and Nancy Cunard, who after a disastrous marriage specialized in doing things perhaps because they were things no woman would have been expected to do. Edith Sitwell's 'The Dancers' has all de la Mare's command of rhythm and more than a dash of Edgar Allan Poe's *Masque of the Red Death*. Helen Hamilton gives short shrift to women who mocked men in civilian clothing on the buses:

> These twice-insulted men,
>   What iron self-control they show,
>   What wonderful forbearance!. . .
>
> You shame us women.
> Can't you see it isn't decent,
> To flout and goad men into doing,
>   What is not asked of you?

Winifred M. Letts gives equal measure to those who condemn a deserter in her poem 'The Deserter', and is well aware also of the irony found in much male writing of the proud mother who does not realize how despicably her son died.

Inevitably, given the practicalities of women's social position and perceived role in 1914–18, women's poetry is more concerned with children than comparable men's writing; indeed, it would be very hard to be less concerned with children than most of the famous male writers. In Teresa Hooley's 'A War Film' a woman is thrown into panic by seeing a film of the Mons retreat, and runs home to her son:

My little son . . .
Yet all those men had mothers, every one.

How should he know
Why I kissed and kissed and kissed him, crooning his name?
He thought that I was daft.
He thought it was a game,
And laughed, and laughed.

Other women poets worry about boys playing with toy guns and soldiers. The sentiments may be simple, but they are not simplistic, and the better women poets seem bent on avoiding sucked sugar stick at all costs.

Certain themes are common between men's and women's verse. The wounded feature widely in the writing of both, more so with women because of the number of nurses who wrote from first-hand experience. Women poets seem less willing than their male counterparts to go one stage beyond the actual wounded into apportioning specific blame for the injuries, either to generals, profiteers or those who stay at home and support the war. Indeed, generals come out well from a study of women's verse, if only by process of omission. Pity and disgust are present in equal measures in both genders, and fascination with the maimed and those who go mad. Like men, women use the environment in which they exist to describe their reaction to the war. Front-line scenery is exchanged for the street, the drawing room or the munitions factory, but nature and pastoral variations feature largely in both camps. Women poets are as keen to use colloquial language as their male counterparts; many damn those of their own kind who hand out the white feathers, as they damn in equal measure profiteers or those who support the war through self-seeking vain-glory.Others, such as Jessie Pope, seem actively to support the white-feather brigade.

The differences between male and female war poetry are sometimes to do with the fact that at least some of the female poetry was written with hindsight and after the war had finished. An impression, though not one based on any particularly deep analysis, is that the female poetry is more balanced and less heightened in tension and tone than that written by men under the stress of active service and combat conditions. This does not make female poetry any less effective, merely different in tone. The overwhelming difference between the two genders seems to me to be the awareness of time and the endless vista of loneliness opened up before so many women. It is summed up for me in Gabrielle Elliot's 'Pierrot Goes to War':

> Bugles, ghostly bugles, whispering down the wind –
> *Dreams too soon are over, gardens left behind.*
> *Only shadows linger, for love does not forget –*
> *Pierrot goes forward – but what of Pierette?*

We have fallen into the trap of believing too often that the only valid experience of war is that of those who fought it. The evidence is on the cover of every new anthology that comes hot off the presses, usually seeking to make as its first claim that its contents were penned by those who experienced combat at first hand. It is easy to forget that wars are fought also by those who make the munitions, tend the wounded and have to face life without those they love, and that those who do not actually fight can experience war and its pain as vividly as those who hold a rifle in their hands. Women's poetry is war poetry as much as is Owen's or Sassoon's. It is often a picture taken from a different vantage point; it is perhaps not surprising that its conclusions are very often the same.

There is, I think, a growing realization that the poetry of the First World War is more than Owen, Sassoon and Rosenberg. There is profit in this, provided the impression is not given that there were others who did better than Owen, Sassoon and Rosenberg what they did so well. What lies beneath the most famous authors is not a pile of dead rivals, but a range of alternative visions as varied and as rich in character as the men who fought the war. If my personal preference is for the women's verse written on or about the war, it is because women's poetry is a significant body of work the existence of which I did not suspect until a few years ago, and which seems to me to offer both an alternative and a confirmatory view of the war to that presented by the trench poets.

CHAPTER SEVEN

The Famous Five

Owen, Sassoon and the Single Man

I first read Wilfrid Gibson's *Collected Poems* after spending nearly a fortnight immersed in the poetry of Sassoon and Owen, preparatory to writing an article on Owen's 'Strange Meeting'. Coming after such total immersion, Gibson's work was a profound shock, not because of its description of bloody incidents or trench horrors, but because it was clearly written by an older, married man with an awareness of what it meant to have children. The poets I had been brought up on – Owen, Sassoon, Rosenberg, Graves, Blunden and Sorley – wrote entirely from the perspective of the young, single male, and it was that voice which I had come to associate with the war, and which I saw as representative and typical.

In many respects that assumption was reasonable; the majority of recruits were relatively young single men. In other respects it was not. The fact that a large number of older men volunteered and were conscripted is evident if one looks only at the literary roll of honour, with Edward Thomas and Hector Hugh Munro ('Saki') being middle-aged, and Sassoon no longer in the first flush of youth. Many BEF and territorial soldiers were far from youthful, and the effect of high casualties was to increase the number of older men joining up or being conscripted, as well as increasing the number of the very young. It is not even true that war poetry was written predominantly by those under twenty-five years of age. Brian Gardner's marvellous anthology of First World War poetry, *Up the Line to Death*, is an extremely representative work, and nearly sixty per cent of the authors listed in his biography were born before 1890.

But a majority of the best poets of the war were either very young

(Owen, Rosenberg, Graves, Sorley) or were single men who wrote with a similar perspective on life (Sassoon and Brooke). Part of that perspective is the upper and middle-class convention of a man marrying late, in his thirties or even forties, in direct contrast to the working-class convention of men marrying young. It is therefore quite a shock if one's vision of a war has been formed by Owen and Sassoon, to find Gibson on the deck of a crowded troopship with a fellow soldier, the final lines of the poem being,

> He comes from Flanders home to his dead wife,
> And I, from England, to my new-born son.

In Gibson's poetry, marriage is the normal state. In the poetry of Owen, Sassoon, Brooke, Rosenberg and Graves, marriage is the socially-acceptable means whereby victims are produced. Women are the producers of the victims. To add insult to injury, women do not have to fight themselves. Children are symbolic figures in Owen's and Sassoon's work, innocent but uncharacterized victims, whilst parents are those who send the boy off to die horribly in '*Dulce et Decorum Est*', or who are described in 'S.I.W.':

> Father would sooner him dead than in disgrace, –
> Was proud to see him going, aye, and glad.
> Perhaps his mother whimpered how she'd fret
> Until he got a nice safe wound to nurse.

The guilt of the older generation, of those who stayed at home and of women are frequent topics in Sassoon's work, as in 'The Fathers':

> Snug at the club two fathers sat,
> Gross, goggle-eyed, and full of chat.
> One of them said: 'My eldest lad
> Writes cheery letters from Bagdad.
> But Arthur's getting all the fun
> At Arras with his nine-inch gun.'

Gibson is kinder, by and large, to parents who wave their sons off to war than are Owen and Sassoon. Most poets who were parents themselves felt and wrote differently from those who were childless. There is a personal bias in this. I know I became as a teacher rather more understanding of parents when I had children myself. After being a parent one realizes why parents make so much fuss. Perhaps that is why poems such as Owen's 'S.I.W.' have always caused me to feel a slight irritation. Does Owen really believe that most fathers pack their sons willingly off to war? Does he not realize that if revenge on a parent was needed then killing their child more than pays off any debt? I suspect he never did, because nothing short of a miracle or telepathy could have given the rather self-worshipping son of a doting mother the experience he required to realize precisely what is invested by a parent in a child. Gibson did not have the talent of Owen, nor anything near Owen's power, but I think this at least he did understand.

> He went, and he was gay to go;
> And I smiled on him as he went –
> My boy! 'Twas well he didn't know
> My darkest dread, or what it meant –
>
> Just what it meant to smile and smile
> And let my son go cheerily –
> My son . . . and wondering all the while
> What stranger would come back to me.

In Owen's 'S.I.W' the smile is the rictus of a youth who puts a rifle in his mouth and pulls the trigger, so the parents hear 'Tim died smiling'; in Gibson, the smile is the artificial cloak a parent puts over his darkest fears, a neat illustration of the respective outlook of both poets. Father and son relationships occur frequently in Gibson's poems, with the anguish being shared equally. Owen's 'The Parable of the Old Man and The Young' sums up one view of the relationship between the generations:

> Offer the Ram of Pride instead.
>
> But the old man would not so, but slew his son,
> And half the seed of Europe, one by one.

In Gibson's poetry, as with Oxenham and Service, it is not quite so simple, and the sower and the seed are both victims of a tragedy they did not write and cannot control. The fact that Owen's and Sassoon's vision is restricted to that of the young, single man is one of the many reasons behind the power and strength of their writing. Youth translates into simplicity of viewpoint and energy, whereas the work of the older poets can be more diffuse and show fewer certainties; Edward Thomas's work is one example. In fairness to Sassoon, it should be noted that his poem 'The Hawthorn Tree' is the exception which proves the rule; in it he does seem to show a genuine sympathy for a father.

Owen, Sassoon and Homosexuality

If the most famous poetry of the war is the product essentially of a middle-class, single and male viewpoint, then it is also in large measure the product of poets who were homosexual, or at some time in their life were strongly influenced by homosexual feelings: Brooke, Owen, Sassoon, Graves and possibly Sorley are among the more obvious, though Graves's homosexuality seems to have been discarded by the end of the war. For many years the sexual bias of the trench poets was to me a matter of sublime indifference; in moral terms it still is, but in terms of a literary judgment on their work and an understanding of its power it seems to me to be increasingly important.

Wilfrid Gibson is again a pointer. His poem 'Long Tom' seems to drive home the fact that the major trench poets were writing from one very particular viewpoint. In many respects it is an inconsequential little piece. Like so much of Gibson's work, it takes a theme – the soldier seen in sleep – that has been beaten almost to death by other and more famous poets:

> He talked of Delhi brothels half the night,
> Quaking with fever; and then, dragging tight
> The frowsy blankets to his chattering chin,
> Cursed for an hour because they were so thin
> And nothing would keep out that gnawing cold –
> Scarce forty years of age, and yet so old,
> Haggard and worn with burning eyes set deep –
> Until at last he cursed himself asleep.
>
> Before I'd shut my eyes reveille came;
> And as I dressed by the one candle-flame
> The mellow golden light fell on his face
> Still sleeping, touching it to tender grace,
> Rounding the features life had scarred so deep,
> Till youth came back to him in quiet sleep:
> And then what women saw in him I knew
> And why they'd love him all his brief life through.

A very different version is given in Sassoon's 'The Dug-Out':

> Why do you lie with your legs ungainly huddled,
> And one arm bent across your sullen, cold,
> Exhausted face? It hurts my heart to watch you,
> Deep-shadow'd from the candle's guttering gold;

And you wonder why I shake you by the shoulder;
Drowsy, you mumble and sigh and turn your head . . .

You are too young to fall asleep forever;
And when you sleep you remind me of the dead.

Both poems take a sleeping figure and comment on the face in repose revealed by the golden light of a candle; Sassoon's poem ends on an explicit reference to death, Gibson's with an implicit one ('brief life'). So much for the similarities. The differences between the two poems sum up some of the most distinguishing features of the most famous war poets.

Sassoon's poem could be addressed to a lover. It is charged with a heightened sensuality, driven by five references to physical features ('legs', 'arm', 'face', 'shoulder', 'head') and three references to physical posture or movement ('legs ungainly huddled', 'one arm bent', 'turn your head'), all in the space of eight lines. The poem's strength lies in its sensuality and the total absorption of the poet with his subject, an absorption that reduces the world to one man gazing at another. That loving vision also gives the poem a lasting tenderness which makes it extremely moving. It is difficult to believe it is driven by a platonic vision of friendship, something which becomes clearer when it is compared with Gibson's treatment of the same theme.

Gibson's mention of 'Delhi brothels' plunges us immediately into the brutal, desensitized world of the professional soldier, presumably an intentional plunge into freezing water so that the following transfer into the warm bath of his sleeping 'tender grace' can have more impact. The man in Gibson's poem is not beautiful; he is fevered, foul-mouthed, 'haggard and worn'. The attraction is not the attraction of the poet towards his subject, but the attraction of women to the man, drawn to him by a tenderness that is only revealed in sleep.

Gibson's poem is about heterosexual attraction; Sassoon's poem is about an attraction, a bonding even, felt by one man for another. Gibson's poem is far less physical in its description, mentioning only 'chin', 'eyes' and 'face', and far less sensual. Sassoon's poem carries the implication of a very strong bond between the poet and the sleeping figure; in his poem only these two exist. Gibson's poem branches out into a web of relationships, with the poet taking a far more passive role as observer; he is almost the narrator in a Conrad novel, commenting dispassionately on events. This has the effect of weakening the poem, and removes from it that same tenderness that gives Sassoon's poem its power.

The sensuality applied to the male form in Owen's poetry can at times be almost overwhelming. Paul Fussell describes the desire of the bullet in Sassoon's 'The Kiss' and Owen's 'Arms and the Boy' to 'kiss' and 'nuzzle' the bodies of an adolescent boy as 'quasi-erotic'. There seems to me very little indeed to justify the use of the word 'quasi' in these poems, any more than in Owen's 'Greater Love' where the imagery is blatantly that of the sexual act. At the same time the word 'erotic', and Fussell's even clumsier 'homo-erotic', do a disservice to both Owen and Sassoon. John Donne had the arrogance and impudence to write of his God as he might write of his lover, and so produced some of the finest religious poetry ever written. From the same stable comes the power of the greatest war poetry ever written. Owen and Sassoon do not write erotic poems: they do not titillate, or see man as a physical object alone, or confuse the spasms of desire and physical love with any-thing that lasts. Instead they write love poems about the soldiers with whom they served and who they saw slaughtered, love poems where the overwhelming emotion of love totally demotes any need to talk of physical consummation. The tenderness and over-whelming desire of the man in a heterosexual relationship to protect his love are transferred to the officer's care and compas-sion for his men in Sassoon's 'Banishment':

> I am banished from the patient men who fight.
> They smote my heart to pity, built my pride . . .

> . . . Love drove me to rebel.
> Love drives me back to grope with them through hell;

These love affairs are consummated by death. The awareness of beauty, fragility and decay are all present in Sassoon and Owen's writing, as they are in the greatest love poetry. The purgatory of being parted from one's lover, the guilt, fear and remorse are pre-sent too, albeit in different form from the conventional love lyric, in Sassoon's 'Sick Leave':

> Out of the gloom they gather about my bed.
>   They whisper to my heart; their thoughts are mine.
>   'Why are you here with all your watches ended?
>   From Ypres to Frise we sought you in the Line.'

One of Owen's greatest love poems, and one of the greatest poems of the war, is 'Futility'. It is based on alternating images of heat and cold and has the physicality and sensuality of Owen's best work,

> Are limbs, so dear achieved, are sides
> Full-nerved, still warm, too hard to stir?

The explosion at the end is not an explosion of anger but of pity, compassion and loss. It would not be out of place as a lament spoken over the dead lovers at the end of *Romeo and Juliet*.

I do not know if Owen's and Sassoon's homosexuality was the catalyst that worked upon their poetic sensibility to produce their greatest work, or if it was merely one of many features. I suspect it was the former, and that their work can only be fully appreciated if it is seen as love poetry and not war poetry.

Rupert Brooke proved that an ability to develop strong relationships with men did not necessarily preclude the forging of equally strong relationships with women. Possibly because of their sexuality, but just as likely because of their upbringing and background, Owen and Sassoon are often as unsatisfactory when writing about women as they are moving when writing about men. All too often women are merely a convenient punch-bag. Owen can patronize women dreadfully:

> Whereas most women live this difficult life
> Merely in order not to die the death
> And take experience as they take their breath,
> Accepting backyards, travail, crusts, all naif;

and uses them as an object of ridicule and hatred, as with the young wife 'getting her fun' while her husband falls apart in 'The Dead Beat' and the women who hand out flowers in 'The Send-Off'. Girls ignore the disabled man in 'Disabled':

> Tonight he noticed how the women's eyes
> Passed from him to the strong men that were whole.

In 'The Kind Ghosts' Britannia (female) sleeps on,

> Her wall of boys on boys and dooms on dooms.

Sassoon is also vitriolic about women. He has moments of tenderness – 'brown-eyed Gwen' in 'In the Pink' and 'that lonely woman with white hair' in 'The Hero' – but these are offset by a poem such as 'Glory of Women'.

You love us when we're heroes, home on leave,
Or wounded in a mentionable place.
You worship decorations; you believe
That chivalry redeems the war's disgrace.
You make us shells.

Women are condemned for thinking only about their own particular man in 'Their Frailty', and condemned for their total
triviality and fawning worship of generals in 'Return of the
Heroes'. Sassoon's bitterness towards women is contained in only
a relatively small number of poems, whilst Owen's seems rather
more spread across his work. For both poets women are at best an
irrelevance, at worst a main part of the unthinking mass of people
at home responsible for supporting and prolonging the war. In
literary terms this hardly matters, any more than it matters that
neither poet understands children nor their parents; it is a small
price to pay for the blend of tenderness, compassion and outrage
that Owen and Sassoon cull from the war. But it does point to a
rather more important issue, the fact that for too long Owen and
Sassoon have been seen as presenting historical truth about the
war as distinct from emotional and artistic truth.

In many respects Owen and Sassoon make bad historians. They
are fixated by their own suffering and that of the men with whom
they served, and so cannot appreciate or understand the suffering
felt by those who bore children only to see them slaughtered.
Facing as they were the near-certainty of their own extinction, they
were not given the time to realize that a mortal's only claim to
immortality is children, and therefore did not understand that to
see one's child die is to see oneself die as well.

Owen and Sassoon are unrepresentative in many other ways.
They do not reflect the fact that front-line soldiers were arguably
more patriotic than those at home in 1918. Their vision of comradeship, the most potent and binding force of the war, is a limited
one. They perceive and express the bonding that exists between
themselves and the victims of the war, but often fail to show the
intense bonds of sympathy between the men themselves, and the
outwardly light and easy comradeship that is brilliantly described
in Frederick Manning's *Her Privates We*. In their desire to prove
that Someone Had Blundered neither poet looks to the root causes
of the blundering, or suggests a way out.

Neither is the slightest bit concerned about the reasons for fighting the war, despite the fact that a belief in resisting German
militarism was the only thing that kept some soldiers going.
Neither show the rewards of war nor come near to catching

Charles Carrington's comment that no one who had not under-stood the hell of combat could understand the heaven of leave. Neither show any awareness of the tremendous, almost over-whelming excitement felt by so many young officers, nor does their poetry reflect the huge bouts of boredom found interspersed with the concentrated moments of terror. Owen's 'Exposure' is the exception that, possibly, proves the rule. There is a vicious, satir-ical humour in both men, but no reflection in their poetry of the humour that made life possible for many in the trenches, nor of the coarse foul-mouthedness of the ordinary soldier.

Owen and Sassoon are therefore very bad historians. So was Shakespeare in almost every play he wrote, but the fact that Hal and Hotspur never did fight each other in history does not make *Henry IV Part I* any less great a play. The only danger comes if the roles of historian and artist are confused. The reputation of the war poets has suffered at times because they have been so closely associated with one particular and specific war. There is now almost no one alive who fought in that war. When the last survivor dies will perhaps be the time to recognize that Owen and Sassoon are not poets of the First World War, or even trench poets, but poets of war. Their power and artistry lies in the fact that they describe the human predicament as seen in war from one particu-lar, intense viewpoint, and their work and reputation need to be unlocked from the prison of four-and-a-half years between 1914 and 1918. They have also contributed strongly to the myth of the war as endless suffering, and been one of that myth's strongest foundations.

Wilfred Owen

Wilfred Owen is generally recognized as the greatest English poet of the First World War. Generations of critics have united in see-ing one poem in particular, 'Strange Meeting', as his finest. Writing in 1921, John Middleton Murry commented,

> The name and genius of Wilfred Owen were first revealed by the publication of his finest poem, 'Strange Meeting', in the anthology *Wheels* in 1919.[1]

In 1993 Merryn Williams wrote,

> Some time later he wrote his most famous poem, 'Strange Meeting', which, if all his other work had perished, would still have made his reputation. Sassoon called it his 'passport to

immortality', and recently *The Guardian* named it 'the poem of the century'. I do not quarrel with this verdict.[2]

Owen's reputation began to be established by the late 1920s, mainly because of the power of his poetry. Subsidiary factors helped him along the way. His cause was espoused by two of the most powerful poets to survive the war, Siegfried Sassoon and Edmund Blunden. Sassoon in particular proved a very loyal friend, and one who showed a different form of heroism from that which won him the MC by acknowledging that Owen was the greater poet.

Secondly, Owen had spent time in France before the war, and Dominic Hibberd proved that the influence of French poetry led to Owen's unusual use of para or half-rhyme, sometimes referred to as 'consonantal rhyme', where the preceding and final consonant are retained but the intervening vowel changed, as in 'swill/swell'. In using pararhyme Owen made himself the only war poet writing during the war who was anything other than traditional in his use of form. When T.S. Eliot revolutionized poetry by publishing *The Waste Land* in 1922 the revolutionary approach to form that had been the main point of Imagist anthologies moved from being fringe to being Establishment. A war poet who could claim to have a 'modern' approach to form was therefore doubly attractive.

Thirdly, Owen had the time to scribble a proposed preface or foreword for a book of his war poems. That preface contained the words:

Above all this book is not concerned with Poetry. The subject of it is War, and the Pity of War. The Poetry is in the pity.[3]

If an angel had descended on Owen to show him the best way to post-war popularity it could not have led him to better words. By his use of capital letters Owen derided 'Poetry' as something artificial and irrelevant, and by implication made his verse something altogether more real and telling. Owen set himself up as the spokesman for all that was real and meaningful. By his concentration on the word 'pity' he not only highlighted the most powerful emotion in his poetry but also staked a claim for pity to be seen as the only proper response to the war from succeeding generations. In the 1920s and 1930s that vision of the soldier as victim and the war as tragic waste came to represent exactly how the intellectual élite believed the war should be seen.

Fourthly, Owen had the good fortune to fall foul of W.B. Yeats.

Just when the war poets were reaching their apogee of popular acceptance. Yeats decided to exclude them from *The Oxford Book of Modern Verse* in 1936. In the days when the BBC banned records such a ruling could be guaranteed to increase sales significantly above what would have been expected if the record had been played all day and night. So the furore over Yeats' action fanned the flame of Owen's fame even further. Yeats justified the exclusion on the grounds that 'Passive suffering is not a theme for poetry'.[4] The exclusion caused an outcry, leading Yeats to comment in a private letter that he considered the work of the war poets 'all blood, dirt and sucked sugar stick'.[5] Yeats had the decency to comment about the war poets:

> There is every excuse for him [Owen] but none for those who like him.[6]

Fifthly, an evident progression in Owen's poetry allowed him to become almost an emblem for the poetic development visible in the war. He started off by writing highly romantic verse with a heavy and luscious influence from Keats and Shelley in particular. The famous meeting with Sassoon at Craiglockhart led to his poetry becoming far harsher and more realistic, with several poems written in the manner of Sassoon: colloquial language, savage satire and a 'hammer blow' final line – 'Dulce et Decorum Est', 'The Chances', 'The Parable of the Old Man and the Young' and 'The Letter' are usually seen as the best examples of the style. If Owen's second phase is often seen as him facing up to the reality of the war, then his third phase is an attempt to transcend the limitations of Sassoon's style and move completely into his own voice, best seen in such poems as 'Strange Meeting', 'Futility', 'Anthem for Doomed Youth', 'Miners' and 'Spring Offensive'. These poems can have an element of obscurity, focus with terrible power on the theme of pity and are unique in their poignancy and flavour. They also appear far more objective than much of his earlier work. Seen in this light, it is as if Owen by his movement from subjectivity to objectivity symbolizes the wider movement in poetry between 1914 and 1923.

Sixthly, and without intending any disrespect to a very great poet, Owen was easy to market. As Brooke had been in 1914, so was Owen in 1918, his life and death almost designed to make him an icon. He did not attend public school or university, powerful recommendations in the rebellious post-war backlash against the Establishment, yet he was clearly intelligent and well, if largely self, educated. Owen was certainly not working class, but neither was his family secure middle or upper middle class: placed in the peculiar English limbo of lower middle class, he could to an extent be seen as all things to all men.

It did not stop there. Owen opposed the war bitterly, and had been invalided home with shell-shock, thus gaining all the credentials of the victims he portrayed so vividly. Yet he also won the MC for an act of outstanding bravery and was a thoroughly professional officer. He was thus similar to Sassoon, able to appeal to both left and right without making either camp feel guilty. The manner and timing of his death also made very good copy, something he shared with Brooke and Rosenberg. Brooke, the 'young Apollo', died romantically in classical seas and was buried on a Greek island, the type of ending that a Hollywood scriptwriter might beg for. On a more raw and ironical note, Isaac Rosenberg, almost comic in his inability to conform to military standards and cursed with bad luck, was killed on April Fool's Day, 1 April, 1918.

Owen's death was equally apt, timed so that the telegram announcing it was received by his parents as the bells rang out to celebrate the Armistice. How fitting that the man who had dedicated his life to speaking for the men he commanded, and who had written more powerfully than any other about the reality of death on the Western Front, should in the closing days of the war go to join those dead millions for whom he spoke. It was almost as if Owen's death in the front line bestowed the final legitimacy upon him, and gave him the final authority to speak and write as he did. Unlike Sassoon and Graves, Owen did not live on trying for years to recapture the strength of his war verse, tinkering with it, dropping it from his *Collected Works* and moving between anger and frustration at the world's tendency to see him as a war poet. With the circumstances of his death the weaknesses in his poetry almost became strengths, the bubbles in the glass that shows it has after all been hand-blown by a craftsman.

A minor myth of the war is that surrounding Owen's 'Strange Meeting'. On a personal level I have never been able to share the general excitement felt for this poem. Its intensive use of half-rhyme may give it a ghostly, half-finished feel, very apt for a poem about unfinished lives, but the insistent and unrelenting need for a rhyme drags the diction and sometimes the sense out of line. The poem is a slave to its half-rhyme, the technique being thrust to prominence and taking a disproportionate amount of the reader's attention. Diction and sense must take second place to rhyme, as in the lines,

> Now men will go content with what we spoiled,
> Or, discontent, boil bloody, and be spilled.

196

'Spoiled' and 'spilled' is a good half-rhyme, but 'spilled' is a rather meagre and ineffectual word for the slaughter Owen needs to convey. To find a rhyme for 'progress' Owen has to write,

> They will be swift with swiftness of the tigress.

Tigress? It is a perfectly valid image of destructive speed, but only a few lines earlier Owen has made it clear that he is referring to 'men'; the choice of gender is dictated by technical rather than poetic need, and artifice interferes with expression to an unwelcome extent.

'Strange Meeting' also acts as a check-list of some of Owen's least valuable features. Its diction is archaic, artificial and often affected. Owen retreats into words and phrases such as 'Titanic wars', 'made moan' and 'sullen hall'. He caps it all in the lines,

> To miss the march of this retreating world
> Into vain citadels that are not walled.
> Then, when much blood had clogged their chariot wheels,
> I would go up and wash them from sweet wells,
> Even with truths that lie too deep for taint.

Various critics have pointed out that no soldier in Europe had gone to war in armour for several hundred years before 1914, but on the outbreak of war volumes of poems had the soldier donning his armour and, for good measure, taking his sword or spear in hand to assault the foe. Owen's sudden delving into archaic biblical imagery is equally unconvincing and is perhaps an attempt to give a rather spurious authority to his poem. Chariots may take the poem out of the context of the particular 1914–18 war, but they do not give it universality. Rather, they merely transfer it from one specific time to another. One wonders again if the need to rhyme 'sweet wells' dictated the choice of 'chariot wheels' as the relevant image. Whereas the effect of Owen's poetry is, more often than not, to bring us closer to some of the harsher aspects of the war's reality, 'chariot wheels' serves merely to take us further away. The chariot is an emblem for a type of warfare far removed from the bolt-action rifle and gas attacks, and with its Roman associations is an image of honour, glory and victory, precisely the glorious image of warfare that Owen seems to wish to avoid. In other poems and in the work of other authors biblical imagery can give depth and historical perspective; here it merely suggests straining after effect.

'Strange Meeting' also shows two other features of Owen's

work: an intense obsession with self, and a lack of any stringent intellectual structure. Most of the poem is taken up by a lament from the main speaker that he will no longer be able to change the world as a result of his death in action. Just as Brooke's patriotic sonnets are really about Rupert Brooke, rather than about England, so the speaker in 'Strange Meeting' shows particular pique at the chronic unfairness of his not being allowed to live and save the world. Any reader who has stood in the French graveyards and seen the crosses stretch for miles might well feel that this speaker can appear remarkably vain and precocious. There are hints of Tom Sawyer's frame of mind when he attended his own funeral, and Twain's marvellous caricature of adolescent self-obsession. The speaker will wash blood from chariot wheels and reveal truths too deep for taint, but he will only do so when a great deal of blood has been spilt. The dead are merely the means whereby the prophet gains honour. Presumably the effect would not be nearly as great if he acted before anyone got killed. There is supreme arrogance in the statement that because the speaker has died 'men will go content with what we spoiled'. I doubt that Owen really means to say that he or his imagined speaker are the only people capable of interpreting the horrors of war to posterity, but that is what he says. 'Strange Meeting' glorifies the poet and his sense of mission, which comes dangerously near to patronizing all the non-poets who died in the war or who survived it trying to make the post-war world a better place.

As might be expected in a poem written by Owen, 'Strange Meeting' has areas of sheer brilliance to match its weaknesses. Perhaps we should treat it as it has been said we should treat a Dickens novel, as a work of art that is great almost because of its weakness, rather than being great despite them. The first ten or thirteen lines of the poem are as vivid and disturbing as anything else written about the war. That we are in a dream vision is conveyed instantly, and for once the half-rhyme trap works to advantage. I can no more explain the power of 'groined/groaned' rhyme than Rosenberg could explain what he meant by 'the same old druid Time has ever' in 'Break of Day in the Trenches'; sometimes critics have just to point out that it works, and therefore does not need mending or explaining. By line thirteen we know that we are in hell, that the protagonists are removed from battle and probably dead, and that they know each other. The poem then goes on a long digression in which the main speaker bemoans his own death as robbing the world of something particularly splendid. It then gets back on course in the fortieth line, with the famous line,

I am the enemy you killed, my friend.

The point is clear. Owen the soldier has killed Owen the poet, and if this view is taken then the poem becomes a masterly and moving portrayal of a soul whose inner turmoil reflects the external tumult of war. If, to misquote Yeats, rhetoric comes from the conflict with others and true art from the conflict within ourselves, then the ending of 'Strange Meeting' is a perfect dramatization of one of the greatest internal conflicts to affect the war poets, the conflict which in another context led Owen to describe himself as a pacifist with a seared conscience. There is no answer to this conflict, except death, which in tragic fashion is seen as a release from suffering. Owen resists the urge to preach or conclude, ending the poem instead on 'Let us sleep now . . .'. The humility and sparseness of the final lines is in direct contrast to the fulsome, wordy and pretentious mouthings of the speaker between lines fifteen and forty-nine, whose certainty of self and inherent superiority would be offensive even if spoken by the Messiah.

'Strange Meeting' is structured rather like Marlowe's *Dr Faustus*, with a beginning and an end that make the middle look even more awful than it is. Yet the poem's popularity has something to do with changing fashions in poetry, and in particular the dominance exerted in the post-war period by T.S. Eliot. 'Strange Meeting' can be subject to multiple interpretations and contains irony. It is at times obscure, an obscurity which might be seen as wilful, and the main speaker could at a pinch be seen as one of Eliot's famous 'objective correlatives'. Its setting is that of a waste land, its mood one of sombre pessimism and its outlook bleak. Small wonder that post-war critics hailed it as the best of the bunch.

As a footnote to 'Strange Meeting', I am not aware that any connection has been made between Owen's poem and Sassoon's 'Enemies', written in January, 1917. The central figure harks back to the opening of 'Strange Meeting', where the dead soldier, a friend of Sassoon's,

stood alone in some queer sunless place
Where Armageddon ends.

Suddenly there 'throng round' the soldier the Germans Sassoon shot in his friend's name. They meet and talk, and the short poem ends.

> And still there seemed no answer he could make.
> At last he turned and smiled. One took his hand
> Because his face could make them understand.

There is the dream vision in a dark place removed from war; the conversation with dead enemies; the absence of an answer; a final vision of some form of reconciliation in an atmosphere of hopeless waste. Both poems represent the schizophrenic nature of the soldier-poet who kills and yet revolts against that killing. I wonder if 'Enemies' might not be the starting point for 'Strange Meeting'.

It can be argued that too much war poetry has been judged on the basis of how much it anticipated post-war poetry movements rather than on its own intrinsic merits. All the major war poets were brought up as members of an essentially Romantic tradition of writing, and the Georgian poets are the clearest symbol of that type of poetry. 'Strange Meeting' itself, for all its pseudo-Modernism, is a variation of the Romantic dream vision, and its obscurity firmly in the mould of Keats and his statement about truth and beauty.

It is possible that even without the push of the war the school of poetry represented by the Imagists would have edged out the Georgians, replacing subjectivity with objectivity, emotion with intellectual directness and sentimentality with irony, as well as treating form with the same cavalier disregard for fashion as the Georgians treated content. In any event, the war made that move inevitable. It is sometimes assumed that irony broke upon British poetry in 1916 like the plague on London in 1665. In fact the image is a valid one: irony, like the plague, had been around long before, but after the war achieved a strength and prevalence it had not reached for many centuries. As Paul Fussell has pointed out, the war posed too many questions, and after it a thinking observer might find it hard to see the world in anything but multiple and sometimes conflicting meanings; the literary equivalent of that uncertainty and the inevitable response to it is the ironic mode of writing. Similarly, the war gave much food for thought. Post-war taste demanded poetry which at least gave the impression of thinking; Romantic poetry seems to favour feeling.

Geoffrey Thurley has argued in his book *The Ironic Harvest* that all truly great literature must at some stage commit itself fully to its subject, and that no ironic vision, however good and powerful, can muster that commitment. In irony there always has to be an alternative. Whatever the truth of that argument, there has been a tendency from the outset to praise irony and objectivity where they appear in war poetry. Almost inevitably this produces a slightly distorted view of a group of poets for whom irony was at best a secondary technique, and helps create the myth that the predominant mode of writing was ironic. I would argue that Owen, and all the war poets, have too often been judged as the start of a new era rather than the culmination of an old one. To me they seem to be in some cases a final, tragic flowering of the English Romantic movement, in other cases firmly in a continuing tradition of English Romanticism.

In Owen's case, a modern article summed up the attitude found in many comments on Owen's work:

> This lingering Romanticism is often mentioned reproachfully, as though it were a survival of earlier bad habits from which Owen, dying young, had not yet freed himself.[7]

In fact Owen's achievement is similar to that of Keats and Wordsworth, where the sheer power of a personal vision can make it both personal and universal. Dennis Welland comments on this feature in Owen's greatest poem, 'Spring Offensive':

> the poetic imagination has transmuted the experience of others, giving it at once universality and yet the quality of an intensely personal vision.[8]

The Romantic pedigree of 'Spring Offensive' is impeccable. The men are about to launch an offensive, and Owen comments on the soldiers' ability to live for the moment, to feed, to loose their packs and sleep. There is more than a hint of Wordsworthian identification with the common man in all Owen's poetry, and here it has advanced to the extent of there being no distinction between officers and men. In his use of nature imagery Owen shows how much he had learnt from the Romantic tradition, and also how much he had refined it. Central to Romanticism is the tendency to heighten experience, and central to Georgian poetry was the tendency to use nature as the jumping-off point for the sublime moment of insight. Owen combines both techniques, replacing the Georgian profligate use of imagery with two central images – sky and grass. Many of the soldiers cannot sleep, but,

> face the stark blank sky beyond the ridge,
> Knowing their feet had come to the end of the world.

One yearns to read 'the end of their world', which the words 'stark' and 'blank' tell us it will be for many of the soldiers. The sky is blank, unyielding, taciturn; it tells the soldiers nothing. The poem then shifts to the long grass, seen as a symbol of life and summer.

> . . . oozed into their veins
> Like an injected drug for their bodies' pains

but at the same time the grass is a threat:

> Sharp on their souls hung the imminent ridge of grass.

Over the ridge lies the enemy, and shell-fire and death, so the ridge of grass becomes a suspended guillotine blade. Just as the grass can be soothing and life-giving and a source of destruction, so the sky changes mood in the line:

> Fearfully flashed the sky's mysterious glass.

Glass is unyielding, cold and hard. It should be transparent, but it has become hard and impenetrable, with Owen making unique cutting images out of both sky and grass.

The soldiers 'ponder the warm field', the buttercups bless their boots coming up, and the brambles clutch them like sorrowing arms. Then the attack is launched. The sun becomes 'like a friend with whom their love is done'. They are exposed on the 'open stretch of herb and heather'. From being impenetrable, 'the whole sky burned/ With fury against them'. Earth is seen as setting cups for their blood, with the grass, the 'green slope', 'charmed and deepened sheer to infinite space' becoming a vast slide to oblivion.

The images of grass and sky have been sustained, but turned on their heads as the poem progresses and made to represent the unspeakable violence and destructiveness of combat. Have the men alienated nature by their violence? Or is nature simply a mirror of mankind, reflecting back whatever mankind imposes on nature? The poem ends with a meditation on those who evade death and the effect of that avoidance on them, turning the whole poem into an examination of the heightened moments of attack, death and survival. It is a very successful attempt to describe in verse the vast complex of emotions that affected those who went 'over the top', a complexity that defeated many prose as well as verse writers.

It is tempting to point out that 'Spring Offensive' does not use the personal pronoun, 'I', that it depends for much of its effect on a manipulation of imagery, and that there is considerable irony in nature turning from beneficence to destruction. A harbinger for the 1920s and a triumph of Imagism? Hardly. Pararhyme is discarded and replaced by conventional, albeit irregular, full rhyme. The lines are bound together by controlled use of assonance and alliteration, a technique central to Keats's work – 'Sharp on their souls', 'Fearfully flashed', and the use within the space of two lines of 'Marvelling', 'May', 'murmurous' and 'midge' are some examples. Nature provides the store of imagery. The Romantic heightened sensibility is visible in a poem devoted to an exploration of an ultimate heightened experience of men facing death.

The universality of the poem is not based on any theme or conclusion from experience, but is an emotional truth drawn from individual observation. There is beauty in the versification, even on such an appalling subject, a sense of wonder, and no attempt to grasp the issues intellectually. Man is seen as bonded to nature in a way that is as palpable as it is unexplained. The poem has the intensity and the imagination of all great Romantic literature. Romanticism is concerned with an extreme assertion of the self and the value of individual experience, as well as with a sense of the infinite and the transcendental; when I came across those words scribbled in note form with no heading or accreditation (in fact they are from *The Oxford Companion to English Literature*) I automatically assumed they were a critic commenting on 'Spring Offensive', and filed them accordingly. The profundity of much Romantic writing comes from its reaction to the Enlightenment and its belief that not all things can be explained by man; 'Spring Offensive' is a great poem not least because it is prepared in the best tradition of Romanticism to describe that which it cannot explain.

It is difficult not to compare 'Spring Offensive' with Charles Sorley's much earlier poem, written before he had faced active service, 'All the Hills and Vales Along'. In Owen's poem there is the ironic contrast between the sleeping or resting men and the hell they are about to face. In Sorley's poem the men are singing on the march,

> And the singers are the chaps
> Who are going to die perhaps.

Both poems contrast the men's mood and their fate. In Owen's poem, brambles and buttercups seek to bless the men, while in Sorley's poem,

> From the hills and valleys earth
> Shouts back the sound of mirth,

Yet in Owen the earth suddenly sets cups for the men's blood, while in Sorley,

> Earth that blossomed and was glad
> 'Neath the cross that Christ had,
> Shall rejoice and blossom too
> When the bullet reaches you.

Rhythmically the poems are totally different, but the similarities in their treatment of nature make me wonder if Owen was, by 1918, familiar with Sorley's work. I am not aware of Owen mentioning Sorley in his letters, nor of him owning Sorley's work, but both Sassoon and Graves were fierce admirers of Sorley, and it seems impossible that one or both of them would not have mentioned him to Owen.

Siegfried Sassoon

Just as much critical attention has been devoted to 'Strange Meeting', so a disproportionate amount of attention has gone on Owen's satirical poems. '*Dulce et Decorum Est*' has become what Masefield's 'Cargoes' was to my generation, the one poem no schoolchild will ever be allowed to miss. Numerous other poems are written in the style of Sassoon, with a reliance more often than not on a final one or two-line hammer blow to ram the point home. There seems no doubt that Owen began writing in this style in emulation of Sassoon. Satire is essentially destructive, and as such imposes strict limitations on itself. In general Owen's satirical poems strain at the leash more than Sassoon's. The use of the Latin tag 'Dulce et Decorum Est' is a clear attempt to make Owen's protest apply to all wars, though it is not clear that this is achieved; the imagery and diction of Owen's poem, with its gas attack and 'five-nines', is more clearly that of the First World War than in almost any other poem he wrote.

Similarly, 'The Parable of the Old Man and the Young', by using a biblical story, goes along the same path as Graves's 'Goliath and David' and some of Rosenberg's poetry. Setting the poem in the biblical past gives the impression of a universal rather than a local experience, and the war is invested, in theory, with a timeless significance. Despite these efforts, and the immense skill Owen brings to what is a surprisingly difficult technique and form, the wider nature of his sensibility at times comes near to reducing the impact of the satire. Sassoon's style works best when it is hard, clipped and focused. Owen's primary emotion, pity, is sometimes too soft and gentle to sit easily by the hard bite of satire. For a start, Owen cannot resist concentrating on the individual – the son in 'The Parable of the Old Man and the Young', Jim in 'The Chances', the letter-writer in 'The Letter', Tim in 'S.I.W.', the gas victim in 'Dulce et Decorum Est'. This gives the poems their own power, but differentiates them from Sassoon's work, where if there is a central figure he is often more universalized and less of an individual, and as a result becomes more representative.

Sometimes Sassoon achieves this wider scope by the simplest of techniques, as when he makes two soldiers, Harry and Jack, comment in 'The General' rather than one individual. Sassoon also has an eye for local detail that Owen ignores, possibly because Owen is always seeking to set his sights higher. Sassoon is less proud, and indeed delights in inserting homely, peacetime detail into poems that drive home the horror of war. There are those in 'Does It Matter?' who

> . . . come in after hunting
> To gobble their muffins and eggs.

Davies, in 'In the Pink', has had his drink of rum and tea. The soldier in 'The One-Legged Man' surveys

> A homely, tangled hedge, a corn-stalked field,
> And sound of barking dogs and farmyard fowls.

The sight that causes thanksgiving to leap in the heart of the 'Stretcher Case' is

> Large, friendly names, that change not with the year,
> Lung Tonic, Mustard, Liver Pills and Beer.

This homeliness of detail does not appear to Owen's satirical work, whose sense of the poet's high purpose might see in such detail a potential loss of dignity.

Sassoon's satirical poems are highly effective, but in one sense it is a pity that they have received so much attention. They play into the hands of those who see the poetry of the war as one-dimensional and lacking in any intellectual depth. Some of these poems fall apart once they are subjected to any close examination. In 'Blighters' he invites the tanks to storm a music-hall audience, while in 'Fight to a Finish' his trusty fusiliers turn on the yellow pressmen and parliament. The first response to the war, suggesting that the violence of the front is perfectly acceptable if brought home and applied to civilians, is a poem of pure hate, its emotions as unreasoning and unthinking as the very ones Sassoon sets out to satirize. 'Fight to a Finish' is simple fascism, arguing that moral and ethical problems are best solved with bayonet and rifle.

Many of Sassoon's other satirical poems are also hymns of hate. Their effect is one of huge initial shock, but the shock can leave an unpleasant aftertaste. In 'The Bishop' there is no attempt to place any form of interpretation on the immense complexity of the war. It is reduced to one equation: men are dying and suffering, and therefore it must stop instantly. The cause of the war is the support given to it by the Church. In other poems, the war is either caused or carried on by women, by the Establishment, by the older generation or by senior generations. All these figures, individually and collectively, are stupid, ignorant and callous. The poems are a graffiti daub, violent, powerful but one-dimensional. It is no accident that they are among the poems most commonly used in schools. They have a childish simplicity in which characters are either black or white, issues can be answered in terms of yes or no, and it would all be so simple if only people could see the simple truth.

If there is anything wrong with the attention given to Sassoon's satirical verse it is that it has possibly drawn attention away from some of his more lasting and deeply-textured poems. I have been lecturing on First World War poetry for nearly twenty years, and have always read as my opener Sassoon's 'To Any Dead Officer'. I know the poem better than I know any other work of literature, and yet it still moves me as much as it did when I first read it. It is a poem with a remarkable history. One school of opinion believes that Sassoon was cynically manipulated by those who wanted a sacrificial victim in the cause of pacifism. Whatever the background, he did compose his famous 'Declaration Against the War', which for all its sincerity is an appallingly pompous, naive and strident piece of writing, public oratory at its worst. Drained of emotion, facing public disgrace and a dangerous and uncertain future, Sassoon turned and wrote 'To Any Dead Officer' almost without pause.

> The words came into my head quite naturally. And by the time I went to bed I had written a slangy, telephonic poem of forty lines. I called it 'To Any Dead Officer', but it was addressed to one whom I had known during both my periods of service in France [Lieutenant E.L. Orme of the Second Battalion, Royal Welsh Fusiliers, killed in action on 27 May, 1917]. Poignant though the subject was, I wrote it with a sense of mastery and

detachment, and when it was finished I felt that it anyhow testified to the sincerity of my protest[9]

Written as a relaxed monologue, its understatement achieves more than any high pleading. The very ordinariness of the dead officer and the experiences to which he has been subject heighten the pathos, until the climax of the final lines, to me ranking among the most moving of the whole war:

> I'm blind with tears,
> Staring into the dark. Cheero!
> I wish they'd killed you in a decent show.

These lines reveal in stark clarity the way in which the war has changed all conventional moral structures. In normal life any death is to be regretted, particularly that of a young man. In the war, what matters is not death, which is inevitable, but the manner of it. Sassoon's dead officer does not even have a victory to show for his death, and by the strange alchemy that works on all great writing that fact underwrites and reinforces the tragic waste of the war.

The relaxed monologue form does Sassoon sterling service. One of his finest poems, and one of the finest of the war, is 'Repression of War Experience', with the build-up to the final madness handled with consummate skill:

> Hark! Thud, thud, thud, – quite soft . . . they never cease –
> Those whispering guns – O Christ, I want to go out
> And screech at them to stop – I'm going crazy;
> I'm going stark, staring mad because of the guns.

Poems such as this owe a considerable debt to John Masefield, and as with much of Owen's work they show the best features of Romantic verse. The heightened sensibility is built and structured throughout the poem to a moment of supreme climax. The individual experience is recorded so well that it acquires an element of universality. Diction, imagery and form are outwardly simple but highly effective.

Equally powerful are those poems where Sassoon is haunted by the pull of comradeship, such as 'Sick Leave', 'Banishment', 'Reward', 'Return' and 'Aftermath'. In these poems anger is secondary to sadness, and the poetry is more that of love than hate. These poems where dead soldiers exert more power than the living are a neglected area of Sassoon's work. Passionate intensity

lights up several poems, sometimes directed at individuals who,
are only thinly characterized, if at all, as in 'The Death-Bed':

> Light many lamps and gather round his bed.
> Lend him your eyes, warm blood, and will to live.
> Speak to him; rouse him; you may save him yet.
> He's young; he hated War; how should he die
> When cruel old campaigners win safe through?
>
> But death replied: 'I chose him.' So he went.

At other times Sassoon is quite unequivocal about his reasons for
being in the front line:

> Love drove me to rebel.
> Love drives me back to grope with them through hell;

Sassoon is rather more convincing when he writes with love than
anger. Unfortunately it is his anger that has come to typify his
work.

Robert Graves

Robert Graves has been a less powerful mover behind the myth of
the war, at least as a poet: he removed his war poetry from his
Collected Poems after 1927, but a new lease of life was given to it
with the posthumous publication of *Poems About War*, edited by
his son. The fifty-four poems included in the selection are by and
large very disappointing, so much so that one might support
Graves in his original decision to bury his war poetry. The problem is that Graves never really finds his own voice for dealing with
the war. There is plenty of evidence from Sassoon and others who
knew Graves during the war that his technique of survival was to
think as little about the war as possible, almost to try and block it
out of his mind. If this was his approach it was hardly one that
would lead to great poetry. As it is Graves's writing falls into a
number of different styles.

A small number of poems form a block of shock-horror poetry,
rubbing the nose of the reader firmly into the blood, guts and
stench of the war. The most powerful example is 'A Dead Boche',
which is no more nor less than a description of a rotting German
corpse. Other examples are 'The First Funeral', 'Limbo', 'The
Trenches' and, to a lesser extent, 'Through the Periscope'. Other
poems contain elements of violence. When Graves and Sassoon

first met, Sassoon criticized Graves's poetry for being too violent and realistic; the poems in question now appear very tame stuff indeed, as in 'The Morning Before the Battle':

> I looked, and ah, my wraith before me stood,
>> His head all battered in by violent blows:
> The fruit between my lips to clotted blood
>> Was transubstantiate, and the pale rose
> Smelt sickly . . .

And with experience of active service Sassoon was soon to outdo Graves in the reality department. Perhaps reality is at the root of the problem in Graves's war work: more often than not he seeks to sideslip out of it at the earliest opportunity, as in the poem 'It's a Queer Time':

> Or you'll be dozing safe in your dug-out –
> A great roar – the trench shakes and falls about –
> You're struggling, gasping, struggling, then . . . hullo!
> Elsie comes tripping gaily down the trench,
> Hanky to nose – that lyddite makes a stench –
> Getting her pinafore all over grime.
> Funny! because she died ten years ago!
>> It's a queer time.

If not drifting from the war into fantasy Graves is more usually found retreating at the first opportunity into memories of a pre-war pastoral idyll. His verse letters are particularly prone to this tehnique, as in 'To R.N.' where a position held in the snow where 'in scrapen holes we shiver' moves almost immediately to

> Sleek fauns and cheery-time,
> Vague music and green trees.

It is as if Graves is desperate to comfort himself with a vision of nature as it was, yet he suffers from the Georgian failing of finding an inspiration in nature's beauty that is not always conveyed to the reader, but which it is expected the reader will understand. Graves is not certain enough to face up to the war directly and consistently through the whole length of a poem, nor certain enough to ignore it almost completely, as does Edward Thomas. The result is an unsatisfactory foot in both worlds. The war in some of Graves's poetry is rather like the mosquito that some believe killed Rupert Brooke, something one would like to ignore and treat as a passing irritant, but which clearly carries the capacity to breed death. Graves at times also writes in the manner of a far more relaxed age. Perhaps there was a time when a poet could waste a line by asking what he was going to say:

> But this Welsh sunset, what shall I say of it?

but in the context of the war such a line is rather too close for comfort to Wordsworth's climactic lines:

> I've measured it from side to side,
> 'Tis three foot long, and two foot wide.

It would be surprising if an author of Graves's power did not produce at least some excellent war poetry. 'To Lucasta On Going To The Wars – For The Fourth Time' and 'Two Fusiliers' are powerful and effective evocations of comradeship. 'The Patchwork Quilt' is a short poem centred on the image of a conventional patchwork quilt, with parts consisting of 'muddied khaki scraps' and other war debris. Both it and the frequently anthologized 'Dead Cow Farm' are poised on the edge of myth, of the type Graves would make so much of in his post-war work. Certain other poems show his fascination with childhood, and his ability to achieve quite complex effects with simple rhythms and rhymes. Wilfrid Gibson and Walter de la Mare are two possible influencing factors in this style, best seen in 'The Adventure', 'I Hate the Moon' and 'A Child's Nightmare'. For me the most successful of Graves's war poems is 'Goliath and David', written on the occasion of the death of Graves's great friend David Thomas. The poem retells the story of David and Goliath in taut, spare verse, with only the ending changed:

> . . . but David, calm and brave,
> Holds his ground, for God will save.
> Steel crosses wood, a flash, and oh!
> Shame for beauty's overthrow!

When Graves admits to his emotion, and when he can find a narrative form that allows him to distance himself just a little from that emotion, the result is an exceptionally powerful poem. Unfortunately the examples of this are very rare.

Graves seems to me to be an example of a poet whose time had not yet come in 1914. Sassoon had written pleasantly enough before the war, as had Owen, but I can see nothing in their pre-war verse that marked them out for greatness. After the war Sassoon wrote very little of lasting merit, and his post-war reputation was based on his prose, not any further poetry. At the risk of committing blasphemy, I am unconvinced that Owen would have been the great poet, had he lived, that so many have predicted. His poetry is based on one theme, or rather the joint theme of suffering and pity, and much of it draws its best imagery from one landscape, that of the war. He does not have the pastoral vision of Thomas or Blunden, which could contain and hold war poetry while giving hope of moving on after the experience was over. He does not have the Judaic vision of suffering which allowed Rosenberg to insert the war into a developing sensibility, instead of making it his only sensibility. He does have the negative side of a Keatsian vision, where the mere fact of the poet's existence can sometimes be seen as meaning that what he has to say is important, even where he has nothing to say. It is possible to argue that Sassoon and Owen were made for and by the war, and that it provided for them a catalyst that no other experience could have done. It certainly burnt out one of them as a poet, and may, had he lived, have done the same for the other.

Graves is different. Myth, childhood, a love of classical models and a strong Welsh or Celtic vision of nature are visible in his pre-war writing, and he was not able with any consistency to turn these inherent strengths into poetry that matched or could cope with his war experience. Psychologically he may have adopted a reined-in attitude that made creative writing difficult; he was certainly psychologically damaged by the war, possibly as a result of repression, and this amateur psychoanalytical insight is helped on the way by how long it took for the experience to work through into a form in which Graves could write about it, in *Goodbye to All That*. Where *Poems About War* lets Graves down is in not printing some of his tortured, anguished post-war work. This does not mention the war, but its ravaged psychological landscape describes the war far more effectively than many more pictorial representations. I am thinking particularly of 'The Pier Glass', which to me could have been called 'Repression of War Experience' just as much as Sassoon's poem of that name.

Isaac Rosenberg

It seems remarkable that in 1970 Isaac Rosenberg could still be described as 'the undiscovered genius of the First World War'. When I was refused permission to write my PhD thesis on Rosenberg in 1972 on the grounds that I was not a Jew I did not realize what a favour was being done to me; in between starting that thesis and finishing it no less than three full biographies were written on him.

Rosenberg has always been different. He was Jewish, poor and from a working-class background, outwardly at the opposite end of the social spectrum from Sassoon, Graves, Brooke, Blunden and the other famous war poets. He joined up and served as a private and was a gifted artist, the whole package leading up to a picture of a man who seemed to have nothing in common with the stereotype image of the First World War poet.

This apparent difference has not always worked to Rosenberg's advantage. The tendency has been, for wholly understandable reasons, to set Rosenberg up as a figure somehow representative of the working classes and Judaism. This is unfortunate. Rosenberg may technically have been of working-class origins, but Jewish culture and intelligence are more than capable of breaking through the barriers of the English class system, and work to laws of their own. Thus though Rosenberg's family were not rich he was still able, through the generosity of others, to go to the Slade School of Art, something not usual for boys from English working-class families. He was also able to visit South Africa as the result of support from the Jewish community in London.

What Rosenberg became was not the working-class hero, but something more closely resembling what we would now describe as a Bohemian; poverty-stricken certainly, but mixing in fringe artistic circles. Though not a figure blessed with much luck, he was fortunate enough to receive massive support from two leading fig-ures of the Georgian establishment, Gordon Bottomley and Lascelles Abercrombie, and the patronage of Edward Marsh. He used his Jewish cultural and religious inheritance both consciously and unconsciously, and suffered from anti-Semitism in the army, but he does not seem to have been orthodox in his observance; indeed, Rosenberg was typical or representative of very little except himself, and if he is to be compared with anyone then the nearest starting point would be another poor London artist/poet, William Blake. Both have an acute eye for visual detail, both write within the Romantic dream vision tradition, and both seek to create or elaborate on ancient myth with a strong mystical element in their work. Much of the problem with Rosenberg's poetry seems to be that he has not worked out fully the myth he is intending to create or recreate.

The result is poetry of remarkable and singularly unfruitful obscurity, larded with exclamations of 'Ah!' and 'O!', with very little to inform the reader what the poet is exclaiming about. Large acreages are written at an unrelenting full volume. We know the poet is excited, but do not know what he is excited about, and Rosenberg cannot tell us.

This makes the outstanding war poetry he wrote even more remarkable, and the experience of reading through Rosenberg's *Collected Works* is like that of the diamond miner who wades through a ton of sludge to find the glistening jewel lurking at the bottom of the pan. Because Rosenberg's good poetry is so very good it is sometimes not realized how very few in number the effective poems are. 'The Dead Heroes'; 'Spring 1916'; 'God'; 'Marching: As Seen From the Left File'; 'The Troop Ship'; 'August 1914'; 'From France'; 'Break of Day in the Trenches'; 'The Immortals'; 'Louse Hunting'; 'Returning, We Hear the Larks'; 'Dead Man's Dump'; 'Through These Pale Cold Days'; 'On Receiving News of the War'; with perhaps 'In War' and 'Daughters of War' – fourteen to sixteen poems in total that seem to be of lasting merit, with perhaps a handful more to be added by an editor with a different taste.

Those poems are remarkable. The emphasis on Rosenberg as an ethnic and social hero has diverted attention away from the fact that very many of his poems rely for their effect on superb handling of images drawn from nature, a pointer to the extent to which Rosenberg is, after all, very much a part of the English Romantic tradition, but also different in a way that gives a tremendous excitement to his verse. One of his most remarkable poems is 'On Receiving News of the War', written in Cape Town in 1914. There is more than a hint of Hardy in the opening stanza:

> Snow is a strange white word.
> No ice or frost
> Has asked of bud or bird
> For Winter's cost.

Hard winter is a part of nature's plan, Rosenberg suggests, and then goes on to suggest that war is in the same mould:

> In all men's hearts it is.
> Some spirit old
> Hath turned with malign kiss
> Our lives to mould.

The final stanza then goes on to express a conventional desire for war to cleanse society, albeit in a highly unconventional style,

> O! ancient crimson curse!
> Corrode, consume.
> Give back this universe
> Its pristine bloom.

The poem has all the hallmarks of Rosenberg's best work. It is impersonal, and wherever Rosenberg is tempted to use the personal pronoun his poetry becomes dangerously susceptible to overheating. The theme of the poem is power, and the question of who holds power over mankind and the universe. It is not a theme he pursues with the intensity and single-mindedness of Owen's concern with pity, but the issues of power and control of human life appear in some of his most effective work. The poem also starts off indirectly, revealing its aim only in the last two lines.

'Spring 1916' is another poem which leads with a powerful image on the natural world. Spring, the time for rebirth, has been transformed by the war:

> Slow, rigid, is this masquerade
> That passes as through granite air;
> Heavily – heavily passes.
> What has she fed on? Who her table laid
> Through the three seasons? What forbidden fare
> Ruined her as mortal lass is?

Other versions of this poem have 'as through a difficult air' in place of 'as through granite air'. In this poem the questions are an emblem for things which can never be answered, not (as they so often are in Rosenberg's lesser work) the strident shriek of a poet who knows neither the answers not the proper question. Another poem with strong links to nature is 'August 1914', ending as it does on one of the strongest images of the war:

> Iron are our lives
> Molten right through our youth.
> A burnt space through ripe fields
> A fair mouth's broken tooth.

A variation of the same image occurs in 'Dead Man's Dump':

> . . . the swift iron burning bee
> Drained the wild honey of their youth.

Though flawed across its length, 'Dead Man's Dump' contains some of Rosenberg's most powerful writing. If it is, as some believe, Rosenberg's best work, it bears comparison with the poem that many would see as its equivalent in Owen's canon, 'Spring Offensive'. Both poems are obsessed by the moment of death, the feelings of those who die and the feelings of those who have gone to the brink and returned:

> What of us who, flung on the shrieking pyre,
> Walk, our usual thoughts untouched,
> Our lucky limbs as on ichor fed,
> Immortal seeming ever?

Some of the most moving lines in 'Dead Man's Dump' are again based on the use of nature imagery:

> Burnt black by strange decay
> Their sinister faces lie,
> The lid over each eye,
> The grass and coloured clay
> More motion have than they,
> Joined to the great sunk silences.

Where Rosenberg differs from so many of his contemporaries is that he has no pre-existing vision of either a beneficent God or a world designed for man's convenience. The war does not shock him in the way that it shocks Owen, Sassoon and Graves, middle-class young men brought up in an atmosphere of privilege and a culture which had faced its last foreign invasion in 1066. That culture does not write poetry is proven, however, by the links between Rosenberg and Sorley. There is in this a strange bond of sentiment between Rosenberg whose earth,

> . . . had waited for them,
> All the time of their growth
> Fretting for their decay

and Sorley's

> Earth that never doubts nor fears,
> Earth that knows of death, not tears,
> Earth that bore with joyful ease
> Hemlock for Socrates,

It is perhaps not so much Judaism that creates this vision as an absence of belief in a kind God. There are surprising links between Jew and gentile in other areas. Sorley and Rosenberg share an unholy excitement about the war, an excitement Sorley sums up in the rhythm of 'All the Hills and Vales Along'. In Rosenberg's case the excitement overwhelms even the personal desire for survival, so that his work contains hardly any of the self-pitying poems that were the staple of so many young war poets desperately in need of something to justify their potential annihilation. Sorley can instruct those who follow after him to forget his existence, as in 'When You See Millions of the Mouthless Dead'. That poem, and Rosenberg's 'Dead Man's Dump', are among the few works that convey the sheer scope and intensity of the killing on the Western Front. The difference between the two poets, of course, is that Sorley wrote nearly all his poems before he had seen active service.

The importance of nature imagery is carried through nearly all Rosenberg's most valuable work. Near-books have been written on 'Break of Day in the Trenches', which to me remains still the most entirely perfect poem written about the war. The opening line is justifiably famous:

> The darkness crumbles away –
> It is the same old druid Time as ever.

Rosenberg was clearly worried that Marsh would object to 'druid Time', as both Marsh and the other Georgians had combined in an attempt to make Rosenberg write less obscure verse; Marsh's response is not on record – Rosenberg found it hard to keep his own paintings, never mind other people's letters.

A rat leaps across Rosenberg's hand, and he muses in dryly ironic mode that it will be shot for showing the 'cosmopolitan sympathies' that allow it to touch both German and English hands. In fact, as Rosenberg realizes, the rat is better suited for life than the men it runs by.

> It seems you inwardly grin as you pass
> Strong eyes, fine limbs, haughty athletes
> Less chanced than you for life.

It is here one notices the real difference between Rosenberg and his contemporaries. He has distanced himself from the war in a way that intense personal identification with their men never allowed Sassoon or Owen to do. That distancing gives his work its unique flavour, and its willingness to imply rather than to state outright. It is tempting to see in Rosenberg's magnificent imagery a variation of Imagist technique, and a foreshadowing of Eliot's powerful combined use of imagery and irony. Yet the images are drawn from the normal store of Romantic verse, from

Like a blind man's dream on the sand
By dangerous tides,
Like a girl's dark hair for she dreams no ruin lies their,
Or her kisses where a serpent hides.

to

Poppies whose roots are in man's veins
Drop, and are ever dropping:
But mine in mine ear is safe,
Just a little white with the dust.

The irony here seems to me to be comparable with that shown in Hardy's 'The Darkling Thrush', just as Rosenberg's search for the dark power that controls human life bears comparison with Hardy's 'Immanent Will' or the forces exposed in 'The Dynasts'. Rosenberg announces his own impending death in these lines as clearly as if he had arranged to be shot in front of us. The base of the image is the fact that poppies grew where the ground had been recently disturbed, most often by an artillery bombardment or where a mass grave had been dug. Therefore quite literally the roots of poppies could be in men's veins, but the additional effect of the image is to bind the whole natural world, man and poppy, into one being, and the clear message of death comes about in part because Rosenberg has plucked the poppy, as the war will soon pluck him. The white dust is, of course, funereal, suggesting desolation over mile after mile of land, and not just the one individual. Again Rosenberg shows his interest in the moment of death. He asks the rat,

What do you see in our eyes . . .
What quaver, what heart aghast?

and this almost clinical interest in the ultimate transcendental moment serves again to distance the poet from the emotion he is portraying. In the preface to *Lyrical Ballads* Wordsworth announced that the techniques of poetry served in part to distance the author from emotion, allowing emotion to be recollected in tranquillity, as if the strength of the poet's passion required a filter before it could be handled safely by the author or seen by the reader. In 'Break of Day in the Trenches' Rosenberg, perhaps more than any other war poet, has managed to find the filter that lets his emotion be viewed dispassionately without losing any of its passion or individual fire.

I cannot share Rosenberg's enthusiasm for his 'Daughters of War', a poem he laboured over more than almost any other, and which he tried both to explain and justify to Edward Marsh. It is a dream vision in which mighty female figures,

> . . . force their males
> From the doomed earth.

Images are thrown at the poem in almost random order and the overstatement renders part of the verse ridiculous. Femininity, birth and regeneration obsessed Rosenberg but his tendency to stridency and fondness for convoluted syntax and strings of exclamations let him down here as they do in so many poems. To offset that poem there are the lines from 'Dead Man's Dump' that I believe to be among the most powerful of the war:

> Their shut mouths made no moan,
> They lie there huddled, friend and foeman,
> Man born of man, and born of woman,
> And shells go crying over them,
> From night till night and now.

As an elegy for the dead of the First World War there is no finer. In five lines Rosenberg compresses the themes of whole poems by other authors: the finality of death; death as a release; the comradeship of death; the equality of death; the appalling range and scope of the loss; its place in an eternal round of suffering, warfare and death. The final triumph of these lines is the shells, man-made agents of destruction, 'crying' for the loss. In one line Rosenberg accomplishes much of what Owen tries to say in 'Anthem for Doomed Youth' where rifles and artillery are the soldiers' only funeral dirge. The tragedy of the mass slaughter becomes the pity of the individual's death, whereas it is more common for the individual to act as emblem for the masses.

'Returning, We Hear The Larks' is one of two perfectly-crafted, mature poems by Rosenberg. Its subject is, yet again, based on nature, and is a favourite theme of amateur and professional poets: the existence of birdsong amid scenes of unthinkable devastation. Reaction to this was not confined to poets: a French soldier wrote to *Le Matin* in 1915 remarking how the larks in spring had sung above the trenches. For most poets, including Sassoon in 'Everyone Sang', the simple contrast between death and devastation and the beauty of the song is enough. For Rosenberg it is not. The contrast is detailed:

> But hark! joy – joy – strange joy.
> Lo! heights of night ringing with unseen larks.
> Music showering on our upturned list'ning faces.

Then come remarkable final images – a dreaming blind man, a girl with a serpent in her hair. It is a consummate vision not of the larks, but of the sky from which their song drops, the beauty that can hide a storm of death as easily as it produces music, the impersonal, arbitrary nature of what falls on the men. Rosenberg can infuriate by not seeming to know what he is writing about; at times he can convert that and make himself the spokesman for all the ironies of war that can never be explained.

Rosenberg had little time for conventional form, but this does not make him an Imagist, or even an occasional experimenter such as Owen; it is rather that he is not concerned about form but only about words, words which he can marshal to marvellous effect or cause to tumble out in an uncontrollable torrent that drowns the poem. His imagery is one key to his poetry, using larks, rats, 'grass and coloured clay', 'broken mouths', the poppy and 'ripe fields': this is not the imagery of a Judaic poet, nor a working-class boy. It is the imagery of a Georgian poet brought up in the tradition of English Romanticism. In Rosenberg's case that tradition is tempered by a Judaic vision of past suffering and persecution, and a painter's eye and intelligence that can make sublime imagery out of relatively conventional materials. One secret of his success is that he does not feel the need to detail the landscape of the trenches, but instead uses such detail only where it helps to create a specific effect:

> Dragging these anguished limbs, we only know
> This poison-blasted track opens on our camp –
> On a little safe sleep.

Compare this with the lengthy narrative and descriptive build-up Owen feels obliged to give in 'Dulce et Decorum Est'. The absence of shock in Rosenberg's response is presumably one reason why he refrains from the travelogue of the front where so many of the weaker poets stop almost before they have started. It is also, ironically, one reason why so few of Rosenberg's poems achieve real quality: the work of Sassoon and Owen, and many of the minor poets, is padded out with graphic narrative or descriptive work that is perfectly vivid and acceptable, but which at the same time can be repetitive and achieves little more than rubbing the reader's nose in the dirt and reality of warfare. Rosenberg makes only the mildest gesture in the direction of this style, as in the melo-dramatic 'In War' and 'The Dying Soldier', but it removes from his canon a type and style of poetry that fills out the work of many other poets. Sorley has suffered from something of the same feature.

It would be incorrect to hail Rosenberg as a genius for the wrong reasons, just as it would be wrong to applaud Rupert Brooke for being handsome and well connected. These things have to do with contemporary fame, but have nothing to do with lasting poetic merit. Brooke does not need his good looks or his London con-nections to ensure him a place in the hall of fame, any more than Rosenberg needs his Judaism and unorthodox background to ensure his. Rosenberg is an arrant Romantic and a true inheritor of the tradition of William Blake, even down to sharing a very con-siderable personal eccentricity.

Edward Thomas, Edmund Blunden and Charles Sorley

The myth of the war states not that poetry about 'blood and dirt' is bad, but rather that any poetry not about blood and dirt is bad. I count just over 140 poems in my edition of *Collected Poems* by Edward Thomas, and on my reading the number of those poems which make any direct reference to the war are in single figures. None contains any harsh description of the front line. There are also a handful of poems about death which do not mention the war, but which, given Thomas's status as a serving soldier, have usually been seen as war poems. Thomas was killed in the war, but largely managed to ignore it in his poetry. Yet he has over the years become firmly associated with the war, and attracted an immensely strong personal following, including a society that has for years organized events and walks devoted to perpetuating his memory and enlarging the number of people familiar with his work.

I have included Thomas in this chapter precisely because he is not, in the strict sense of the word, a war poet. He is a nature poet, the inheritor of a pastoral, Romantic tradition that went back hundreds of years and was a far stronger presence in war poets in general than has often been supposed. That tradition allows

Thomas, like Rosenberg but for very different reasons, to take the war in his stride. Quite simply, nature is more important. Sassoon and Graves often wanted to believe this, but their horror at the carnage overwhelmed their capacity to place the war in context.

Thomas is important in his own right, and also as a symbol of the fact that the world did not come to an end in 1914. He is the most impressive spokesman of a group of poets who similarly took the war in their stride, and who for that reason have perhaps not been afforded their due credit. I think particularly of Edmund Blunden and Charles Sorley. Blunden declined in popularity in the 1930s in part because a rather archaic diction associated him with the worst manifestations of the Georgian movement. This association is grossly unfair, though at first glance there is a rather old-fashioned appearance and flavour to some of Blunden's war writing. He did himself no favours either by some of his work in the 1930s, which in comparison with the war work is rather lacklustre. It is, nevertheless, possible to see the same tradition that Blunden, Thomas and Sorley followed operating in contemporary British poetry, in authors as far apart as the early Ted Hughes, R.S. Thomas and Norman Nicholson.

Thomas's 'As the Team's Head-Brass' is the record of a conversation between the author and a ploughman, engaged in his ancient craft. At each end of his run the ploughman exchanges a few words with the poet, largely about the war. One of the ploughman's mates has been killed in France, and so a fallen tree has not been moved. If he had stayed,

> . . . Everything
> Would have been different. For it would have been
> Another world.

Yet the rest of the poem denies the concept of war as making a monumental change. The lovers who disappear into the wood at the start of the poem emerge again, a symbol of renewal, regeneration and the continuation of the eternal truths.

> I watched the clods crumble and topple over
> After the ploughshare and the stumbling team.

The clods crumbling and toppling can clearly be an image of death, but it is also an image of continuity, and a reminder that in Thomas's work the cycle of nature, its absorption of death and its need for death before renewal can take place, is never far away. Thomas's is no cosy view of a world order where the birds sing sweetly and the sun always shines. Nature holds a truth, but it is one that mankind can only see through a glass darkly, and the awareness of its beauty is tempered by an awareness of its savagery and violence. In Edmund Blunden's 'Rural Economy' the front is 'life's farm', and the rural economy is the fact the blood spilt in the battle can be seen as fertilizing the earth:

> Why, even the wood as well as field
>   This thoughtful farmer knew
> Could be reduced to plough and tilled,
>   And if he planned, he'd do;
> The field and wood, all bone-fed loam,
> Shot up a roaring harvest home.

There is more cynicism and shock in this than in Thomas's work, with Thomas lacking the capacity to be surprised, but both poets suggest that war is as natural as death; nature has a power that the war can suspend but never destroy. Blunden is suddenly hauled back into normal times by the sheer beauty of an autumn day:

> Your countenance still ripe and kind
>   Gazes upon me, godlike day,
> And finding you again I find
>   The tricks of time all thrown away.
> The recollected turns to here and now
> Beneath the equipoising glory of your brow.

Thomas, an older man, does not need to say that an autumn day is part of the universal language of life, and one whose statement can for a while at least counteract war and its impact; it is implicit in his writing that war may come and man may die, but nature lasts. There is anger in Blunden's poetry, and again one suspects the anger of a young man who on occasion feels betrayed by his faith. Nature can deceive, can make believe that all is as it used to be:

> Grass thin-waving in the wind approached them,
> Red roofs in the near view feigned survival,
>   Lovely mockers, when we
>   There took over.

> There war's holiday seemed, nor though at known times
> Gusts of flame and jingling steel descended
>   On the bare tracks, would you
>   Picture death there.

Many of you soon paid for
That false mildness.

At the same time Blunden's poetry tends to return to the fact that basic truth can only be found in nature, not in the aberration that is the war, as when he finds peace with a friend when the men are at rest:

> Not seldom, soft by meadows deep in dew,
> Another lit my soul with his calm shine.
>   There were cadences and whispers
>   In his ways that made my vespers –
> A night-piece fitting well that temple blue
> Where stars new trembled with delight's design.

Nature never quite loses its regenerative power in Blunden's poetry, though it is not an active agent in restoration; rather the natural resilience of the men takes strength from 'green grass thriving' and,

> Clad so cleanly, this remnant of poor wretches
> Picked up life like the hens in orchard ditches,

Blunden's childhood and instinctive roots in a pastoral world allow him to see beyond the immediate horror, as in 'Premature Rejoicing':

> There sleeps Titania in a deep dug-out.
> Waking, she wonders what all the din's about,
> And smiles through her tears, and looks ahead ten years,
> And sees her Wood again, and her usual Grenadiers,
>   All in green.

In 'War Autobiography' Blunden relates how he clung to sanity by always perceiving the lasting world that lay behind the war. This extract also suggests the reassurance that an awareness of nature's cycle can bring to the poet; after dark there will always be day:

> War might make his worst grimace
> And still my mind in armour good
> Turned aside in every place
> And saw bright day through the black wood.

However, Blunden is too good a poet for the reassurance that nature provides to come easily to him, and part of his strength is the variety and richness he brings to his treatment of nature. He admitted that by 1916 the war had come near to overwhelming him:

> The grimness of war began to compete as a subject with the pastorals of peace.[10]

While the war never drowned his love of nature or admiration for its richness, it changed him as a man and as a poet. As he wrote in 'Old Homes', his pastoral vision may have been 'A herb of grace to keep the will from madding', and his post-war work described how his vision of nature saved him from torment:

> Beyond estranging years that cloaked my view
> With all their wintriness of fear and strain;
> I turned to you; I never turned in vain . . .
> . . . in your pastoral still my life has rest.

But the 'rest' was only relative, and, though he stopped short of madness, he became extremely depressed and full of restlessness. Blunden was drawn back to the battlefields time and again after the war ended, and never quite lost the guilt that he and many others felt that they had survived when so many had died. Nature provided continuity, 'perspectives from which to cope with immediate horrors',[11] but the coping left him scarred.

He was 'haunted by war's agony'. Those scars can be seen in his vision of nature, where honesty drives him to deny at times his own creed and show nature as a far from regenerative force. Anyone who wishes to see just how complex a pastoral mode of writing can become in the hands of a very accomplished poet should read 'Vlamertinghe: Passing the Château, July 1917', where the use of flower imagery is some of the most compelling and complex of any war poem. At other times his use of natural imagery to describe weapons of war suggests that nature and war are natural partners, sharing a vision of torment. Bullets are 'steel born bees' and the slaughter of the Somme is 'summer's bravery changed to autumn chill'; the mood here is not that winter will always be replaced by summer, but that summer will always be replaced by winter, a change from optimism to stark pessimism, bringing the feeling that all brightness and hope are useless, the happy times merely making the drop to misery even harder to bear. At times the impression that war is central to nature is very strong, the 'ancient, crimson curse' that Rosenberg sees as being in the hearts of all men. Blunden's explanation in 'Return of the Native' is that man

> . . . struck the Sun,
> And for a season turned the Sun to blood.

Blunden's extensive use of nature imagery in war poetry is unusual for the period, in that nature is used to illustrate the war, not merely to act as a contrast to it. One of the more interesting features of his later work is his use of war imagery in post-war nature poetry, a startling example being 'Perch Fishing'.

A notable feature in Thomas's work is the melancholy he summons from the simplest images and verse form. I struggle to find a word to describe the mood expressed in so many of his poems, his awareness of the infinitesimal nature of human life, the huge currents of sadness and change that swirl around us, the knowledge that will forever be denied humans. Thomas wrote, in 'No One Cares Less than I':

> 'No one cares less than I,
> Nobody knows but God,
> Whether I am destined to lie
> Under a foreign clod,'
> Were the words I made to the bugle in the morning.
>
> But laughing, storming, scorning,
> Only the bugles know
> What the bugles say in the morning,
> And they do not care, when they blow
> The call that I heard and made words to early this morning.

There is in Thomas's work a mood that is also found in Sorley, and which he ascribed to 'some forgotten restlessness'. The similarity is most clearly seen in Thomas's 'Aspens' and Sorley's 'Rooks'. Thomas's poem has:

> All day and night, save winter, every weather,
> Above the inn, the smithy, and the shop,
> The aspens at the cross roads talk together
> Of rain, until their last leaves fall from the top . . .

And it would be the same were no house near.
Over all sorts of weather, men, and times,
Aspens must shake their leaves and men may hear
But need not listen, more than to my rhymes

whereas Sorley writes:

There, where the rusty iron lies,
    The rooks are cawing all the day.
Perhaps no man, until he dies,
    Will understand them, what they say . . .

Still trouble all the trees with cries,
    That know, and cannot put away,
The yearning to the soul that flies
    From day to night, from night to day.

In Blunden's work the equivalent image is the River Ancre and the
noise of water. There are surprising echoes in Sorley's poem of
Rosenberg's 'Dead Man's Dump': the reference to iron in the first
stanza, the repetition in 'day to night, from night to day'. The gap
between man and nature is as important to the mood of these
poems as the links, and the yearning restlessness of the human
spirit is continually offset against nature, which reflects but is also
beyond that restlessness.

Little changes for Thomas in France. In peacetime,

Roads go on
While we forget, and are
Forgotten like a star
That shoots and is gone.

In wartime,

Now all roads lead to France
And heavy is the tread
Of the living; but the dead
Returning lightly dance:

This is to me a clear statement that the road, like nature, does not
change whatever the fate and aspirations of the humans who tread
on it. The same is true of the road Sorley's men march on:

Tramp of feet and lilt of song
Ringing all the road along.
All the music of their going,
Ringing swinging glad song-throwing,
Earth will echo still, when foot
Lies numb and voice mute.

It is also possible to link Thomas's 'I hate not Germans' from 'This is No Case of Petty Right or Wrong' with Sorley's 'You are blind like us' in his sonnet 'To Germany'. Both poets reject mindless jingoism, and do not need it to justify their own service.

Blunden's and Thomas's poetry grows on the reader. Whereas the work of Sassoon, Rosenberg and Owen has an immediate and dramatic effect, Thomas and Blunden need to be marinated and left to soak in the mind. There are many dramatic and moving evocations of comradeship in the poetry of the war, yet for some reason Blunden's simple, calmly colloquial 'The Watchers' stays in my mind longer than many others:

When will the stern, fine 'Who goes there?'
Meet me again in midnight air?
And the gruff sentry's kindness, when
Will kindness have such power again?

Perhaps the key to Blunden's poem is that it is not set in a moment of tension or high drama, but in the ninety per cent boredom that is part of the experience of soldiering. It also profits from the fact that much of it was written after the war, when dust and minds had settled and a sense of perspective was easier to achieve. The fact that Thomas and Sorley had that perspective without the time to acquire it makes their work even more remarkable.

Blunden also has that rarest of things in the war poets, a sense of humour. He and Thomas share a fascination for rural figures, Thomas's Lob being an attempt to elevate one such to almost mythical status. There is no such grandeur about Blunden's sentry in 'The Guard's Mistake', but there is a glorious conflict not between English and German soldier, but between the 'cowman now turned warrior' who in the depths of rural peace rapidly reverts to cowman and exchanges his rifle for a 'cudgel brown and stout'. The 'crimson-mottled monarch, shocked and shrill' of a staff officer soon turns the cowman back into 'the terror of the Hun', but even at the end there is a delicious dry irony in Blunden's use of the catch-phrase from so many newspapers. Blunden's sentry bears comparison with Thomas's soldier in 'A

Private', though the latter is a more sophisticated and complex poem.

'The Prophet' is a neglected poem, in which Blunden takes an old guide book to the Netherlands and again with delightful irony compares

> . . . the polished phrase
> Which our forefathers practised equally
> To bury admirals or sell beaver hats;

with the reality of Flanders at war. The guide book comments,

> 'But lately much attention has been paid
> To the coal mines'

in an inadvertent reference to the fighting around the slag-heaps and the endless mining in the sector. Blunden is not oblivious to the horror of the mines. He ends one of his more famous poems, 'Concert Party: Busseboom' with the shattering lines:

> To this new concert, white we stood;
>   Cold certainty held our breath;
> While men in the tunnels below Larch Wood
> Were kicking men to death.

A modern critic has commented:

> Blunden's poetry has a deep sanity about it which is impressive even where the style is mannered or contorted. It is a sanity of remembering pasts and holding to them even in the midst of destruction, but it is also at times the sanity of the absurdist,[12]

Blunden, Thomas and Sorley share that sanity, as they share an occasionally absurdist vision. It comes in part from being in touch with a reality that outlasts man, and which does not deign to explain everything it knows. The pastoral vision of all three poets is one in which absurdity comes from our inability to understand, not because nature is inexplicable. Nature gave the war poets a vast store of imagery, allowing them to see war as a cancer on the face of creation or as part of the endless cycle whereby life can only be achieved by means of death. It allowed them to sustain images of contrast, to place suffering in the context of a world where life and death are opposite sides of the same coin, and most of all it allowed them to write poetry that rose above the fact of one war to engage in a wider vision of suffering and death.

In some respects the poetry of Owen and Sassoon was a marvellous and magnificent side-track from the mainstream of British poetry, and the war ensured that a different side road peopled by the Imagists and T.S. Eliot was enlarged into an eight-lane motorway. It may be that poets such as Blunden, Thomas and Sorley have proved themselves to be art of the more lasting tradition, and that all the war poets were able to profit more than has been supposed from the English pastoral and Romantic tradition of nature poetry.

Notes

1 Hibberd, *Casebook*, p. 60
2 Williams, *Owen*, p. 96
3 see all editions of Owen's work
4 *Oxford Book of Modern Verse* (Oxford, Oxford University Press, 1936) p. xxxiv
5 *Letters on Poetry from W.B. Yeats to Dorothy Wellesley* (Oxford, Oxford University Press, 1940) 21 December, 1936, p. 113
6 *ibid.*, p. 6
7 Hibberd, *Owen the Poet*, p. 161
8 Welland, quoted Hibberd, *Casebook*, p. 150
9 Sassoon, *Siegfried's Journey*, p. 54
10 Blunden, *War Poetry*, p. 24
11 Marsack, Blunden *Selected Poems*, p. 3
12 Parfitt, *English Poetry*, p. 51

CHAPTER EIGHT

Debunking the Myth

I cannot remember where I was when Kennedy was assassinated, but I can remember where I was when I first read Andrew Marvell's 'To His Coy Mistress' (in a rather nasty flat in Leeds) and when I first read Paul Fussell's *The Great War and Modern Memory* (for over an hour, in the long-suffering Heffer's Bookshop in Cambridge). Fussell's is a very great book, and is seriously and gloriously wrong in some of the claims it makes. I feel rather like a child when it reaches the awful moment of realizing that its parents are not perfect, and more like that same child when it dares to say so. My reason for daring rather more than a slapped wrist is that Fussell's book, for all that it is a masterpiece and a great destroyer of myths, is now in the situation of contributing to some myths that surely should be laid to rest.

Fussell can be very dangerous when he writes about history. I have already commented on his statement that,

> In the Great War eight million people were destroyed because two persons, the Archduke Francis Ferdinand and his Consort, had been shot.[1]

The First World War was an accident waiting to happen, and historical accidents deserve to be respected as immensely complex events with no single cause, and certainly no cause as simple as that.

To Fussell,

> England began to train her first conscript army, an event which could be said to mark the beginning of the modern world.[2]

The Industrial Revolution marked the beginning of the modern world, and Britain had been training conscripts for its armed forces for hundreds of years, as had most countries with the wealth to raise an army.

These are minor errors, statements made for dramatic effect at a risk of bending the truth. More serious are Fussell's claims that the 'catastrophe' of the Somme was caused in part by class:

> Another cause was traceable to the class system and the assumptions it sanctioned. The regulars of the British staff entertained an implicit contempt for the rapidly trained new men of 'Kitchener's Army', largely recruited among working men from the Midlands. The planners assumed that these troops . . . were too simple and animal to cross the space between the opposing trenches in any way except in full daylight and aligned in rows or 'waves'.[3]

Where does one start? 'Implicit' is a good word for what Fussell wants to do, because one can claim the bias exists even if there is no record of it; it is implicit, unspoken. It is also rubbish. There was deep and bitter resentment against the new army, and it was in part based on class. It changed more remarkably than almost anything else in the war, from Haig downwards. Kitchener's Army was not recruited largely from working men in the Midlands (I wonder if Fussell knows how near those comments have come to having him lynched by ninety-year-olds in the north of England?). It was recruited from the brightest and best that Britain had to offer, many of whom were working men. The planners did not assume they were 'animal', but knew that they had not been trained in offensive warfare and chose to favour artillery as the main prong of the attack, planning to use the troops to mop up the pieces. The planners knew that troops, however willing, tended to go to pieces if separated from their officers. They knew that a night attack, even for highly-trained professional troops, was the most dangerous and accident-prone of any, and that without radio or effective telephone word of mouth was the only guaranteed method of communication between officers and their men.

Fussell finds it 'astonishing' that a sergeant could write,

> In humble, reverent spirit I dedicate these pages to the memory of the lads who served with me in the 'Sacrifice Battery', and who gave their lives that those behind might live.[4]

Such comments can be found in their thousands in any archive of the war, and they do not reflect, as Fussell seems to think, a fatuous ignorance of the war or a mindless jingoism. They represent instead the love that men can feel for each other in the midst of appalling hate, and as such they deserve to be respected and not patronized.

The sporting ethic obsesses Fussell, and the English capacity, in his eyes, to see war as a game,

> In nothing, however, is the initial British innocence so conspicuous as in the universal commitment to the sporting spirit.[5]

Fussell links Rupert Brooke, without citing a poem, with Newbolt's 'Vitae Lampada', a fatuous comparison that makes one glad Brooke died before he could read it, and which links two poets who are wildly different in outlook. He also pillories as 'preposterous' the officer who led his men across no-man's-land kicking a football. His comments reveal a major misreading of history. It is true that a number of popular journals went in for sporting imagery in the early stages of the war, but to take this as a reflection of a wider historical fact is to reach wide-ranging conclusions about the nature of British society by reading the *News of the World*. The sporting approach was not a universal phenomenon and it lasted a very short while; the proportion of poetry that uses war-as-sport is actually very small. There are to my knowledge no poems by Brooke, Sassoon, Owen, Rosenberg, Graves, Sorley or Blunden which mention sport in connection with the war, and a poem that does, such as C.J. Ronald's 'In Memoriam J.H.H.', uses sporting imagery (life as a race) only to acknowledge that war is by far 'a greater game' which ends in death. Some rather silly articles and verse were written at the start of the war using sport as their central conceit, but their number and universality is far less than Fussell would have us believe. As for the officer and the football, Fussell fails to acknowledge that it was marvellous psychology.

General Haig is shot at dawn by Fussell, and one reason for his summary conviction and execution is extremely bizarre.

> In Duff Cooper's immense biography *Haig* . . . neither Graves, Blunden, nor Sassoon makes a single appearance in either text or index, which would suggest that fighting men and their reports on what they have done and seen are as irrelevant to the career of the staff officer as literature itself.[6]

To me it would suggest that poets are not the first people a commander calls on to advise him on how to fight a war. Owen's and Sassoon's poems are not reports from fighting men; they are works of art. In addition, any staff officer who called on Owen and Sassoon to enquire as to their views would have had to be remarkably perceptive. Owen had hardly had any poems published by the time he was killed, and though he was a published poet Sassoon, by his own admission, kept very quiet about his 'other' life, and indeed dismissed it entirely from *Memoirs of an Infantry Officer* for much the same reasons as he kept it quiet at the front. Fussell never really grasps the split personality of men such as Owen, Sassoon, Graves and Blunden, though their separation into soldiers on the one hand and poets on the other is a (and perhaps the) crucial factor in understanding them. The bridge that spans the chasm between the opposites is comradeship, which Fussell tends to confuse with sex.

In a truly remarkable extract he quotes Owen's

There was extraordinary exultation in the act of slowly walking forward, showing ourselves openly,[7]

stating quite clearly that this is analogous to a sexual act of exposure. One of the Fussell's great achievements is to show how the First World War brought irony to British culture, and with it double meanings. He makes the mistake of reading into 'showing ourselves openly' what that means now, not what it meant then. To Fussell, Owen's act is the same as a young man leaving his clothes too far away to be reached in a hurry, then masturbating naked behind bushes near others. Well, yes; the terror of being caught out in a grubby sexual act could be seen as the same as walking out to face death and taking every step with the heightened awareness that it could be one's last, but I probably sound desperately old-fashioned if I say that it cheapens what Owen is trying to say beyond belief, and reduces men to an absurd level where they can only think and feel with their hips. It also ignores the fact that being shot is, perhaps, a little more exciting than masturbating. There are sometimes things more exciting than sex.

For Fussell comradeship is 'homoeroticism', a 'sublimated form of temporary homosexuality'. There is nothing wrong with the 'homo' part of Fussell's favourite word, although I do not believe there is anything temporary about the sexual inclination of Owen and Sassoon, but the 'eroticism' reduces the relationships between men to a carnal level that would indeed make them animals if it were true. Fussell interprets 'comrade' simply as an old-fashioned way of saying 'friend'. To those who shared life and death with their fellow men in the front line, 'friendship' could not begin to describe what they felt.

Fussell is desperately bad on Georgian poetry, seeing it concerned only with dawn and sunset.[8] This is simply untrue, as I hope to have shown in Chapter 1, and Fussell has no concept of the power Georgian poetry brought to bear on the development of a large number of excellent poets. He even gets the time of day wrong; it was moonlight that seemed to obsess the worst Georgian poets.

Fussell comments:

> Simple antithesis everywhere. That is the atmosphere in which most poems of the Great War take place, and that is the reason for the failure of most of them as durable art.[9]

Simple narrative and simple description of war landscapes seem to me far more typical of First World War poetry, and far more damaging, than simple antithesis. I suppose one could say that antithesis is at the heart of Owen's 'Spring Offensive', Rosenberg's 'Break of Day in the Trenches' and Sorley's 'All the Hills and Vales Along', but I would be hard pushed to describe it as simple. The emphasis on antithesis is necessary to prove Fussell's point, which usually comes back down to irony. To prove the point he has stretched it considerably beyond its natural span.

Most of the weaknesses in *The Great War and Modern Memory* derive from two factors: Fussell's tunnel vision with regard to irony, and his interest in the Great War only as something which began things and forced change. In terms of social history the war began some things, finished others and let others continue, but Fussell gives no quarter to those who take the war in their stride:

> But [David] Jones's commitment to his ritual-and-romance machinery impels him to keep hinting that this war is like others.[10]

In many respects it *was* like others. It mixed boredom and terror in unequal measure, it killed a lot of people, many of them tragically young and talented. It broke hearts and bodies, and left roughly the same number alive in comparison to those who died as most other wars. It started ludicrously and ended after far too long. It had some stupid generals and some rather clever ones, some stupid politicians and some who were just trapped, and profiteers, deserters, bad food and soldiers who contracted syphilis and got drunk. Fussell cannot see this. It was larger and greater than any other preceding war, but, in essence, it was not different.

> The war will not be understood in traditional terms: the machine gun alone makes it so special and unexampled that it simply can't be talked about as if it were one of the conventional wars of history.[11]

But it can. What is a conventional war? Was it conventional when Hannibal first used elephants, or primitive man a bronze helmet? Was it conventional when the American Civil War used iron-clad monitors? War kills people: that is what is conventional about war. How it does it may be unconventional, but matters far less. Some of the greatest poetry of the war achieves the status of greatness because it does understand the war in traditional terms, and does see in it an appalling form of normality. Rosenberg's vision of the war as an extension of the persecution that has beset his race throughout history, Blunden's concept of it as something that is part of rather than the death of nature – both these and much more would be lost if the war poets were unable to see it in a wider perspective. Indeed, the poets who fail to do this are those who write the weakest verse.

Fussell's book is exceptional in many areas, not least its treatment of language and charting of the vast changes that the war brought to British society and thinking. Its weakness is to assume that because it changed so much it changed everything, and that the literature of the war can also serve as its history. It is in danger of creating its own false myths in areas that are too important to be part of a falsehood.

Part of the fascination of the First World War is that its full story will never be told, any more than one can tell the full story of any major event in history. I regret the areas that this book has not been able to cover. There are almost as many myths about the war at sea as there are about the war in Flanders. It is a pure flight of fancy to state that Jellicoe could have lost the war in a day; when British battle-cruisers at Jutland blew up it had as much to do with the Royal Navy's willingness to remove flash-proof shutters to speed up rate of fire as it had to do with weak armour. HMS *Lion* was probably not saved by the man who was decorated for doing so; the German ships were very hard to sink, but it was not their design but the bad performance of British armour-piercing shells that meant fewer German than British ships were sunk at the Battle of Jutland.

There are whole new books to be written on the poetry of the campaigns outside Europe, and the campaigns themselves, as well as on the poetry of the home front and the theatrical and musical response to the war. There are powerful and influential authors who have hardly been touched on in this work – Robert Nichols, David Jones, Ivor Gurney, Herbert Read. Many generals beg the process of myth-deconstruction, not least Sir Henry Rawlinson, Maxse, Monash and Plumer. I have not looked at the remarkable flowering of dialect poetry produced by the war, and in particular the work of Violet Jacob.

The question remains why the First World War exerts such a myth-creating power, and why after so much horror it remains a central symbol of British and European culture. One of the clichés is that it was a literary war, and one of the great myths of literature is tragedy. According to Aristotle tragedy requires a nobly-born protagonist who is neither wholly good nor wholly bad, and who is brought to destruction after much pain and suffering through a weakness in his own character that in a different time and place might have never even been noticed. Tragedy arouses in heightened intensity the twin emotions of pity and terror, and expels them in a moment of *catharsis*. Death, evil and suffering are unleashed into a closed world and become uncontrollable, until evil turns on and destroys itself. After the tragic *dénouement*, where the death of the hero is seen as a release from pain, society is purged and regeneration can begin.

The European powers were mighty in their strength and wealth. They were neither wholly good nor wholly bad, and were brought to near-destruction by powers of ambition, greed and aggression that had always been there but which had never before led to destruction on such a scale. The war evoked pity and terror like no other, and when peace was declared there was an almost animal venting of emotion in the streets of Britain. It unleashed untold suffering on Europe, a suffering that went out of the control of any human agency and which toppled some monarchies and shook other nations to their roots. And of course, when it was all over, the world had been made safe, and the war to end all wars had been fought.

Tragedy is the deepest myth of all, going back to pre-history, the need for a sacrificial victim and the purging of society. By accident, or by the design of a god whom Thomas Hardy might have recognized, when the countries of Europe fought the First World War they followed the tragic myth as if it had been written for them. Unfortunately for us all, it was not actors and a mock death that died in Flanders and across the world, but a whole generation. Perhaps the problem with our century is that in 1918 we replaced Hamlet with Fortinbras.

Notes

1 Fussell, *The Great War and Modern Memory*, pp. 7–8
2 *ibid.*, p. 11
3 p. 13
4 p. 23
5 p. 25
6 p. 85
7 p. 271
8 p. 55
9 p. 82
10 p. 150
11 p. 153

Select Bibliography

This bibliography is a little wayward. I have listed in each case the edition I have actually used in preparing this book, which is not always the most modern and is usually the cheapest. The list is not intended as a complete guide to reading on or about the First World War; it is rather a list of the works I have personally found most helpful. For reasons of space I have not included articles, with the exception of the epoch-making edition of 'Stand'.

Bibliography

Reilly, Catherine, *English Poetry of the First World War. A Bibliography* (London, George Prior Publishers, 1978)

Biography, Autobiography, and Letters of Literary Figures

Blunden, Edmund, *Undertones of War* (Penguin, Harmondsworth, 1984)

Brooke, Rupert, ed. Keynes, Sir Geoffrey, *The Letters of Rupert Brooke* (London, Faber & Faber, 1968)

,ed. Harris, Pippa, *Song of Love. The Letters of Rupert Brooke and Noel Oliver* (London, Bloomsbury, 1991)

Cohen, Joseph, *Journey to the Trenches. The Life of Isaac Rosenberg, 1890–1918* (London, Robson Books, 1975)

Cook, William, *Edward Thomas: A Critical Biography* (London, Faber, 1970)

Corrigan, D. Felicitas, *Siegfried Sassoon, Poet's Pilgrimage* (London, Victor Gollancz, 1973)

Farjeon, Eleanor, *Edward Thomas: The Last Four Years* (Oxford, Oxford University Press, 1979)

Fido, Martin, *Rudyard Kipling; An Illustrated Biography* (New York, Peter Bedrick, 1986)

Fussell, Paul, ed., *Sassoon's Long Journey* (London, Giniger/ Faber & Faber, 1983)

Grant, Joy, *Harold Monro and the Poetry Bookshop* (London, Routledge & Kegan Paul, 1967)

Graves, Richard Perceval, *Robert Graves: The Assault Heroic* (London, Macmillan, 1987)

Graves, Robert, *Goodbye To All That* (Harmondsworth, Penguin, 1960)

ed. O'Prey, Paul, *In Broken Images: Selected Letters of Robert Graves 1914–1946* (London, Hutchinson, 1982)

Gurney, Ivor, ed. Blunden, Edmund, *Poems of Ivor Gurney 1890– 1937* (London, Chatto & Windus, 1973)

Hassall, Christopher, *Edward Marsh, Patron of the Arts* (London, Longman, 1959)

Rupert Brooke (London, Faber & Faber, 1964)

Hibberd, Dominic, *Wilfred Owen. The Last Year* (London, Constable, 1992)

Hurd, Michael, *The Ordeal of Ivor Gurney* (Oxford, Oxford University Press, 1978)

Lehmann, John, *Rupert Brooke: His Life and Legend* (London, Quartet, 1981)

Liddiard, Jean, *Isaac Rosenberg: The Half Used Life* (London, Victor Gollancz, 1975)

Marsh, Sir Edward, *A Number of People; A Book of Reminiscences* London, Heinemann, 1939)

Marsh, Jan, *Edward Thomas. A Poet For His Country* (London, Paul Eleck, 1978)

Moorcroft Wilson, Jean, *Charles Hamilton Sorley. A Biography* (London, Cecil Woolf, 1985)

Isaac Rosenberg. Poet and Painter (London, Cecil Woolf, 1975)

Mosley, Nicholas, *Julian Grenfell, His Life and the Times of His Death 1888–1915* (London, Weidenfeld and Nicolson, 1976)

Owen, Wilfred, ed. Owen, Harold and Bell, John, *Wilfred Owen: Collected Letters* (London, Oxford University Press, 1967)

Rosenberg, Isaac, ed. Parsons, Ian, *The Collected Works of Isaac Rosenberg* (London, Chatto & Windus, 1979)

Sassoon, Siegfried, ed. Hart-Davies, Rupert, *Siegfried Sassoon: Diaries 1915–1918* (London, Faber, 1983)

Memoirs of an Infantry Officer (London, Faber, 1965)

Siegfried's Journey (London, Faber & Faber, 1945)

The Old Century and Seven More Years (London, Faber & Faber, 1986)

Seymour-Smith, Martin, *Robert Graves: His Life and Work* (New York, Holt, Rinehart and Winston, 1982)

Sorley, Charles Hamilton, ed. Spear, Hilda D., *The Poems and Selected Letters of Charles Hamilton Sorley* (Dundee, Blackness Press, 1978)

ed. Sorley, W.R., *The Letters of Charles Sorley* (Cambridge, Cambridge University Press, 1919)

Stallworthy, Jon, *Wilfred Owen* (London, Oxford University Press and Chatto & Windus, 1974)

Swann, Thomas Burnett, *The Ungirt Runner. Charles Hamilton Sorley, Poet of World War I* (Connecticut, Archon Books, 1965)

Thomas, Edward, ed. Thomas, R.G., *Letters from Edward Thomas to Gordon Bottomley* (Oxford, Oxford University Press, 1968)

Thomas, Helen, *As It Was and World Without End* (London, Faber, 1972)

Webb, Barry, *Edmund Blunden. A Biography* (New Haven, Yale University Press, 1990)

Critical Works

Bergonzi, Bernard, *Heroes' Twilight. A Study of the Literature of the First World War* (London, MacMillan, 1980)

Blunden, Edmund, *War Poets 1914–1918* (London, Longmans, 1964)

Caesar, Adrian, *Taking It Like A Man. Suffering, Sexuality and the War Poets* (Manchester, Manchester University Press, 1993)

Clark, Keith, *The Muse Colony. Rupert Brooke, Edward Thomas, Robert Frost and Friends, Dymock 1914* (Bristol, Redcliffe Press, 1992)

Crawford, Fred D., *British Poets of the Great War* (Selinsgrove, Susqehanna University Press, 1988)

Field, Frank, *British and French Writers of the First World War: Comparative Studies In Cultural History* (Cambridge, Cambridge University Press, 1991)

Fussell, Paul, *The Great War and Modern Memory* (New York and London, Oxford University Press, 1975)

Graham, Desmond, *The Truth of War: Owen, Blunden, Rosenberg* (Manchester, Carcanet Press, 1984)

Hibberd, Dominic, *Owen the Poet* (Athens, University of Georgia Press, 1986)

Hynes, Samuel, *A War Imagined: The First World War and English Culture* (London, Bodley Head, 1990)

Johnston, John H., *English Poetry of the First World War. A Study in the Evolution of Lyric and Narrative Form* (London, Oxford University Press, 1964)

Kerr, Douglas, *Wilfred Owen's Voices* (Oxford, Clarendon Press, 1993)

Longley, Edna, *Poetry in the Wars* (Newark, University of Delaware Press, 1987)

Mallon, Thomas, *Edmund Blunden* (Boston, Twayne, 1983)

Parfitt, George, *English Poetry of the First World War: Contexts and Themes* (London, Harvester/Wheatsheaf, 1990)

Fiction of the First World War: A Study (London, Faber & Faber, 1988)

Press, John, *A Map of Modern English Verse* (Oxford, Oxford University Press, 1969)

Rogers, Timothy, *Georgian Poetry 1911–1922. The Critical Heritage* (London, Routledge & Kegan Paul, 1977)

Rupert Brooke. A Selection and Reappraisal (London, Routledge & Kegan Paul, 1971)

Ross, Robert H., *The Georgian Revolt: Rise and Fall of a Poetic Ideal 1910–1922* (London, Faber & Faber, 1967)

Rutherford, Andrew, *The Literature of War. Five Studies in Heroic Virtue* (London, Macmillan, 1978)

Silk, Dennis, *Siegfried Sassoon* (Salisbury, Compton Russell, 1974)

Silkin, Jon, *Out of Battle: The Poetry of the Great War* (London, Oxford University Press, 1978)

'Stand', *The War Poets* (Volume 4, No. 3, nd)

Stead, C.K., *The New Poetic: Yeats to Eliot* (Harmondsworth, Penguin, 1964)

Thurley, Geoffrey, *The Ironic Harvest. English Poetry in the Twentieth Century* (London, Edward Arnold, 1974)

Welland, D. S. R., *Wilfred Owen: A Critical Study* (London, Chatto & Windus, 1969; revised and enlarged edition, 1978)

Williams, Merryn, *Wilfred Owen* (Bridgend, Seren Books, 1993)

Fiction

Aldington, Richard, *Death of a Hero* (London, Consul Books/World Distributors, 1965)

Barbusse, Henri, *Under Fire* (London, J. M. Dent, 1969)

Carrington, Charles C., *Soldier From the Wars Returning* (London, Hutchinson, 1965)

Kipling, Rudyard, *The Complete Stalky & Co* (Oxford, Oxford University Press, 1987)

Manning, Frederick, *Her Privates We* (London, Peter Davies, 1964)

, *The Middle Parts of Fortune* (unexpurgated version of *Her Privates We*) (London, Buchan & Enright, 1986)

Waugh, Alec, *The Loom of Youth* (London, Methuen, 1984)

History

Asprey, Robert B., *The German High Command At War: Hindenburg and Ludendorff and The First World War* (Little Brown, 1993)

Beckett, Jane and Cherry, Deborah, ed., *The Edwardian Era* (London, Phaedon Press and Barbican Art Gallery, 1987)

Chandos, John, *Boys Together. English Public Schools 1800–1864* (New Haven and London, Yale University Press, 1984)

David, Daniel, *The 1914 Campaign, August-October, 1914* (New York, Military Press, 1987)

de Groot, Gerald J., *Douglas Haig, 1861–1928* (London, Unwin Hyman, 1988)

Farrar-Hockley, A.H., *The Somme* (London, Pan, 1983)

Gardner, Brian, *The Public Schools* (London, Hamish Hamilton, 1983)

Gathorne-Hardy, Jonathan, *The Public School Phenomenon* (London, Hodder & Stoughton, 1977)

Haig, Douglas, ed. Boraston, J.H., *Sir Douglas Haig's Despatches, December 1915–April 1919* (London, Dent, 1979)

Harris, John, *The Somme: Death of a Generation* (London, Hodder & Stoughton, 1976)

Horne, Alistair, *The Price of Glory. Verdun 1916* (Harmondsworth, Penguin, 1964)

Keegan, John, *The Face of Battle. A Study of Agincourt, Waterloo, and the Somme* (Harmondsworth, Penguin, 1978)

Laffin, John, *British Butchers and Bunglers of World War I* (London, Alan Sutton, 1988)

Liddell Hart, B. H., *History of the First World War* (London Pan, 1972)

Liddle, Peter H., *The 1916 Battle of the Somme. A Reappraisal* (London, Leo Cooper, 1992)

MacKenzie, Jeanne, *The Children of the Souls: A Tragedy of the First World War* (London, Chatto & Windus, 1986)

Mangan, J. A., *Athleticism and the Victorian Public School* (Lewes, Falmer Press, 1981)

Marwick, Arthur, *The Deluge. British Society and the First World War* (London, Macmillan Paperback, 1965; revised edition, 1991)

, *Women at War 1914–18* (London, Fontana, 1977)

Middlebrook, Martin, *The Kaiser's Battle* (Harmondsworth, Penguin, 1983)

Nowell-Smith, Simon, ed., *Edwardian England 1901–1914* (London, Oxford University Press, 1964)

Parker, Peter, *The Old Lie. The Great War and the Public School Ethos* (London, Constable, 1987)

Prior, Robin, and Wilson, Trevor, *Command on the Western Front: The Military Career of Sir Henry Rawlinson 1914–1918* (Oxford, Blackwell, 1992)

Read, Donald, *Edwardian England 1901–15. Society and Politics* (London, Harrap, 1972)

Reeves, Maud Pember, *Round About A Pound A Week* (London, Virago, 1979)

Rich, P. J., *Chains of Empire. English Public Schools, Masonic Cabalism, Historic Causality, and Imperial Clubdom* (London. Regency Press, 1991)

Simon, Brian, and Bradley, Ian, *The Victorian Public School. Studies in the Development of an Educational Institution* (Dublin, Gill and Macmillan, 1975)

Shrosbree, Colin, *Public Schools and Private Education: The Clarendon Commission, 1861–64, and the Public Schools Act* (Manchester, Manchester University Press, 1988)

Smyth, Brigadier the Rt Hon Sir John, Bt, VC, MC, *Leadership in Battle 1914–1918* (Newton Abbot, David & Charles, 1975)

Sommer, Dudley, *Haldane of Cloan* (London, Allen & Unwin, 1961)

Stevenson, John, *British Society 1914–1945* (Harmondsworth, Penguin, 1984)

Terraine, John, *Douglas Haig: The Educated Soldier* (London, Leo Cooper, 1990)

The Smoke and the Fire: Myths and Anti-Myths of War 1861– 1945 (London, Sidgwick & Jackson, 1980)

White Heat: The New Warfare 1914–1918 (London, Sidgwick & Jackson, 1982)

Travers, Tim, *How The War Was Won. Command and Technology in the British Army on the Western Front, 1917–1918* (London, Routledge, 1992)

Waites, Bernard, *A Class Society At War* (Leamington, Berg, 1987)

Warner, Philip, *Field Marshal Earl Haig* (London, Bodley Head, 1991)

Winter, Denis, *Death's Men* (Penguin, Harmondsworth, 1978)

Haig's Command. A Reassessment (Harmondsworth, Penguin, 1992)

Abercrombie, Lascelles, *The Poems of Lascelles Abercrombie* (Oxford, Oxford University Press, 1930)

Barnes, Leonard, *Youth at Arms 1914–1918* (London, Peter Davies, 1933)

Blunden, Edmund, *The Poems of Edmund Blunden* (London, Cobden-Sanderson, 1930)

ed. Marsack, Robyn, *Edmund Blunden: Selected Poems* (Manchester, Carcanet, 1982)

Bottomley, Gordon, *Poems of Thirty Years* (London, Constable, 1925)

Brooke, Rupert, ed. Keynes, Geoffrey, *The Poetical Works of Rupert Brooke* (London, Faber & Faber, 1946)

Chesterton, G.K., *Collected Poems* (London, Methuen, 1937)

ed. Cross, Tim, *The Lost Voices of World War I* (London, Bloomsbury, 1989)

Day, Jeffery, *Poems and Rhymes* (London, Sidgwick & Jackson, 1919)

ed. Gardner, Brian, *Up The Line To Death* (London, Methuen, 1986)

Gibson, Wilfrid, *Collected Poems 1905–1925* (London, Macmillan, 1933)

ed. Giddings, Robert, *The War Poets* (New York, Orion, 1988)

Graves, Robert, *Poems About War* (London, Cassell, 1988)

Gurney, Ivor, *Poems of Ivor Gurney 1890–1937* (London, Chatto & Windus, 1973)

ed. Hibberd, Dominic, and Onions, John, *Poetry of the First World War* (London, Macmillan, 1986)

ed. Hussey, Maurice, *Poetry of the First World War* (Harlow, Longmans, 1973)

ed. Jones, P., *Imagist Poetry* (Harmondsworth, Penguin, 1972)

Kipling, Rudyard, ed. Kaye, M.M., *The Complete Verse* (London, Kyle Cathie, 1990)

Mackintosh, E.A., *A Highland Regiment* (London, John Lane, nd)

War the Liberator (London, John Lane, 1918)

ed. Marsh, Edward, *Georgian Poetry 1911–1912* (London, The Poetry Bookshop, 1912)

Georgian Poetry 1913–1915 (London, The Poetry Bookshop, 1915)

Georgian Poetry 1916–1917 (London, The Poetry Bookshop, 1917)

Georgian Poetry 1918–1919 (London, The Poetry Bookshop, 1919)

Georgian Poetry 1920–1922 (London, The Poetry Bookshop, 1922)

Owen, Wilfred, ed. Stallworthy, Jon, *The Poems of Wilfred Owen* (London, Chatto & Windus, 1990)

ed. Parsons, I. M., *Men Who March Away: Poems of the First World War* (London, Chatto & Windus, 1965)

ed. Powell, Anne, *A Deep Cry* (Aberporth, Palladour Books, 1993)

ed. Reilly, Catherine, *Scars Upon My Heart. Women's Poetry and Verse of the First World War* (London, Virago, 1981)

Rickword, Edgell, ed. Hobday, Charles, *Collected Poems* (Manchester, Carcanet, 1991)

Rosenberg, Isaac, ed. Bottomley, Gordon and Harding, Denys, *Collected Poems* (London, Chatto & Windus, 1974)

Rutter, Major Owen, *The Song of Tiadatha* (London, Philip Allan, 1935)

Sassoon, Siegfried, ed. Hart-Davis, Rupert, *Siegfried Sassoon, The War Poems* (London, Faber & Faber, 1983)

ed. Silkin, Jon, *The Penguin Book of First World War Poetry* (Harmondsworth, Penguin, 1979)

Sorley, Charles Hamilton, *Marlborough and Other Poems* (fifth edition, Cambridge, Cambridge University Press, 1919)

ed. Moorcroft-Wilson, Jean, *The Collected Poems of Charles Hamilton Sorley* (London, Cecil Woolf, 1985)

ed. Stephen, Martin, *Never Such Innocence. A New Anthology of Great War Verse* (London, Buchan and Enright, 1988; third enlarged edition as *Poems of the First World War*, Everyman, 1993)

Thomas, Edward, *Collected Poems* (London, Faber & Faber, 1949)

War Memoirs, Magazines and Journals

Beaver, Patrick, ed., *The Wipers Times* (London, Macmillan, 1988)

Beresford, Christine and Newbould, Christopher, ed., *The Fifth Gloster Gazette. A Chronicle, Serious and Humorous, of the Battalion while serving with the British Expeditionary Force* (Stroud, Alan Sutton, 1993)

Brown, Malcolm, ed., *The Imperial War Museum Book of the First World War* (London, Sidgwick & Jackson, 1991)

The Imperial War Museum Book of the Western Front (London, Sidgwick & Jackson, 1993)

Chapman, Guy, *A Passionate Prodigality* (London, Buchan & Enright, 1985)

ed., *Vain Glory. A Miscellany of the Great War 1914–1918 written by those who fought in it on each side and on all fronts* (London, Cassell, 1968)

Coppard, George, *With a Machine Gun to Cambrai* (London, MacMillan Papermac, 1986)

Crozier, Brigadier General F. P., *A Brass Hat in No Man's Land* (London, Jonathan Cape, 1930)

Dunn, Captain J. C., *The War The Infantry Knew 1914–19* (London, Sphere, 1989)

Edmonds, Charles (pseudonym of Carrington, Charles), *A Subaltern's War* (London, Peter Davies, 1929)

Fraser, Hon. William, ed. Fraser, David, *In Good Company. The First World War Letters and Diaries of the Hon. William Fraser, Gordon Highlanders* (Salisbury, Michael Russell, 1990)

Glover, Michael, ed., *The Great War Sketches and Journals of Captain Henry Ogle, MC* (London, Leo Cooper, 1993)

Harris, Ruth Elwyn, *Billie, The Nevill Letters 1914–1916* (London, Julia MacRae Books, 1991)

Laffin, John, ed., *Letters From the Front 1914–18* (London, Dent, 1973)

Uddle, Peter, ed., *The Soldier's War 1914–1918* (London, Blandford Press, 1988)

Macdonald, Lyn, ed., *1914–1918. Voices and Images of the Great War* (Harmondsworth, Penguin, 1988)

1915 (London, Headline, 1993)

Messenger, Charles, *Terriers in the Trenches. The Post Office Rifles at War, 1914–1918* (Picton Publishing, 1982)

Middleton Murry, J., *The Evolution of an Intellectual* (London, Richard Cobden-Sanderson, 1920)

Moynihan, Michael, ed., *People at War: 1914–1918* (Battle Standards Series, Newton Abbot, David and Charles, 1988)

Nesham, Felicite, *Socks, Cigarettes and Shipwrecks. A Family's War Letters 1914–1918* (Gloucester, Alan Sutton, 1987)

Ogle, Captain Henry, *The Fateful Battle Line* (London, Leo Cooper, 1993)

Orr, Philip, ed., *The Road to the Somme. Men of the Ulster Division Tell Their Story* (Belfast, Blackstaff Press, 1987)

Panichas, George A., ed., *Promise of Greatness. The War of 1914–1918* (London, Cassell, 1968)

Pryor, Alan, and Woods, Jennifer K., ed., *Great Uncle Fred's War: An Illustrated Diary 1917–1920* (Whitstable, Prior Publications, 1985)

Quinn, Tom, *Tales of the Old Soldiers* (Stroud, Alan Sutton, 1993)

Stepmann, Harry, *Echo of the Guns. Recollections of an Artillery Officer 1914–1918* (London, Robert Hale, 1987)

Stuart Dolden, A., *Cannon Fodder. An Infantryman's Life on the Western Front 1914–18* (London, Blandford, 1981)

Tennant, Norman, *A Saturday Night Soldier's War, 1913–1918* (Waddesdon, The Kylin Press, 1983)

Vansittart, Peter, *Voices From The Great War* (Harmondsworth, Penguin, 1983)

Vaughan, Edwin Campion, *Some Desperate Glory. The Diaries of a Young Officer, 1917* (London, Leo Cooper, 1987)

Woolf, Ann, *Subalterns of the Foot. Three World War I Diaries of Officers of the Cheshire Regiment* (Worcester, Square One, 1992)

Index

253